THE PROTESTANT PARISH MINISTER: A BEHAVIORAL SCIENCE INTERPRETATION

by
SAMUEL W. BLIZZARD (1914-1976)

With the assistance of
Harriet B. Blizzard

Introduction by
Hart M. Nelsen
Pennsylvania State University

SOCIETY FOR THE SCIENTIFIC STUDY OF RELIGION
MONOGRAPH SERIES, NUMBER 5, STORRS, CONNECTICUT
ISBN 0-932566-04-9

Library of Congress Number: 85-50402
International Standard Book Number: 0-932566-04-9

TABLE OF CONTENTS

Page

LIST OF TABLES iii
SERIES EDITOR'S INTRODUCTION. v
FOREWORD vii
PREFACE. ix
INTRODUCTION. 1
I.   Research on an Occupational Group 19
II.   The Minister 29
III. Characteristics of the Protestant Parish Clergyman,
      and His Organizational Setting. 39
IV.   The Master Role 51
V.   The Integrating Roles 65
VI.   The Practitioner Roles 83
VII. The Practitioner Roles: Time Management .97
VIII. Role Conflict 117
IX.   The Minister's Concept of the Church 135
X.   Relationships Within the Whole of Professional Practice 147

APPENDICES
A   Acknowledgements. 156
B   Parish Minister's Time Allocations (1955) 159
C   A Comparison of Clergy Time Allocation to
     Practitioner Roles Reported in Two Surveys 163
D   A Comparison of Clergy Daily Time Allocations. 165
E   Forty Types of Ministerial Activity (as ranked by
     Hartshorne and Froyd-1944) Distributed Among the
     Russell Sage Practitioner Roles 167
F   Personal Job Analysis. 169
G   One-day Diary 181
     References 185
     Bibliography 189

TABLES, FIGURE, CHARTS

TABLE   PAGE
1   Emotional maturity continuum. 41
2   Awareness of desired change 42
3   Professional mobility 44
4   Criteria for effectiveness and success. 45

5   Effectiveness and success ranked 47
6   Denominational affiliations 49
7   Master role orientation. 53
8   Master role typology 56
9   Integrative role distribution 66
10 Primary and secondary integrative roles. 77
11 Integrative role continuum. 78
12 Normative evaluation of practitioner roles. 87
13 Most enjoyed practitioner role 88
14 Most effective practitioner role 90
15 Practitioner roles ranked by clergy evaluations. 90
16 Evaluation of practitioner role 92
17 Intercorrelation of role evaluations 92
18 Evaluation of practitioner roles by denomination 94
19 Time allocation to practitioner roles. 100
20 A comparison of the rankings of practitioner role evaluations 102
21 Time spent in total work day by age. 103
22 Time allocation for selected parish activities. 110
23 Number of evident role conflicts held by ministers 123
24 Distribution of role conflict types 124
25 Church orientation themes 137
26 Church orientation typology 141
27 Relationship of practitioner role evaluations to
    master and integrative roles 149
28 Correlation of master role with specific integrative
    role by role evaluation 149
Figure 1   Practitioner role interaction pattern 86
Chart 1   Role conflict model 121
Chart 2   Role interaction patterns. 122
Chart 3   Apparent role conflict model 128

Series Editor's Introduction

The Protestant Parish Minister: A Behavioral Science Interpretation is the fifth monograph in the Society for the Scientific Study of Religion Monograph Series. The series intends to make available significant work on religion from a variety of scientific disciplines and perspectives.

As Hart Nelsen's excellent introduction to Blizzard's work and its impact makes clear, the study of ministers owes a tremendous debt to Samuel Blizzard. Blizzard's articles from the project that resulted in this posthumous book have inspired and greatly enriched a large number of studies of ministers and their roles. I hope that the availability for the first time of the entire work will stimulate still more research, for Blizzard's creative theoretical concepts can help us understand the role of the minister at a time when new influences from the social environment present the ministry with new challenges and pose exciting new research problems for those who would understand this important societal role.

James R. Wood
Indiana University

FOREWORD

Samuel Wilson Blizzard, researcher-author of this report, completed collection and analysis in 1957 of the data which informed his work. As a sociologist and theologian, Blizzard studied Protestant parish ministers from the perspective of what these professional men and women felt about themselves, their ministries, and their environment. The concepts derived from his material have since been used by others in further research. (See Review of Religious Research 23, December 1981.)

Revisions of his manuscript were made by Blizzard in 1968 and 1971; but illness prevented completion of chapters 11 and 12, and much of the theory suggested for these chapters was not substantiated. It should be kept in mind, however, that at the time when the data were analyzed some of the rather sophisticated types of multivariate analysis were not possible, due to limited or nonexistent computer facilities. Further exploration of the data with current technology might yield different results for those chapters. His death in 1976 prevented the further refinement and conceptualization of his theories which he had desired.

In an effort to make the data available to educators, parish ministers, seminarians, and other scholars, it was decided to publish chapters 1-10. All unpublished material has been placed with the Blizzard papers in Speer Library, Princeton Theological Seminary, Princeton, New Jersey. This includes chapters 11 and 12, a methodological appendix, all revisions of the manuscript, an extended bibliography, and all raw data.

Acknowledgements for all phases of data collection and analysis (1953-1957) have been placed in the appendices. (See Appendix A.)

For the current effort in getting this volume ready for publication, I am deeply indebted to six persons who gave much advice and encouragement: Dr. Jackson Carroll, Hartford Theological Seminary; Dr. James I. McCord and Dr. Hugh T. Kerr, Princeton Theological Seminary; Dr. Dean Hoge, Catholic University; Dr. Hart M. Nelsen, Pennsylvania State University; and Mrs. Jane Blizzard Gorman.

Harriet B. Blizzard
1984

PREFACE

This book is intended as a behavioral science contribution to an understanding of the ministry. Material for study was obtained from the self-images of 1,111 Protestant parish ministers with a view to making generalizations about their professional behavior. These ministers were selected from the alumni of five seminaries, and from 22 additional Protestant denominations.

The self-image data are not ends in themselves—interesting and revealing as they may be—but a means to an end. That end is to contribute to a better understanding of how the prospective minister may be more adequately trained for service, and how ministers now in practice in the Protestant parishes of the United States may be more effective.

It is the author's desire to help rather than to hinder, to be constructive rather than destructive, to explore rather than to be definitive. It is hoped that the analysis will provoke discussion, encourage examination and further research, and eventuate in a clearer understanding of what the ministry is.

Samuel Wilson Blizzard
1971

INTRODUCTION

MINISTERS AND THEIR MILIEU: SOCIALIZATION, CLERGY ROLE, AND COMMUNITY

Samuel Blizzard's *The Protestant Parish Minister* has a specific focus: the description of the roles clergy hold, the gaining of some understanding of why they hold those roles, and the elucidation of conflicts they experience as they engage in their roles. With funding from the Russell Sage Foundation, Blizzard collected the data for this study during the mid-fifties, from alumni of five Protestant seminaries and from 22 additional Protestant denominations. He was one of several scholars engaged by the foundation to study how social science could be used in training professionals.

Blizzard quickly published the heart of the findings in several periodicals read by clergy, seminary faculty and administrators, and other church leaders,[1] rather than in journals read primarily by social scientists. I believe he chose this initial placement because he was intent on reaching the clergy, on helping them to develop both relevant ministries and positive self-images. He viewed the parish ministry as having undergone considerable change, and he undoubtedly envisioned related changes occurring in roles held by clergy, seminary preparation for the ministry, and perceptions by the laity of the goals and duties of ministers. These early publications, then, were his way of providing for ministers a behavioral interpretation of their profession.

But, as Bouma (1981:211) has remarked, Blizzard was a "border broker between social science and theological education." He needed also to reach those outside the profession of the ministry, including his fellow social scientists. They were to be the target audience for the book that would be the vehicle for interpreting the data in a more integrated fashion, that would permit him to expand on role theory vis-a-vis the parish minister.

His dream of bringing the book to fruition during his lifetime was not to be realized. The ill health that plagued him prior to his death in 1976 prevented him from finishing the volume. Fortunately for us all, Sam's widow, Harriet, persisted in the hard work, making the difficult editorial decisions necessary to turn his manuscript into a publishable form. She was aided in this task by several people, especially Jackson Carroll and Dean Hoge. The publication of the book form of his study means that scholars of the ministry have this seminal work in a more usable reference format and no longer have to rely on the initial series of short articles.

I am most pleased to have been asked to write this introduction for a number of reasons. Some of my own research has utilized Blizzard's conceptualization of clergy roles and quite early in my career I benefited from his course on the ministry as a profession. Much more important, I am convinced that Blizzard's research implicitly

---

[1]The most important of these articles are: "The Minister's Dilemma," *The Christian Century*, Vol. 73, April 25, 1956, pp. 508-9; "Role Conflicts of the Urban Protestant Parish Minister," *The City*, Vol. 7, September, 1956, pp. 13-15; "The Protestant Parish Minister's Integrating Roles," *Religious Education*, Vol. 53, July-August, 1958, pp. 374-80; "The Parish Minister's Self-Image of His Master Roles," *Pastoral Psychology*, Vol. 9, December, 1958, pp. 25-32; and "The Parish Minister's Self-Image and Variability in Community Culture," *Pastoral Psychology*, Vol. 10, October, 1959, pp. 27-36. His practitioner, integrating, and master roles (from most to least specific, or from most practical or functional to the most theoretical) are in the first, third, and fourth articles above (in order). (For a complete list of Blizzard's papers, see Harriet Blizzard [compiler], 1981:214.)

demands that the scholars of the eighties take up the research agenda that he unveiled: the implications of changing expectations for the clergy on the part of parishioners and community members as well as the clergy themselves—how clergy are socialized to want to be clergy or to feel a call, how parishioners interact with ministers, how community members perceive clergy, and how social control is instituted in regard to the behavior of clergy and clergy spouses.

The above topics only begin to introduce this research agenda. Blizzard's focus was explicity on the minister's behavior (how she or he used time), goals, role conflict, and so on, but from time to time he noted the importance of the surrounding religious culture and the social context of the ministry, what is in many ways the other side of the study of the ministry and an area that has hardly begun to be explored. Moreover, the substantial amount of time since Blizzard's work and the fateful stream of events that has sometimes seemed to tear and twist beyond recognization our cultural foundations intensify the importance of replicating that work in the eighties and conducting parallel research on lay perceptions and expectations for ministers.

I shall explore here the ways in which other scholars have woven Blizzard's role concepts and findings into their own work. The very volume of the literature involved testifies to the enduring value of Blizzard's work, but it also complicates the task at hand. I can only hope to commit few sins of omission. The order I will attempt to impose on these works will be in terms of how Blizzard measured and used his three levels of roles and how others have done so, parishioners' expectations of clergy, and the basic question of clergy roles and professionalization (or deprofessionalization) of the ministry. Inevitably, the discussion must begin with Blizzard's own interpretation of the three levels of clergy role.

MASTER, INTEGRATIVE, AND PRACTITIONER ROLES

At the surface, "role" signifies engaging in behaviors that are learned and then performed in conjunction with the status a person has. Thus the ministry as a whole can be viewed as a status, and appropriate behaviors might run the gamut from performing ritual to providing comfort. There would also exist specialities within the ministry: armed services and hospital chaplaincies, counselors, televangelists, and so forth. More importantly, some agreement can be reached as to what constitutes the role. Not only are individuals required more or less to perform the set of behaviors making up the role, but there exists "external validation" for the role whereby "the behavior is judged to constitute a role by others whose judgments are felt to have some claim to correctness or legitimacy" (Turner, 1962:30). In other words, there are shared behavioral expectations for the individuals who take on these roles. A name for the position, in this case "clergy" (or in its context: Reverend, Rabbi, Father, et cetera), invokes the meanings (Stryker and Gottlieb, 1981:321; also Turner, 1962:30).

The taking on of roles simplifies interaction; normally, one knows what to expect from the other party (on attribution theory and symbolic interactionism in this regard see Stryker and Gottlieb, 1981). But with the label and social expectation can also come difficulties in blending together seemingly incompatible expectations of behavior. As Stryker and Gottlieb write (p. 449): "the central problem in interaction is to assume or to create complementary or mutually compatible roles for self and others involved in interaction."

Stryker and Gottlieb then present interrelated questions about actors [read clergy and laity] casting and presenting themselves and the other; these questions fit into the research agenda not yet taken up, to which I earlier referred.

Master Role

Blizzard approached clergy role by asking how the clergyperson perceives the ministry being alike or different from other occupations. The "master role" is Blizzard's most inclusive concept and is the subject of the fourth chapter. The minister was asked how his or her work was related to the church or the people with whom he or she interacted and to other occupations.

Ideological (theological) and functional orientations provide two major frames of reference for the master role. The former is more church (ideology) oriented and the latter centers more on actual function. For example, the clergyperson might define herself or himself as a mediator between God and person or as a servant of God. From the functional perspective she or he might represent someone who serves the spiritual needs of parishioners or who is a leader of leaders or simply as someone who has a product of real worth. About three-fourths of Blizzard's respondents endorsed either or both the theological and functional perspectives of the master role. Younger ministers, more recent products of seminaries and hence more likely to conceptualize in theological terms, were more likely to have the ideological orientation to the master role, while older ministers were more geared to the functional view. Age was an important predictor in Blizzard's study, and his unfinished research agenda would have us focus on what happens during a ministerial career: do concerns with running churches over the years and as part of having increasingly larger churches in a successful career lead to a different presentation of the master role? Is it simply that continuing education of clergy is insufficient or fails to reinforce theological concerns? Or, is "the real world out there," where the ministry is enacted, different from the one to which seminarians are socialized? Denomination was an important predictor of the type of master role held. By starting with the minister's master role and not taking it as given, but looking for significant predictors such as age and denomination, Blizzard provided evidence that his view of clergy role was not simply descriptive. He was not just looking for what clergy do as related to their role: he viewed clergy role as varying and as in flux, with role conflict a possibility.

Integrative Roles

While as many as one-fourth of Blizzard's subjects lacked a master role, less than one-tenth lacked an integrative role, Blizzard's next level of conceptualization of how a minister sees himself or herself. This type of role is the subject of Chapter Five. These roles are goal-oriented and less abstract than master roles. Ministers may work with the same groups—community leaders and organizations, parishioners, the larger church bodies, and so forth—but toward different ends. Whom the minister works with might also be influenced by the minister's goal, for example, not all ministers will choose to join the Rotary.

Through content analysis of the themes used by ministers to describe their work, Blizzard specified 12 integrating roles[2] (plus the general practitioner role, consisting of no identifiable integrative role or when the individual held three or more integrating roles—this accounted for 9 percent of his respondents). These 12 were grouped under two headings: *traditional integrative roles*—believer-saint, scholar, evangelist, sacramentalist, and father-shepherd; and the *contemporary integrative roles*—the interpersonal-relationships specialist, the parish promoter, social actionist or social problem solver, educator, subcultural specialist, community religious leader (or representative of the church-at-large), and the churchman (denominational politician). Four of these roles—father-shepherd, interpersonal-relations specialist, parish promoter, and social actionist—were primary for almost two-thirds of the clergy and these all essentially involve "inter-personal, intra-group, and inter-group relations." An additional one-sixth subscribed to the believer-saint and evangelist orientations which Blizzard considered ideologically oriented. That leaves only one-fifth of the clergy for the other roles, including the scholar, a role emphasized by many seminaries; yet, with the exception of the general practitioner role none of these is primary for more than one in 25.

I have not defined each of these specific integrative roles because of space limitations and because Blizzard fully described each in a convincing fashion. In Chapter Five Blizzard noted denominational differences in the holding of one or another role. In the tenth chapter he related integrative roles to master roles—for example, the believer-saint is theologically and functionally oriented, and the interpersonal relations specialist is functionally oriented. The evangelist, parish promoter, and general practitioner are neither theologically nor functionally oriented. Perhaps the question used by Blizzard to secure material that provided the master role orientations lacked an even more pragmatic orientation, one that did *not* have a people-oriented or service ethic. Perhaps these individuals are not oriented to abstract conceptualization of the ministry (see Converse, 1964, on levels of conceptualization).

Practitioner Roles

At the most specific level of Blizzard's schema of clergy orientations are the practitioner roles. As we will see later in this introduction, not only has this level been the most utilized by researchers as they have built on Blizzard's research, but it formed the basis for one of his accounts for role conflict—what the minister saw as most important versus how he or she spent his or her time as clergy. Blizzard reported this source of role conflict in *The Christian Century* (see footnote 1); as Carroll and Wallace report in their introduction to a special issue honoring Blizzard (*Review of Religious Research*, December, 1981), Blizzard noted that this piece "is probably the most significant article that I have written, judging by the extent to which it has been reprinted and debated in counter-articles." Clergy role conflict has come to be identified with conflicting time and norma-

[2]Blizzard originally had 14 integrative roles—13 plus the general practitioner. In this book he deletes the " 'lay' minister" which he described in his article in *Religious Education*. This role was anticlerical: "The minister . . . wants to 'be just like everyone else.' " He reported that one in twenty-five had this role. I would speculate that Blizzard concluded that this orientation was a reflection of role conflict involving the traditional-personal versus the contemporary-personal spheres (see chapter 8). He probably viewed it as constituting conflict and not a role per se. With more "nonstipendiary clergy" (secularly employed)—see Bonn and Doyle (1974)—this type of conflict might be more in evidence. Are those engaged in "tentmaking ministries" subject to identity problems because they are not gainfully employed as clergy? Blizzard's study concentrated on the parish ministry; data should now be collected from nonparish ministers as well as those serving pastorates and these should include stipendiary and nonstipendiary clergy.

tive demands (as reported by this piece) rather than as conflicting integrative roles or other bases for role conflict. In my opinion this overemphasized the importance of the practitioner roles.

The sixth and seventh chapters discuss practitioner roles. In Chapter Six the ministers' orderings of practitioner roles—normative (the level of importance she or he assigned each task), satisfaction (personal enjoyment in performing the task), and effectiveness (his or her performance evaluation)—are given. From first to last in terms of average rank on these three evaluations were the roles of preacher, pastor, teacher, priest, administrator, and organizer. Blizzard evaluated the preacher, priest, and teacher practitioner roles as traditional, the pastor role as neotraditional, and the administrator and organizer roles as contemporary. In the administrator role the minister is an executive, or the manager or director of the parish; in the organizer role he or she is involved in numerous organizations in the community and groups within the parish. Of those evaluating the practitioner roles, 64 percent found the preacher role to be most important, 22 percent the pastor role, and the remainder chose other roles. Significantly, only 4 percent chose either the administrator or the organizer role.

The seventh chapter deals with time management. Here we learn that fully half of the minister's day is devoted to the contemporary roles of administrator and organizer, quite in contradiction to the ordering of these roles noted in the previous paragraph. This is the dilemma of the minister that Blizzard reported in *The Christian Century* and which has come to be identified as Blizzard's role conflict within the ministry. The minister's workday has the practitioner roles ordered one way; the clergy's normative and motivational views order the practitioner role quite differently. Furthermore, seminary preparation was inadequate for this more functional aspect of the ministry; there was little training and positive sanctioning for these two contemporary roles.

Blizzard's practitioner roles were not new to him; others employed many of the same terms or noted the activities but used different terminology. Blizzard referred to the work of May (1934) and Hartshorne and Froyd (1945) so that he could compare time allocation in the mid-1950s (his data) with those in earlier time periods. Nauss (1972:148) in comparing Blizzard's and May's findings wrote that "Blizzard's research tended to indicate that there had been little essential change in basic functions over a twenty-year period." Yes, the minister was still doing the same tasks as Nauss states, but, no, time allocation had changed considerably. Appendix C shows the comparative data; clearly, there was a shift by the mid-1950s for the administrator and organizer roles to take considerably more time from the clergy's workday.

Numerous researchers mentioned one or another task that was included in Blizzard's list. For example, in discussing the role of the rabbi in American society, Goldstein (1953) provided one listing—teacher, scholar, educator, preacher, prayer leader, pastor, organizer, administrator, and ambassador of goodwill—"the term *rabbi* is denotative for a many-roled occupation" (p. 32)—and he also noted that "the rabbi usually has a cultural definition of his role, whereas the members of a congregation have their own personal and private notions of what a rabbi ought to do, each one with his own bias and emphasis" (p. 36; also see Blass, 1977). To provide another, but later, example, I cite Wilson's (1959) well-developed study of the role conflict implicit in the Pentecostalist ministry. That role is marginal, being relatively new and lacking distinctive ideological support (p. 504). In this sense Blizzard's work was not that unusual; others had noted or were observing that the clergy and parishioners were not always in agreement with one another about the oughtness of the minister's job.

It is at the more descriptive level where similarities with Blizzard's practitioners are found. The influential Study of Theological Education in the United States and Canada (Niebuhr, 1956) provided a description of what the minister does in contemporary society, and Niebuhr (1956:80) suggested a term for the new mix of ministerial duties in the urban society, which was "pastoral director." This smacks, of course, of Blizzard's organizer and administrator roles. There was also Fichter's (1954:123-37) analysis of the social roles of the Catholic parish priest, including the administrative role, which referred to "the fact that he must be an organizer and manager of the social relations and structures which center in the parish" (p. 129) and the "businessman" role, which involved the raising and administering of funds.

The mid-1950s, then, was a period when the minister's job and training were under scrutiny and Blizzard's forte was applying a social science perspective and methodology for the careful study of the minister's roles. He succeeded where others fell short because not only did he present clear data that showed that normatively the minister wanted one thing but functionally was doing something quite different, hence, "the minister's dilemma," but he further developed the notion of role conflict. I will not summarize the difficulties in how the minister conceived his or her role (in addition to problems in time allocation). They are found chiefly in Chapter Eight. For example, "the believer and the scholar are forced to deal with the less spiritual aspects of the ministry. Or, the specialist in matters of interpersonal and intergroup relations is critical of the pious expectations that are made of the minister."

Before I turn to how subsequent researchers have measured clergy roles, I will briefly note that Blizzard lacked the computer-facilities that we now take for granted. He had no software packages that enabled factor-analysis. His analysis of the data was generally not multivariate. He especially used open-ended questions—his advisory committee insisted on this—and his examination began with a content analysis of the responses. His assigned scores and/or categories were then punched onto McBee cards and these were hand-tabulated. Such processing does not readily permit data reduction in the sense of factor analysis and scale building. Hadden (1965:20) has asked if a more parsimonious set of categories could be derived than was introduced by Blizzard; clearly, Blizzard was limited by his method of tabulation.

Blizzard's work was especially good for exploratory purposes. He turned up a whole host of role conflicts that we should pursue. The kind of role conflict especially experienced by younger pastors is not that experienced by those more seasoned, as noted in his book. Knowing the types of conflicts each experiences, we can develop sufficiently good indices and contextual variables, as well as measures dealing with placement, or career mobility, to develop a more dynamic understanding of the experiences of today's clergy. Furthermore, we have a quite different setting today than we had in the 1950s; the job market is not good for clergy today and one has the impression that churches typically are smaller. There are fewer vacancies and less opportunity to move on to larger churches (see Carroll and Wilson, 1980). Role conflict could be exacerbated in the modern-day setting consisting of older clergy serving smaller churches than their career would suggest.

It is understandable that Blizzard did not compare male and female clergypersons as he described roles held, because the percentage of ministers who were women was not substantial when he collected his data (for data here and a thorough review of literature, see Carroll, Hargrove, and Lummis, 1983). Now that percentage is increasing, and it would be valuable to know whether clergywomen are more likely to choose some roles rather than others and how their choices compare to those of clergymen. Lehman (1980a; also see 1980b, 1981) found that the laity are more likely to prefer a man for some clergy tasks than for others. In general there probably exists more role conflict for clergywomen when they embrace the traditional rather than the contemporary integrative roles. Blizzard's role schema should prove to be valuable in examining conflict experienced by female clergy.

LATER MEASUREMENT OF CLERGY ROLES

Almost all researchers who have utilized Blizzard's concept of clergy role have operationalized it by using the most specific level of practitioner. These are the tasks ministers do, or the means to ends, rather than directly reflecting clergy goals. Such analyses are behavior-centered, then, and they tell us less about the ministers' motivations. We lack studies that operationalize the three levels and that use these measures to predict, for example, orientation to social activism, intentions or desires in regard to changing parishes or leaving the ministry, and feelings of effectiveness. Typically, only one level is used for predicting a particular dependent variable. Bouma (1981:209) writes that "much of the value of Blizzard's model has been lost to ministry studies because most of those studies that have used his model have not paid attention to the relationships between the analytical types of roles (Master, Integrative, and Practitioner) specified by the model." Simply to operationalize Blizzard's roles at the practitioner level is surely to lose the theoretical grasp his model provides.

An ambitious attempt to operationalize clergy roles was undertaken by Webb (1968, 1974; also see Webb and Hultgren, 1973). This was built on the work of Blizzard and Kling (1959). The scales were designed to tap interest in performing activities; Webb writes (1968:10), "for any particular occupation the activities or tasks actually performed define the *occupational role* or role behavior." Webb's Inventory of Religious Activities and Interests focuses on ten role segments—counselor, administrator, teacher, scholar, evangelist, spiritual guide, preacher, reformer, priest and musician. The one labeled "spiritual guide," according to Webb and Hultgren (p. 312), is a master role scale, while the other nine are practitioner role scales. The *list* (but not the questions soliciting the information) more closely resembles Blizzard's integrative roles than it does his practitioner roles. The instrument has not been utilized in the research by others, although I believe it might have utility, especially if one wants to combine the two levels (practitioner and integrative).

Perhaps the most frequently used list of items by which researchers have built indices for clergy roles, sometimes explicitly utilizing Blizzard's list of practitioner roles, is that from Jud, Mills, and Burch (1970:158). There the authors asked how much the minister usually enjoys each of ten particular activities. These items were utilized by Hoge, Dyble, and Polk (1981) and they informed the instruments developed by Glass (1976) and Blanchard (1981). Similar lists have been prepared containing perhaps a dozen or two items that focus on practitioner roles; another example would be Newman's (1971).[3]

The researchers have been successful in operationalizing clergy roles at the practi-

---

[3]Earlier I referred to the mid-1960s study reported by Hadden (1965). He and his associates used 30 items developed by Kling (1959) and they supplemented these items with additional ones suggested by Blizzard's dimensions which were not covered by the Kling items (see Hadden, 1965:20). For another use of these 52 items see Longino and Kitson (1976).

tioner level. My intent is not to question any of these instruments but, rather, to empha-size the specificity of the measurement (practitioner rather than integrative or master roles). Etzioni and Lehman (1967:6-7) discussed the fact that researchers often substi-tute the measurement of means for the measurement of goals because the former are often easier to measure. It is possible that clergy role measures would be better predictors of such dependent variables as the minister's intent to remain in his or her present church or in the ministry itself, if these role measures were at the integrative rather than practitioner level.

CLERGY ROLES AND SOCIAL ACTIVISM:

USE OF INTEGRATIVE AND PRACTITIONER ROLES

The 1960s saw an increase in social activism among the clergy. Researchers asked who among the clergy was active and why. Activists were seen as "more likely than others to accept the legitimacy of a prophetic social witness as a part of a Christian ministry" (Winter, 1977:179; also see Winter, 1970, 1971; and Winter, Mills, and Hen-dricks, 1971). Two well-known studies in this area were by Hadden (1969) and Quinley (1974). The latter notes (p. 167) that "the minister may include in his definition of his professional role areas of expertise that are not recognized by the layman. Active leadership on social and political issues is likely to fall into this category." The Campbell and Pettigrew (1959) study of Little Rock clergy in a time of racial crisis observed that "Blizzard [did] not find a 'community reformer' or 'social critic' role in the ministry." They noted the importance of reference systems[4] in understanding clergy reaction (or lack of action); the minister who was oriented to his parish was less likely to support desegrega-tion.[5]

Blizzard's practitioner roles lacked social activism, and it is to this level of role that Campbell and Pettigrew and others looked when they asked if there was something about clergy role that might lead to or hinder social action. Blizzard noted, for example, that clergy might practice practitioner roles for different purposes; one might preach to convert, another to be prophetic. Blizzard's integrative roles included social actionist or problem solver. Using data from Protestant clergy serving churches located in five ma-jor cities, Nelsen, Yokley, and Madron (1973), first subjected to factor analysis the re-sponses to 56 items designed, with Blizzard's help, to measure Blizzard's integrative roles. Five factors resulted, and these were labeled the traditional role (combining the

---

[4]Hoge, Dyble, and Polk (1981a; also see 1981b) use both clergy roles (measured by the practitioner level) and reference system variables to predict clergy orientation to remaining in the present pastorate and to remaining in the ministry. (Also see Nelsen and Everett, 1976.) The variables used by Hoge et al., measuring vocational com-mitment, also have to do with effectiveness and satisfaction. It should be pointed out that in his book Blizzard gives significant attention to effectiveness and satisfaction. Chapter three introduces this topic and it is then picked up again in the chapters in regard to role: in chapter four (the master role), chapter five (the integrative role), and chapter six (the practitioner roles). On ministerial effectiveness and morale also see the work of Nauss (1972, 1983), Luecke (1973), and Dudley and Cummings (1982).
[5]On organizational variables affecting desegregation, see Wood and Zald (1966) and Wood (1970).

believer-saint, evangelist, and father-shepherd), counseling (interpersonal relations specialist), administrator (parish promoter), community problem solving (social activist), and religious educator. These five roles would have embraced almost 90 percent of Blizzard's respondents (Nelsen et al., 1973:378-9). The results of the factor analysis have been replicated in later studies (Nelsen, 1975; Nelsen and Baxter, 1981; Walsh finds the same factors for Presbyterian clergywomen). Second, the social activism role index was shown to be positively related and the traditional role inversely related to protest orientation. When theological and political views of clergy are controlled, only the activist role is significantly related to activism. This instrument is of interest because it focuses on integrative rather than practitioner roles.

Reilly (1975) focused on the practitioner level and added items on "involvement with groups working for racial justice," community activities, and so forth. Her roles were priest and teacher, prophet, pastor, administrator, organizer, priest-ritual, much like Blizzard's practitioner roles except with the addition of the prophet (activist) role.[6]

Whether one should expect to find activist practitioner tasks or activist interests as goals, with various practitioner tasks related to the goals (the integrative roles listed by Blizzard), cannot be settled at this time. Perhaps new developments in seminary and urban institute education have introduced new concerns and skills (see Winter et al., 1971; Luecke, 1970). Or, perhaps this represents differences in the construction of scales, techniques, and levels of measurement (practitioner versus integrative). In much the same way that Roof (1979:36-7) has analyzed having several dimensions of religion versus having one general dimension, concluding that pragmatic considerations can properly determine the number (and specificity) of measures used. We might conclude that the level of measurement should be decided relative to the dependent variable under analysis and the causal sequence that is hypothesized. Similarly, whether one should use five integrative roles or Blizzard's thirteen should depend upon theoretical considerations.

TIME EXPECTATIONS OF PARISHIONERS

As noted, the finding for which Blizzard is especially known involves time allocation—that the minister wants to spend his or her time one way but the position functionally demands a different ordering, namely, that the minister spend a higher percentage of time on administering and organizing practitioner activities than he or she desires. This finding was also reported by Coates and Kistler (1965) in a study of metropolitan clergy. (For a review of ministry studies see Schreuder, 1970; also see the three volumes of *Ministry Studies* edited by Ted Mills and published from 1967 to 1970).

Glock and Roos (1961) secured Lutheran parishioner data on perceptions and attitudes toward clergy time allocation. First, parishioners viewed clergy as spending the greatest amount of their time on sermon preparation, followed, in order, by work for the church at large, attending church meetings, office work, giving people advice, calling on nonmembers, calling on members, and his or her own recreation. They were most likely to approve of what the minister was doing if he or she was "perceived as devoting

---

[6]On the roles of Catholic clergy, besides Fichter (cited earlier) see Kelly (1971) and, more recently, on staying in or leaving the priesthood see, Schoenherr and Greeley (1974).

considerable time to visiting members and nonmembers, as not spending much time on office work, and as striking a reasonable balance in the amount of time spent in sermon preparation, work for the church at large, attending church meetings, and giving people advice" (p. 173). Glock and Roos concluded (p. 175) that ministers and laity "are not far apart in their preferences" and that "it is the preaching and pastoral functions which are the most traditional to the church and it is here that primary commitment—both ministerial and lay—appears to lie." Blizzard presents the rank orders and comes to a similar conclusion. Recent data from Indianapolis (Wood, 1981:35-7) indicated that "members and ministers agree on the basic responsibilities of the minister."

With the exception of the data from Glock and Roos and Wood we lack studies of the interpretation by lay people of clergy roles and time allocation. We have statements from researchers, who generally lack empirical data on the subject, about the changing roles of clergy in American society. I turn to these after I very briefly discuss changes in religious views and behaviors in the 25 years following Blizzard's research.

THE CLERGY ROLE AND CONTEMPORARY SOCIETY

The 1960s and 1970s saw considerable change in religious and other beliefs and attitudinal outlook on the part of Americans, especially youths (see Yankelovich, 1974; Hastings and Hoge, 1981; and for an overview see Riche, 1982). Roof (1982:177) summarizes the impact of the pursuit of personal fulfillment as a new major goal as undermining institutional religious loyalty. Part of the change in goals was "a more basic shift in the locus of moral authority, away from traditional sources to more personal, relativistic considerations" (p. 176; also see Carroll, Johnson, and Marty, 1979; Hoge and Roozen, 1979). The change in the 1960s and 1970s has had repercussions for the clergy—the trend toward specialization (with the question of professionalization) continues, for example.

Writing in 1963, Gustafson claimed (p. 733) that American ministers no longer know what their function is. There are different interpretations of causality by psychology, sociology, mental health professions, and so forth, as well as from the traditional religious perspective, and so "the dilemma of the modern clergyman is that he represents a historical tradition which in many respects is dissonant with contemporary knowledge and with the principles of practical life in the age of technology. He is no longer clear about his authority." (See Wuthnow [1976] for his elaboration of the basic meaning systems predominating in America at this time.)

Gustafson linked religious voluntarism with the expansion of the functions undertaken in the ministry: "The praise of God for his goodness and power does not legitimate a clergyman in the United States. He is expected to be engaged in practical activities that affect the lives of the people in his community or congregation" (p. 732). Gustafson noted that the Catholic priest engaged in less adaptation of his roles than Jewish or Protestant clergy (also see Fichter, 1965:202). Goldner, Ference, and Ritti (1973:122) in commenting on the multiple roles of the priest, from providing the sacraments to helping the poor and providing personal counsel, observe that secularization has included the professionalization of society and the deprofessionalization of the priest. These three authors basically note, then, that the priest is now in a competitive situation, or "the priesthood is challenged both in terms of its proper professional role and of the creation of opportunities to exercise that role" (p. 123). More recently, Sweetser (1983:124-48) gives examples of the growing lay participation in Catholic parish activities, with many of the tasks formerly done by priests now done by the laity. Apparently, then, the Protestant, Jewish, and Catholic clergy are not that different from one another in today's American society.

Harris (1977:45) has described the growing sense of powerlessness clergy come to feel as they realize that their "central place in society" has disappeared. He writes that "the psychological state created by this chain of events is one of increasing non-essentiality. For many clergy it is accompanied by feelings of self-doubt . . . depression, inadequacy, and helplessness which may surface as questions [are raised] about the worthwhileness of the parish ministry or the usefulness of the pastor's work." Even more recently Schuller (1980) has summed up questions about the minister's effectiveness and relevance, with the leaving of clergy for other professional fields, by speaking of the minister as the "wounded healer." According to Goldner et al. (1973:131) the changes that have occurred relative to what the minister does or can do have brought about an increased interpersonalism for the priest: "the main criteria by which the priest is . . . judged, by younger parishioners and fellow priests, are his personal warmth and his ability to create and maintain this Christian Community."[7] (On the interpersonalism within the seminary setting, as a goal as well as a means, see Kleinman [1981], although her work might well not apply to most seminaries. For a perspective of types of seminaries see Carroll, 1971, and Blanchard, 1981.)

From the Readiness for Ministry study it was determined that four of the five top characteristics which people are seeking in their ministers involve the clergy's commitment and faith and are personal qualities. These five are service without regard for acclaim, personal integrity, generosity and setting an example that can be respected, acknowledging limitations and mistakes (recognizing the need for continued growth and learning) and leadership abilities in community building (Schuller, 1980:19). Today's clergyperson is judged not just by what she or he does or does not do but also by what type of person he or she is. Surely this reflects potential role conflict between occupational and personal spheres (see Blizzard's role conflict model, chart 1 in chapter 8).

How does the clergyperson view himself or herself? Glasse (1968:22-3) has written that most people when answering the question "Who am I?" refer to their occupation, and he claimed that the professional clergyperson identifies himself or herself in terms of seminary attended, denominational affiliation, and as a full-time clergyperson. Mills (1969:18) described the "total status of the minister, in which every aspect of his life is expected to serve an exemplary function," and he noted that personal and occupational spheres of life are mixed. In industrial America the private and the occupational worlds are separate, but not for the clergy.

But considerable change occurred over the past quarter-century as people have come

---

[7]This is a far cry from the minister viewed as God's emissary, dispensing the sacraments or preaching for conversion. Fallding (1978:152) claims that the ministry has experienced considerable change since society has industrialized. Revivalism continues in memory for some denominations, but charisma has been routinized and an elaborated ministry has resulted, being characterized, in fact, by the problems in time allocation described by Blizzard and others. This is not to say that some ministers do not rely on authority "from on high" to validate what they do, that is, to reduce stress and role conflict (see Ingram, 1980, 1981 on pastoral power). Where does authority come from if it is not from an understanding clergy and laity alike have about the minister's call or ordination? Is it how the minister does his or her job and in what mode—with warmth? Fukuyama (1972:130) claimed that "it is the denomination rather than the profession which legitimates the minister's occupational status." Ultimately that would be correct as there would exist differences in expectation about clergy roles and about how well trained the pastor is for a specific task.

11

to be less judgmental and as morals have become more private. The self as anchored in institution is giving away to impulse as the locus of self, as one noted scholar has phrased it (Turner, 1976). Institutional religion, as we noted earlier, has lost some of the loyalty it once commanded; especially, younger Americans are less likely to belong to and participate in churches than they were in the 1950s. Younger Americans place considerable emphasis upon privacy (Yankelovich, 1974:57), and participation in public church life can seem counter to this desire. Rather than speculating that clergy are freer than ever before to maximize their own selves, I would speculate that their parishioners are somewhat more willing to admit that ministers "are people too" and should have personal lives while at the same time they continue to some extent to tag onto minsiters expectations they have for ideal people or social relations. (On viewing the pastor as a representative of God see DeLuca, 1980:238; Switzer, 1975:56-58; also see Glasse, 1968:80). Those who are antagonistic to churches are probably as willing as ever to stereotype the clergy. Infrequent attenders give poorer "grades" to clergy than regular attenders; the young give poorer grades, as do those with higher levels of education (Gallup, 1982:82-83). Whether clergy feel freer to be themselves in spite of those with whom they interact or whether they are encouraged to do so, still, we see more news today about clergy engaging in what would once have been considered deviant behaviors by parishioners (many still hold these to be deviant), for example, divorce, adultery, and homosexuality (see news stories by Stout, 1982; Fishburn, 1982; and Trillin, 1982). At the worst, the "mental health" of clergy was discussed two decades ago.

ROLES AS INTERACTIVE

As I noted earlier, clergy roles are not simply tasks to be done, a list representing agreement by parishioners and ministers, with the latter socialized partly by their seminary experience (which brings acquiescence for carrying out these activities). Rather, a role is bound to interaction—it simplifies interaction, it results from interaction, and it facilitates interaction. If there is a criticism to be made of the Blizzard study it is that he lacked parishioner data on expectations regarding roles (see Mitchell, 1967:45). Blizzard does utilize the Glock and Roos data, summarized earlier. Blizzard's sample consisted of clergy; parishioners were not sampled. A broader study, which Blizzard was not commissioned to do, if done today should include both clergy and community residents. I have discussed this omission in Blizzard's design as implicitly suggesting another large research agenda that someone should adopt: the changing role expectations on the part of parishioners and community members.

We need to know more about the interaction between clergy and parishioners. Turner (1978:7) writes that "people are most likely to see the role as the person when they have no opportunity to see the actor in alternative or contradictory roles." Similarly, "the broader the setting in which a role is lodged, the greater the tendency for members of the community to conceive the person as revealed by the role" (p. 9). And, "the more a role exemplifies the goals and nature of the group or organization in which it is lodged, the greater the tendency for community members to conceive the person as revealed by the role" (p. 10). From these and other propositions, I believe it is fairly easy to make the case that the person who is employed as a minister is target for being perceived (stereotyped) as such—as role-centered or defined. This would especially occur in the smaller community. To what degree has such a contemporary role as counselor broken this mold? The broader contemporary versus traditional spheres—that framework within which a minister attempts to work and define himself or herself—has relevance for role conflict, dependent somewhat on the goodness of fit between minister and parish/community (the outlook the parishioners hold). We have just addressed the perception by others of ministers—the degree to which they see person and minister role as one. What about the minister himself or herself? Turner suggests (p. 15) that "the greater the unresolved role strain, the greater the tendency to merge the role with the person." Would it be true that the greater the difficulty in aligning tasks normatively with what one does, the more totally one might define oneself as a minister? That would constitute a costly risk for those entering the ministry.

PROFESSIONALIZATION AND DEPROFESSIONALIZATION

I turn now to a final topic, which is the meaning of "profession" and how the ministry with its various tasks measures up to this concept. The Blizzard findings—that ministers experience role conflict and that there are numerous role orientations and expectations—have been taken to mean that the minister must do many things to validate the occupation. We have already introduced this thesis—that voluntarism and the professionalization of the society had led to the development of more than one or two roles in the ministry. This had led to further loss of authority as clergy vie with other professionals working in the same spheres, especially mental health workers and social workers (on the strain felt by clergy as they interact with social workers, see Cumming and Harrington, 1963; also see Bentz, 1972). This, then, involves a secularization process (Goldner et al., 1973:127) whereby the lines between clergy and parishioners become blurred and where the former come into competition with the latter.

Gannon (1971:68) described the ministry as an occupational conglomerate. The clergyperson "is frustrated by the dilemma of too many associated roles for which he has neither enough skill nor time to perform adequately" (p. 69). Jarvis (1976:355-6) quoted Dunstan as suggesting that the ministry is a learned profession based upon theological excellence. The characteristics of a profession, which we will not list for lack of space (see Gannon, 1971; Hughes, 1963; Barber, 1963; Becker, 1970:87-103), include a knowledge base. As soon as we consider a multifaceted ministry we can ask how seminaries prepare students for the various roles these future clergy will perform. An examination of a seminary curriculum indicates the rather thorough base for Blizzard's scholar role (and also for the preacher role). As Blizzard and others have commented, seminary education lacks attention to organizing and administrative skills. Counseling courses are available in seminary, but extensive clinical experience is not available at the basic professional degree level. The argument can be made that the ministry is in the process of deprofessionalizing as the roles that are exhibited in the parish setting are those for which little education is given in seminary (the most extensive argument along this line is developed by Jarvis, 1975, 1976). The seeking of training in counseling by clergy can be interpreted as their trying to regain a level of respect and authority, specifically that level now held by clinical psychology (see Bouma, 1968, 1981). But the scholar role, for which many seminaries especially train clergy, is held by one out of seventy-five, according to Blizzard's data on integrative roles. Of course, some of the scholarly skills are part of related roles or a minister can hold a secondary integrative role as well as a primary one. My point is that the scholarly training a minister receives is not the basis for most of what he or she does in the ministry.

CONCLUSION

It has been my intent in this introduction to relate Blizzard's work to the 1950s and what followed. In doing so I have referred to other role conflict studies that were being done about the same time or later, and I have observed that Blizzard's study led to questions about the professional status of the ministry. Clearly, new data should now be collected, in part drawing on Blizzard's questionnaire. Do the same integrative roles predominate now? Are the time allocations the same or has the trend toward organization and administration continued? (How many clergy have their own personal computers, or are dreaming about them, as they organize their parish records?) I have referred to the other research agenda that needs to be undertaken—the study of lay orientation toward ministers. The clergy roles result from interaction with parishioners and both clergy and laity need to be studied, that is, roles and role conflicts emerge as clergy and laity interact and this interaction, itself, and its products should be studied. The requirements for the ministry need to inform theological education; to what degree do seminaries teach organization and administrative skills and how do they justify this use of time? Are there new roles that have emerged and are these causing conflict? A vast agenda remains in front of us. Samuel Blizzard's *The Protestant Parish Minister* provides an invaluable schema as we pursue this agenda.

Hart M. Nelsen

REFERENCES

Barber, Bernard
    1963   "Some problems in the sociology of the professions." Daedalus 92 (Fall):669-88.
Becker, Howard S.
    1970 ·   Sociological Work. Chicago: Aldine.
Bentz, W. Kenneth
    1972   "The influence of the community on the mental health role of ministers." Review of Religious Research 14 (Fall):37-40.
Blanchard, Dallas A.
    1981   "Seminary effects on professional role orientation." Review of Religious Research 22 (June):346-61.
Blass, Jerome H.
    1977   "Role preferences among Jewish seminarians." Sociological Analysis 38 (Spring):59-64.
Blizzard, Harriet (compiler)
    1981   "The writings of Samuel Wilson Blizzard." Review of Religious Research 23 (December):214-8.
Bonn, Robert L., and Ruth T. Doyle
    1974   "Secularly employed clergyman: a study in occupational role recomposition." Journal for the Scientific Study of Religion 13 (September):325-43.
Bouma, Gary D.
    1968   "Development and change in occupations: a model and an analysis." Cornell Journal of Social Relations 3:72-84.
    1981   "Samuel Blizzard: sociologist, theological educator, and border broker: an appreciative evaluation." Review of Religious Research 23 (December):205-13.

Campbell, Ernest Q., and Thomas F. Pettigrew
1959   "Racial and moral crisis: the role of Little Rock ministers." American Journal of Sociology 64 (March):509-16.

Carroll, Jackson W.
1971   "Structural effects of professional schools on professional socialization: the case of Protestant clergymen." Social Forces 50 (September):61-74.

Carroll, Jackson W., and Adair T. Lummis
1983   Women of the Cloth. San Francisco: Harper & Row.

Carroll, Jackson W., Douglas W. Johnson, and Martin E. Marty
1979   Religion in America: 1950 to the present. New York: Harper & Row.

Carroll, Jackson W., and Robert Wilson
1980   Too Many Pastors? New York: Pilgrim Press.

Coates, Charles H., and Robert C. Kistler
1965   "Role dilemmas of Protestant clergmen in a metropolitan community." Review of Religious Research 6 (Spring):147-52.

Converse, Philip E.
1964   "The nature of belief systems in mass publics." Pp. 206-62 in David Apter (ed.), Ideology and Discontent. New York: Free Press.

Cumming, Elaine, and Charles Harrington
1963   "Clergyman as counselor." American Journal of Sociology 69 (November):234-43.

DeLuca, Joel R.
1980   " 'The holy crossfire': a job diagnosis of a pastor's position." Pastoral Psychology 28 (Summer):233-42.

Dudley, Robert L., and Des Cummings, Jr.
1982   "Factors related to pastoral morale in the Seventh-Day Adventist Church." Review of Religious Research 24 (December):127-37.

Etzioni, Amitai, and Edward W. Lehman
1967   "Some dangers in 'valid' social measurement." The Annals of the American Academy of Political and Social Science 373 (September):1-15.

Fallding, Harold
1978   "Mainline Protestantism in Canada and the United States of America: an overview." Canadian Journal of Sociology 3:141-60.

Fichter, Joseph H.
1954   Social Relations in the Urban Parish. Chicago: University of Chicago Press.
1965   Priest and People. New York: Sheed and Ward.

Fishburn, Janet F.
1982   "Male clergy adultery as vocational confusion." Christian Century, September 15-22, pp. 922-5.

Fukuyama, Yoshio
1972   The ministry in transition. University Park, Pa.: The Pennsylvania State University Press.

Gallup Organization
1982   Religion in America. Princeton: Princeton Religion Research Center.

Gannon, Thomas M.
1971   "Priest/minister: profession or non-profession?" Review of Religious Research 12 (Winter):66-79.

Glass, C. Conrad, Jr.
1976   "Ministerial job satisfaction scale." Review of Religious Research 17 (Winter):153-7.

Glasse, James D.
1968   Profession: Minister. Nashville, Tn.: Abingdon.

Glock, Charles Y., and Philip Roos
1961   "Parishioners' views of how ministers spend their time." Review of Religious Research 2 (Spring):170-5.

Goldner, Fred H., Thomas P. Ference, and R. Richard Ritti
1973   "Priests and laity: a profession in transition." Pp. 119-37 in Paul Halmos (ed.), Professionalization and Social Change. The Sociological Review monograph 20.

Goldstein, Sidney I.
1953   "The roles of an American rabbi." Sociology and Social Research 38 (Sept.-Oct.):32-7.

Gustafson, James M.
1963   "The clergy in the United States." Daedalus 92 (Fall):724-44.

Hadden, Jeffrey K.
1965   "A study of the Protestant ministry of America." Journal for the Scientific Study of Religion 5 (Fall):10-23.
1969   The Gathering Storm in the Churches. Garden City, N.Y.: Doubleday.

15

Harris, John C.
1977   Stress, Power and Ministry. Washington, D.C.: Alban Institute.

Hartshorne, Hugh, and Milton C. Froyd
1945   Theological Education in the Northern Baptist Convention. Board of Education of the Northern Baptist Convention.

Hastings, Philip K., and Dean R. Hoge
1981   "Religious trends among college students, 1948-79." Social Forces 60 (December):517-31

Hoge, Dean R., John E. Dyble, and David T. Polk
1981a   "Influence of role preference and role clarity on vocational commitment of Protestant minsiters." Sociological Analysis 42 (Spring):1-16.

1981b   "Organizational and situational influences on vocational commitment of Protestant ministers." Review of Religious Research 23 (December):133-49.

Hoge, Dean R., and David A. Roozen (eds.)
1979   Understanding Church Growth and Decline: 1950-1978. New York: Pilgrim Press.

Hughes, Everett C.
1963   "Professions." Daedalus 92 (Fall):655-68.

Ingram, Larry C.
1980   "Notes on pastoral power in the congregational tradition." Journal for the Scientific Study of Religion 19 (March):40-48.

1981   "Leadership, democracy, and religion: role ambiguity among pastors in Southern Baptist churches." Journal for the Scientific Study of Religion 20 (June):119-29.

Jarvis, Peter
1975   "The parish ministry as a semi-profession." The Sociological Review 23 (November):911-22.
1976   "A profession in process: a theoretical model for the ministry." The Sociological Review 24 (May):351-64.

Jud, Gerald J., Edgar W. Mills, Jr., and Genevieve Walters Burch
1970   Ex-Pastors. Philadelphia: Pilgrim Press.

Kelly, Henry E.
1971   "Role satisfaction of the Catholic priest." Social Forces 50 (September):75-84.

Kleinman, Sherryl
1981   "Making professionals into 'persons.' " Sociology of Work and Occupations 8 (February):61-87.

Kling, F. R.
1959   "Roles of parish ministers." Princeton, N.J.: Educational Testing Service, 1-5.

Lehman, Edward C., Jr.
1980a   "Patterns of lay resistance to women in ministry." Sociological Analysis 41 (Winter:317-38.
1980b   "Placement of men and women in the ministry." Review of Religious Research 22 (September):18-40.
1981   "Organizational resistance to women in ministry." Sociological Analysis 42 (Summer):101-18.

Longino, Charles F., Jr., and Gay C. Kitson
1976   "Parish clergy and the aged: examining stereotypes." Journal of Gerontology 31 (3):340-45.

Luecke, David S.
1973   "The professional as organizational leader." Administrative Science Quarterly 18 (March):86-94.

Luecke, Richard Henry
1970   "Protestant clergy: new forms of ministry, new forms of training." The Annals of the American Academy of Political and Social Science 387 (January):86-95.

Marty, Martin E.
1982   "Religion in America since mid-century." Daedalus 111 (Winter):149-63.

May, Mark A.
1934   "The profession of the ministry: its status and problems." The Education of American Ministers, Vol. IV (Appendix B to Vol. II):180-188. New York: Institute of Social and Religious Research.

Mills, Edgar W.
1969   "Career change in the Protestant ministry." Ministry Studies 3 (May):5-21.

Mitchell, Robert E.
1967   "Implications for comparative analysis arising from alternative conceptions of roles: an example from the ministry." Review of Religious Research 9 (Fall):44-7.

Nauss, Allen
1972   "Problems in measuring ministerial effectiveness." Journal for the Scientific Study of Religion 11 (June):141-51.

1983   "Seven profiles of effective ministers." Review of Religious Research 24 (June):334-46.

Nelsen, Hart M.
1975   "Why do pastors preach on social issues?" Theology Today 32 (April):56-73.

Nelsen, Hart M., and Sandra Baxter
1981   "Ministers speak on Watergate: effects of clergy role during political crisis." Review of Religious Research 23 (December):150-66.

Nelsen, Hart M., and Robert F. Everett
1976   "Impact of church size on clergy role and career." Review of Religious Research 18 (Fall):62-73.

Nelsen, Hart M., Raytha L. Yokley, and Thomas W. Madron
1973   "Ministerial roles and social actionist stance: Protestant clergy and protest in the sixties." American Sociological Review 38 (June):375-86.

Newman, William M.
1971   "Role conflict in the ministry and the role of the seminary: a pilot study." Sociological Analysis 32 (Winter):238-48.

Niebuhr, H. Richard
1956   The Purpose of the Church and Its Ministry. New York: Harper & Brothers.

Quinley, Harold E.
1974   The Prophetic Clergy: Social Activism among Protestant Ministers. New York. John Wiley & Sons.

Reilly, Mary Ellen
1975   "Perceptions of the priest role." Sociological Analysis 36 (Winter):347-56.

Riche, Martha Farnsworth
1982   "The fall and rise of religion." American Demographics 4 (May):15-19, 47.

Roof, Wade Clark
1979   "Concepts and indicators of religious commitment: a critical review." Pp. 17-45 in Robert Wuthnow (ed.), The Religious Dimension. New York: Academic Press.

1982   "America's voluntary establishment: mainline religion in transition." Daedalus 111 (Winter):165-84.

Schoenherr, Richard A., and Andrew M. Greeley
1974   "Role commitment processes and the American Catholic priesthood." American Sociological Review 39 (June):407-26.

Schreuder, Osmund
1970   "A review of ministry studies." Social Compass 17 (4):579-88.

Schuller, David S.
1980a   "Basic issues in defining ministry." Pp. 3-11 in David S. Schuller, Merton P. Strommen, and Milo L. Brekke (eds.), Ministry in America. New York: Harper & Row.

1980b   "Identifying the criteria for ministry." Pp. 12-22 in David S. Schuller, Merton P. Strommen, and Milo L. Brekke (eds.), Ministry in America. New York: Harper & Row.

Stout, Robert J.
1982   "Clergy divorce spills into the aisle." Christianity Today. February 5, pp. 20-21.

Stryker, Sheldon, and Avi Gottlieb
1981   "Attribution theory and symbolic interactionism: a comparison." Pp. 425-58 in John H. Harvey, William Ickes, and Robert F. Kidd (eds.), New Directions in Attribution Research, Vol. 3. Hillsdale, N.J.: Lawrence Erlbaum Associates, Publishers.

Sweetser, Thomas
1983   Successful Parishes. Minneapolis, Mn.: Winston Press.

Switzer, David K.
1975   "The minister as pastor and person." Pastoral Psychology 24 (Fall):52-64.

Trillin, Calvin
1982   "U.S. Journal: Boulder, Colo.—let me find a place." The New Yorker, January 25, pp. 80-88.

Turner, Ralph H.
1962   "Role-taking: process versus conformity." Pp. 20-40 in Arnold M. Rose (ed.), Human Behavior and Social Processes. Boston: Houghton Mifflin.

1976   "The real self: from institution to impulse." American Journal of Sociology 81 (March):989-1016.

1978   "The role and the person." American Journal of Sociology 84 (July):1-23.

Walsh, Mary Paula
1984   Role Conflicts among Women in Ministry. Ph.D. dissertation. Washington, D.C.: The Catholic University of America, Sociology Department.

Webb, Sam C.
1968   The Inventory of Religious Activities and Interests. Princeton: Educational Testing Service.

1974   "Transferability of a role-oriented interest inventory from men to women in church-related occupations." Journal of Vocational Behavior 5:347-56.

Webb, Sam C., and Dayton D. Hultgren
1973   "Differentiation of clergy subgroups on the basis of vocational interests." Journal for the Scientific Study of Religion 12 (September):311-24.

Wilson, Bryan R.
    1959   "The Pentecostalist minister: role conflicts and status contradictions." American Journal of Sociology 64 (March):494-504.

Winter, J. Alan
    1970   "The attitudes of societally-oriented and parish-oriented clergy: an empirical comparison." Journal for the Scientific Study of Religion 9 (Winter):59-66.

    1971   "Pastor or prophet? Clergy reaction to hypothetical parish unrest over a clergyman's social activism." Social Compass 18 (2):293-302.

    1977   Continuities in the Sociology of Religion: Creed, Congregation, and Community. New York: Harper & . Row.

Winter, J. Alan, Edgar W. Mills, Jr., and Polly Hendricks
    1971   Clergy in Action Training: A Research Report. New York: IDOC-North American.

Wood, James R.
    1970   "Authority and controversial policy: the churches and civil rights." American Sociological Review 35 (December):1057-69.

    1981   Leadership in voluntary organizations. New Brunswick, NJ: Rutgers University Press.

Wood, James R., and Mayer N. Zald
    1966   "Aspects of racial integration in the Methodist Church: sources of resistance to organizational policy." Social Forces 45 (December):255-65.

Wuthnow, Robert
    1976   The Consciousness Reformation. Berkeley, Ca.: University of California Press.

Yankelovich, Daniel
    1974   The New Morality. New York: McGraw-Hill.

I
RESEARCH ON AN
OCCUPATIONAL GROUP

This is a book about the Protestant parish minister. Its primary purpose is to examine the roles that the minister performs in the church, in the community and in the nation. It is hoped that, if they are able to see themselves in a mirror, ministers will be able to fulfill their roles more effectively.

The secondary purpose of this report is to assist theological educators in understanding the role and situation of the Protestant parish minister in contemporary American society; and it is suggested that this type of material and analysis will lead to an examination of the implications that the minister's situation has for theological education.

There are few observant religious leaders who are not aware that the structure and functioning of American society has changed during the current century. There are many symbols of the complexity of society and the changes that have taken place. One of these is that the metropolitan community has replaced the rural community as a model place to live. Suburban and satellite communities on the periphery of cities have developed rapidly, and the central city has deteriorated. The airplane and the automobile are symbolic of our transportation system. Organizationally, bigness has touched industry, education, government, and religion. The one-room school, the little brown church, the town meeting, the small shop, and the owner-operated business have been replaced by the symbols of a corporate society—supermarkets, collective bargaining, corporation mergers, mass education, television, and multi-clergy churches.

The social and cultural change in present day American society calls for a redefinition on the part of the Protestant clergy of their function and roles. The rapidity with which change is progressing places a premium on personal adaptability and social understanding on the part of the ministers. This situation contributes to the ambiguities of the parish ministers' roles. A relatively serene rural social scene has increasingly been displaced by a fluid but forceful type of mass-communication-dominated society. The highly mobile and complex nature of American society has yielded symptomatic effects in personality structure and in the lack of clarity and homogeneity of values. The problem personality and formalized school relations in our society have considerably changed the situation in which the parish minister functions.

This newer American society has resulted in a change in the expectations that people have of the clergyman. In the past the Protestant parish minister in America has tended to perform his functions as a general practitioner in a small church. Now it would appear that increasingly he is expected to have the skills of a specialist in many areas. Parishioners who are confronted by a complex and chaotic world want to be counseled rather than visited socially by the minister. They look for a perceptive prophet who is able to make sense out of the crises of the current week rather than a preacher that merely assures them that all is well with the world. They seek the help of a priest who uses liturgy, rites, and sacraments in a way that is meaningfully related to the issues of life rather than using them to promote a letter-perfect administration of the church ordinances. They want a professional organizer rather than an amateur promoter. They expect him to be an efficient executive of the business affairs of the parish rather than a *laissez faire* manager.

This was a propitious time to be studying the role of the minister. Concurrent developments which underline this fact are related to significant advances that have been made in two areas of intellectual pursuit—theology and behavioral science.

Theological thinking is experiencing a continual reformation. In the last half century or more the theological world has accommodated itself to the challenge of new thought forms and methods in the humanities and in the natural sciences. The scientific study of literary forms has required a new examination of the Bible. This challenge centered in higher criticism. The challenges of new areas of knowledge in the natural sciences centered in the religion and science conflict. Differing theological answers to new scientific findings about the natural world were devised by the fundamentalist and the modernist, more recently by the neo-orthodox theologian who has attempted to take science and religion seriously so that the integrity of each area of knowledge is respected. The resulting changes in theological thinking would appear to have implications for defining the clergyman's role. Daniel Jenkins, for example, writing about the revived interest in Protestant theology, and referring to the work of Karl Barth, has expressed the hope that Protestantism may recover a new theological understanding of the minister. (Jenkins, 1947:12)

At the same time there is a new interest in the behavioral sciences. Even the indifferent observer of the academic scene is aware that there have been significant developments in psychology, sociology, social psychology, cultural anthropology, economics, and political science during the last several decades. In commenting on these changes, Laswell observes that "no one seriously doubts that the level of technical excellence of American social science rose between World War I and World War II despite the Depression." (Lerner and Laswell, 1951:7) He suggests that "the battle for method is won" so that the emphasis may now be placed on significant problems.

The findings of the behavioral scientist as a result of these developments and the resulting clarifications in our understanding of the social world have implications for the minister as he performs his function in community life. This book is written out of the conviction that developments in social science theory, especially role theory and the theory about the professions, provide a perspective for interpreting the ministry on the basis of both theological and non-theological factors. For the ministry, the meaning of knowledge derived by the methodologies of the social and behavioral sciences has yet to be evaluated. It is this fact that gives relevance to the objectives and goals of this project.

While this book is a behavioral science interpretation of the ministry, it is seen as complementary to a theological interpretation. The theological reformation has given us a new understanding of the ministry from an ideological point of view. The new insights gained from the behavioral sciences give a fuller understanding of the work of the minister and of the environment in which his work is performed. The full contribution of both of these revivals would seem to require their integration. To fully exploit the values of both of these intellectual developments is a neat but not impossible task. The theologian may conceive of the church as a redemptive community, whereas the behavioral scientist may view it as an operating social system.

To explore this possible integration, a research project was designed to relate social science theory to the practice of the ministry as a basic and integral part of theological education. It was initiated by the Russell Sage Foundation; and in keeping with Foundation policy it was a collaborative enterprise among several groups of persons and organizations which exercised national leadership in professional education. The major collaborator, in addition to the Foundation, was Union Theological Seminary, New York. To conduct this research, the author (as a sociologist) was appointed to the Union Theological Seminary faculty as a visiting professor.*

The Foundation had become convinced that "added emphasis should be given to the increasing body of knowledge of human behavior to the end that practitioners in human affairs may have the most reliable basis possible for their work." "Both social science and social practice have made great advances in recent decades; but as they have progressed, there has been costly failure by each to maintain sufficiently close liaison with the other. Research needs to be kept realistic by contact with the practitioners who use its results, and practitioners need to keep informed about the frontiers of research knowledge bearing on their techniques." (Russell Sage Foundation, 1947-48)

To discover the function of the social sciences in theological education two basic, and differing, approaches were proposed. One approach would start with the curriculum as it was and work toward the training needs of the parish minister; another would start with the needs of the minister in the parish and work back to the curriculum.

The function of social and behavior science knowledge in relation to the work of the minister is more widely recognized by the practitioner in the parish than it is by the educator in the seminary. The recognition of this knowledge in the parish tends to be problem-oriented. The minister in his daily practice seeks to resolve his problems in part from resources gained in his professional training and in part from new resources which he gains from his own reading and from colleagues in other professions. The interest of the clergy in movements focused on counseling, the rural community, the inner city, and the church in public affairs, reflects their desire to resolve problems. Many of these problems require behavioral science knowledge, understandings and insights in order to be resolved. The professors in professional schools become aware of social science resources through these movements among the clergy and the problem concerns they express; and they also become aware of social science resources through their reading in the field and in interaction with colleagues in these disciplines on university campuses. Generally, the sources available to the theological educator are oriented to *theoretical* knowledge in the social sciences rather than to problems of the clergy profession.

The subject matter approach would assess the extent to which the social sciences are now a part of the seminary teaching program, and would involve an examination of courses and their descriptions in order to delineate those that use social science knowledge and concepts. In addition, it would involve conferences with professors who were teaching courses that presented social science materials. It is conceivable that in addition to a revision of individual courses and the possible introduction of new courses, a restructuring of certain aspects of the curriculum might be required. It would become an administrative matter rather than a substantive one. Social scientists in some seminaries have been placed in a separate department, and this has resulted in their isolation and a stifling of their integration into the core curriculum of the seminary. In other seminaries the social sciences have been so located in the curriculum as to limit their function to problem-solving and application rather than to permit the building of theoretical foundations.

---

*See Cottrell and Sheldon (1963) and Bloom, et al. (1960) for an analysis of the experience of the Russell Sage Foundation in seeking to develop working relations between the social sciences and other practicing professions, e.g. law, medicine, nursing, education and social work.

There are several features of this approach that would seem to make it appear to be less than promising. In part it is the approach that has been followed over several decades in theological education. The focus has been on the content of the teaching rather than on the purpose of the teaching. There is a tendency in seminaries to view social science either as a new discipline and therefore non-traditional; or as "practical," and therefore not substantive. When the focus is in this direction, attitudes that are unconsciously competitive may be fostered among professors as they conceive the importance attached to the student and his needs. In the Foundation project it was decided that cataloguing and evaluating the present place of social science in the seminary curriculum would provide useful information, but that it would be more productive to do so after the needs of prospective practicing ministers had been analyzed.

The second approach—that of evaluating the needs of the theological student as a prospective practicing clergyman—required that a disciplined analysis be made of the roles of the parish minister. The complexity of the structure of American society and the multiplicity of functions that the parish ministry requires necessitate that the clergy roles be examined in the contemporary situation. It is assumed that analysis of the roles of the minister will reveal the component behavior that each role involves. One may begin assessing the contribution that the social sciences can make by examining questions involving the *intra*-personal relations of the minister. Basic, illustrative questions might concern the minister's own perception of his role, and the manifest and latent conflicts within his own personality with respect to these roles.

The minister, it appears, spends much of his professional time dealing with individuals. Hence knowledge, understanding, and behavioral skills involving *inter*-personal relations, technically informed by psychology, are also pertinent to the work of the minister.

Many of the minister's practitioner roles suggest another contribution that the social sciences may make, namely intra-group and inter-group relations. As conceived here, intra-group relations are concerned with the role of the minister as a member of a group. How does he function in groups so that he respects the structure and dynamics of the group and at the same time works with the group in fulfilling its goals and functions as a unit of the parish? Or how does he function where he may be the presiding officer of a church official board, session, consistory, or vestry?

There are many auxiliary associations in the church that function in relation to the total church. To be specific, in the Presbyterian church there are times when the session and the trustees are at cross purposes because of differing conceptions of their functions and prerogatives. Or in the Methodist churches in rural areas where pastors serve many congregations, conflict sometimes springs up between the Sunday school leaders and the church officers. This kind of interaction also includes inter-group or group-to-group relations in the community and in the denomination. In larger communities ministers and churches are necessarily involved in inter-group relations with social welfare agencies. Through councils of churches there are group-to-group relations with other churches. It is assumed that sociology may have knowledge and understandings of which the parish minister should become aware in order to be more effective in a ministry of redemption and reconciliation in the community.

The church at the local community level, as well as at the state and national level, interacts with political and economic groups. Political science and economics, as specialized behavioral sciences, may inform the clergyman in group structures and dynamics.

A further way in which the social sciences, particularly anthropology, may be used in the training of the clergy is related to the culture of the society in which the church is located and to which it ministers. Church programs in the United States are carried on in the subcultures of the rural, urban, and suburban areas. Some churches minister to those living in the occupational sub-cultures associated with laboring groups, and others minister to white collar workers. Functioning effectively within these sub-cultures, so that the message of the faith is meaningfully related to the values of these sub-cultures, would be achieved through understandings which cultural anthropology offers.

The approach taken in this study is that an analysis of the roles of the minister, using social science theory, would permit an examination of the ways in which the contribution of these sciences to professional education of the clergy could be demonstrated.

Theologically trained Protestant clergymen follow many types of careers. These include being teachers and educators, administrators and executives, chaplains, editors and authors, missionaries, and parish ministers. This project is concerned with only one career type—the clergyman or clergywoman rendering a professional service to local congregations. The parish minister is the most pervasive career type in the ecclesiastical organization. Most seminary resources are devoted to the training of this type of practitioner. Many of those who eventually enter non-parochial careers begin by serving apprenticeships in the parish. We use the nomenclature "parish minister" deliberately. It has an organizational, rather than a geographic connotation, as we conceive it. This permits without prejudice, the analysis of many differing orientations to the ministry; whereas the term "pastoral ministry" tends to represent just one specific orientation.

There are several ways to analyze the role of the minister. Generally these may be classified as the ideological, the descriptive and the functional. Within each of these methods of analysis there is more than one school of opinion. The theologian and the ethicist are frequent articulators of ideological analyses of the minister. Two authors who have made contributions to a theological understanding of the minister are H. Richard Niebuhr (1956) and Daniel T. Jenkins (1947). They and others write from a normative point of view. They are concerned with the "oughtness" of the minister and his work.

The descriptive approach is a methodology for analyzing the minister's role in which the church historian makes a special contribution. Of interest from this perspective is *The Ministry in Historical Perspective* (Niebuhr, 1956). The historians who contributed to this volume have reviewed the varying concepts held about the ministry and have shown the changes that have taken place in these concepts from century to century and from decade to decade. The chronicle of these changes highlight the theological as well as the psychological, sociological, economic, political and cultural factors that have operated in relation to changes in the concept of the ministry. It would appear that consensus about the minister's role is relative to a period in history, and to the culture of the society in which he ministers. In so doing the historian furnishes a description of what the ministry has been in the past. He provides the sociologist with data regarding the social location of the various concepts of the ministry.

The third method of analyzing the minister and his work, the functional method, is the approach taken in this book. The minister is seen as an actor or person interacting within a religious system and in relation to other systems in society. His role is accepted as being essential to the functioning of the religious system in society. Churches differ for a variety of reasons and so do ministers. The functional view attempts to analyze those variables that help explain the varieties of ministers and churches. This is the approach used by the behavioral scientist. It is concerned with what the role of the minister is, rather than what it has been or should be.

A social science analysis of a religious profession requires the adoption of research methods and techniques that may not be a part of the day-to-day academic work of the theological educator or of the parish minister. To keep the theological reader informed about the methodology we employed, and to present it for critical review and evaluation to social science colleagues, we have placed all discussions of research methods in an appendix.* Our central concern is to analyze the role of the Protestant parish minister. Methodology is a necessary means to this end.

Language, or rather the choice of words, is a problem for a researcher seeking to communicate ideas about a profession, especially one that has developed its own highly technical language as is true of theology and of the minister. Technical words may be an efficient and precise means of communication, or they may be a barrier to communication. The author has elected to take a calculated risk. The language of the behavorial sciences is used because of its precision in this type of analysis. It is also the technical language with which the author is most familiar. He also believes that the use of these words may provide a stimulus for a fresh examination of the role of the minister by the theologically oriented individual. Even though this researcher had been trained in a seminary in addition to his graduate training as a social scientist, he learned quickly that technical theological terminology can severely limit and restrict one's opportunities for communication with theological colleagues. While he felt that use of his social science terminology was of decisive importance in contributing his knowledge to theological education, he first had to be able to use the technical language of those whom he served as a consultant. When terms have been used that have theological meanings that coincide with the stated doctrines or theories about religion, it is hoped that they will communicate effectively. They are used to convey meanings that the author believes are part of the clergyman's cognitive apparatus. However, in this research they are constructed inductively on the basis of essay materials received from the clergymen cooperating in the research. They were not deduced from theology or from the stated doctrines of the church. They are functional in the ministry and may be described as the working doctrines of the church.

It will be obvious to the reader that the author writes from a frame of reference oriented to the social and behavioral sciences. Social psychology, sociology and anthropology are the sciences of man that provide the insights about human behavior and culture that are used in the interpretation of the Protestant parish minister in these chapters. At the same time the author considers the various normative views of the ministry to be essential to an understanding of the sub-culture of the minister and to be a part of a theoretical description of the ministry. They constitute one factor that the behavioral scientist includes in an analysis of the work of the minister. The author takes no valuative stance with respect to these views; he has not consciously espoused one, nor consciously rejected another. However, he has tried to include a variety of theological views of the ministry and of the church as expressed by the clergy responses in this analysis.

Research on a specific occupational group, especially one that is concerned with ontological questions such as concern ministers and lawyers, involves the researcher in a sub-culture that has many subtleties. One who has been trained for and has served in the ministry is aware of this sub-culture of the profession. However another factor, objectivity, is involved. I am aware of the tight-rope between subjectivity and objectivity that permits one to be aware of the subtleties of a profession, and yet be free to record with some accuracy one's observations about that profession.

---

*Relevant appendix materials have been placed among the Blizzard papers in Speer Library, Princeton Theological Seminary, Princeton, New Jersey.

Descriptive materials about the minister developed by the historian are of special interest in the development of a theoretical model and the specification of the factors that function in a given situation. However, in dealing with historical material, the behavioral scientist uses concepts for describing data and methods of analyses that differ in some respects from those used by the historian. He uses concepts and methods that are appropriate to an understanding of the *interaction within* a system rather than the *development of* a system.

This is a study of the ministry at one point in time (1953-1957). It is not a study of trends, but is a systematic analysis made over five years. It is possible to draw inferences about trends on the basis of common sense knowledge, but these inferences about trends cannot be validated empirically by data gathered in this project. An historian might show trends by analyzing relevant documentary materials, but no attempt is made to do so here.

Perhaps a major difference in the methods of approach taken by the social scientist, the church historian, and the theologian in a study of the minister and his work is a matter of assumptions or presuppositions. This author took a relative rather than an absolute view of the differing ideological views of the minister within Protestantism. This means that few assumptions have been made about the "oughtness" of the role of the minister. Attention is focused on the *variety* of ideological views, and on how a particular view held by a minister is related to the conduct of his ministry. One view has not been purposefully selected as being more or less desirable than another. From the theological standpoint we would assume that the basic purpose of the church and the basic function of the minister are the same in any age, are universal rather than particularistic, and are derived from the truth revealed by God to the church. We would suggest that the inferences drawn from interpretations of these theological assumptions would vary from time to time and that psychological, sociological, economic, political and cultural factors may contribute to our understanding of this variability. Aside from the general acceptance of the theological assumptions about the mission of the church and the function of the clergy, there would be much variation in opinion about the appropriate means by which the church fulfills its purpose in society. Appropriate and legitimate means may change, as may the performance of the roles by which the minister fulfills his function as a religious leader in the church.

The study of the clergy as a profession has been neglected by both the theologian, who deplores "professionalism," and the sociologist, who thinks the spiritual is not his concern. (Carr-Saunders, 1933:3)

The lack of systematic knowledge about how ministers themselves perceive the role of the minister, and about the expectations that laymen have of ministers, has been a major handicap for the church and general public. It has hindered ministers in being fully effective, parishioners in knowing the full potential of the minister's professional services, theological educators in preparing ministers realistically for the parish, and denominational executives in using clergy manpower resources wisely.

The present research assumes that the clergy are members of a profession that is related to the day-by-day aspects of life. The study is concerned primarily with the role of the minister and his view of his work environment and is not an attempt to analyze his function in the church as a social system.

There are many ways in which the roles of the Protestant parish minister might be observed. The layman in the local church is a fellow participant with the clergyman in the church program. As a participant observer of such interaction, the layman could provide a fruitful source of data. Other potential observers are denominational administrators in the regional and national offices and the theological educator. Finally, the social scientist, as one who is somewhat of an outsider to the system in which the minister functions, is an observer trained in analyzing the interaction that takes place as actors perform their respective roles. Each of these observers would perceive the clergy practitioner from their own vantage point.

Perhaps the term that best describes the role of the researcher-social scientist in this situation is middle-man. He acted as a middle-man in relation to the world of theological education and the social science profession. He was a middle-man in relation to the cooperators in the project, and in the securing of data from the parish ministers. Any technical knowledge and research skill that the social scientist contributed to the enterprise, hinged on the fulfillment of the middle-man role.

In this research the actor being studied, the parish minister, is an observer of his own actions and is a reporter of his own interaction with other actors in the church system. The parish minister, as an informant in research, can make available basic and revealing observations that no outsider can perceive. The data furnished by the clergy are self-images, and have the limitations of any self-portrait together with the advantages of any self-revealing technique. It is limited to the degree that the minister is willing to reveal himself in depth. Related to this limitation is the fact that it is reported from the perspective of the minister and may be a distorted image. It has the advantage of offering insights from within the profession and of being furnished in depth. If the clergy informants are sensitive, frank and open, the advantages would seem to outweigh the disadvantages.

If implications for the function of social science in the seminary were to be drawn from the research, the most meaningful data could be secured from alumni of the institution conducting the study. Therefore the decision was made to study the alumni of Union Theological Seminary, New York. This raised the question of whether these alumni were atypical or were in atypical church situations. To guard against this possibility, four additional seminaries were invited to study their own parish minister alumni: The Christian Theological Seminary, Indianapolis, Indiana; Garrett Biblical Institute, Evanston, Illinois; The Protestant Episcopal Seminary, Alexandria, Virginia; Louisville Presbyterian Theological Seminary, Louisville, Kentucky.

Separate analyses were made of the alumni of each of the five schools and confidential reports were presented to the respective faculties for interpretation and discussion. The preliminary findings included material regarding the minister's role and the environment of his ministry in the church, the community and the society, as well as parish minister alumni evaluations of their own theological education at their respective seminaries. (Blizzard, 1956b)

The project then became a self-examination process for the participating institutions. They were looking at their educational program in the mirror of their own graduates in the parish. A searching look into the mirror can be as rewarding for institutions as for individuals. Self-discovered facts are revealing and make self-evaluation possible, especially when the informants are products of the educational enterprise being examined. As a result of this feedback, Union Theological Seminary informed its alumni and other publics about its own re-examination conference. (Bennett, 1957)

To further broaden the possible applications of the results of the study to Protestant theological education, the National Council of Churches, through the Departments of the Urban Church and the Town and Country Church, was invited to select a representative cross-section of parish clergy. In the past, the respective programs fostered by Departments of Urban Church and Rural Church in Protestant denominations had strongly advocated a unique ministry in areas where cultural variability is evident. In order to test this assumption, ministers from twenty-two denominations were finally chosen to cooperate in the project; and conferences and seminars were the forum for relevant feedback to denominational representatives (Blizzard 1955, and 1956a).

II

THE MINISTER

One may distinguish among many types of clergy careers. Within each religious system there are many sub-systems such as local congregations, regional and national denominational agencies, educational institutions, publishing "companies," missionary agencies, and welfare programs. Religious systems also conduct ministries within or in relation to other systems which they do not control, such as educational institutions, the military, hospitals, and corrective institutions. A clergyman may devote all or a part of his career to any one or more of these religious systems, or to a system that requires a clergyman in its table of organization. Non-parish careers for clergymen include those of missionary, both national and international (Lively, 1958; Schmidt, 1959; Yost, 1959); teachers and professors, presidents and deans in schools, colleges, universities and seminaries; and chaplains with the military, and in prisons, hospitals and educational institutions (Klausner, 1964; Hammond, 1966).

While some clergymen are staff persons in these institutions, others may minister to personnel as non-staff representatives of their denominations. There are many types of specialized administrative positions in denominations and ecumenical agencies such as program executives of boards and agencies, and denominational administrators such as bishop, moderator, president, stated clerk, and district superintendent (Mitchell, 1968; Donovan, 1958; Smith, 1964; Leiffer, 1960). The evangelist, social worker, physician, editor, author, financial specialist, and many other specialized careers are required for religion. Some are attached to nonparochial sub-systems within their denomination, while others conduct ministries in non-religious systems.

The parish ministry, however, is the most frequently chosen career among clergymen. According to The Year Book of the American Churches (Landis, 1960:266-271), in the 22 denominations from which the ministers in this study were selected there were 129,282 clergymen. Of this number 76.4 percent were parish ministers. Other clergy careers apparently required less than one-fourth of the clergy manpower (Scherer and Wendel, 1966; Johnson and Ackerman, 1959:1-32; United Presbyterian Enterprise in Theological Education, 1959). Protestant lay persons (as well as clergymen) tend to think of the ministry in a local church or parish as the ministry. They distinguish between those who are in the "active" ministry and those who are in other types of assignments. They seem to assume that the "active" ministry is more important because this is where the "real work" is done. By contrast, the Catholic "regular" priest is a member of an order or congregation; and the diocesan, or secular clergy, are in parish work. For many Catholics the regular priest has more status than the diocesan priest. The lack of a poverty vow and the continued participation in secular society on the part of the diocesan clergy is thought to be a lesser choice.

Clergymen in local Protestant churches may be senior ministers or they may be associate or assistant ministers (Potter, 1963). In addition, ministers are attached to local parishes as directors of religious education, parochial school teachers, and directors of music. Frequently any one or more of these staff persons are women; and if they are ordained, their career patterns may differ from those of clergymen (Jones, 1963).

Persons employed by the church may not all be ministers. Ordination status for professional personnel is helpful but not absolutely essential, except where preaching and administration of the Sacraments are part of their vocation. Some clergy, who serve as hospital or military chaplains, are employed as religious functionaries in institutions and agencies that are not controlled by a church. They are ministers of religion, and ordination is essential to the performance of their work, even though they are not economically dependent upon the church.

In addition to his ordination status, a clergyman has professional status. Chapman (1944) has traced the status of the ministerial profession in American society from early colonial times. He has concluded that the prestige and the power of the clergy have been reduced with the growth of other professions and the increase of scientific knowledge. Carr-Saunders (1955) differentiates four types of professions: the old and the new professions, the service professions, and the would-be professions. Clergymen, lawyers and physicians are generally recognized as belonging to the old professions; however while they are so recognized, the status of the clergy may not be equated with that of the other professions. In defining the established professions Carr-Saunders notes two characteristics: "their practice is founded upon the theoretical study of a department of learning"; and they "follow a certain mode of conduct which is dictated by the responsible or fiduciary position in which an independent practitioner stands in relation to his client."

With respect to the first of these characteristics, this research on the Protestant parish minister is a study of a profession, and is controlled by the standard of training which its practitioners receive in a specific body of knowledge. The ministers included in this survey were all college *and* seminary graduates, and were typical of the professionally-trained Protestant ministers in the United States in 1955. According to Sperry (1946:176) in 1946, 22 percent of the ministers in the United States were graduates of both college and seminary, 29 percent were graduates of either college or seminary, and 49 percent were graduates of neither college nor seminary. If the same percentage distribution was still accurate in 1955, the ministers in this study were atypical of all Protestant clergy in the United States. In fact, they were a select group from the 22 denominations with which they were affiliated, because the clergy in the denominations as a whole were not uniformly college and seminary trained.

The second of Carr-Saunder's definitions of a professional, that he or she "follows certain modes of conduct" in the practice of the profession (or professional behavior), is the central focus of this analysis.

The professions in American society are being defined or re-defined. This is reflected in the emergence of new professions, as indicated by Carr-Saunders, and by the mobility of professional workers (Reiss, 1955). It is also evident in the changing organizational structure of institutions and agencies to which professionals give leadership. For example, as the size of the local parish increases, it is apparent that the role of the clergy also changes.

Development of an Image

The parish minister is the professional leader of the local church, a social system which is oriented to a theological perspective. The minister is a central actor in the system because he not only symbolizes and articulates the ideology of the church but also performs other essential person- and group-oriented functions. There are other formal and informal leaders in the system, including church officers, members, and such staff persons as assistant minister, organist or choir director, secretary and janitor. They are all actors in the system, whether professional or non-professional.

Each of the several actors in the local church has a role to perform that is essential to the maintenance of this social system. The definitions of their roles vary according to the expectations of persons functioning both within and outside of the system. Denominational heritage, the history of the local church and its practice of religion, and community traditions are a few of the relevant factors that help create and maintain role definitions within the system.

Actors in the local church are also participants in other social systems in the local community and in the larger society. These broader participation patterns affect the way in which their role in the church is performed. Furthermore, actors in other systems, who may have no immediate relationship to a specific local church, contribute indirectly to the role definitions of actors in that church. This would include community leaders and residents, ministers and members of other churches, and all persons and agencies that shape or convey public opinion.

There is much confusion in contemporary usage in American society with respect to the nomenclature used to designate clergymen and to describe their professional behavior. This is reflected in the multiplicity of titles by which different clergymen may be addressed, as Father, Rabbi, Reverend, Pastor, Doctor, and Brother. It is also noted in the variety of terms used to refer to the clergyman, as priest, preacher, rector, and minister. These descriptive terms are used, even in the same context, with more than one connotation, and they vary for several reasons.

First, the traditions of the three major Judeo-Christian faiths appear to require separate symbols to identify their clergy. Professional leaders inherit cultural characteristics that distinguish them as clergy of one tradition rather than another. These differences are reflected in the title of address used in each group. The Roman Catholic clergyman is addressed as Father, and the Jewish professional leader as Rabbi. However, in the Protestant traditions a wide variety of terms, which are particularistic rather than universalistic, may be used to designate and address the clergy.

Second, the rural-urban, regional and ethnic differences in the United States lead to differing usages in the designation of a clergyman. In the past, terms of reference to the clergyman have been rather specific, relatively unstructured, and informal in the culture of the agrarian areas of America. Traditionally, in the rural areas, particularly in the South, the minister has been known as "Preacher," a title that is appropriate in a society in which the major professional service that is rendered is "preaching, christening, marrying, and burying." Among the rural Protestants of German ethnic origin in the middle-atlantic and mid-western states, the most prevalent word used to refer to ministers is "Pastor." It connotes a personal concern on the part of the minister for each parishioner. In urban areas where organized religion is more complex and offers a greater variety of services, more general terms are used to describe a clergyman. In situations where more than one clergyperson is on the staff the title may describe a specialized function.

Third, the clergyman's job is complex. He engages in a wide variety of activities, and this tends to encourage diversity of identification. Because their need is related to a specific role, persons served by a clergyman may not be aware of his many functions. He is a spiritual leader, an ideological leader, a technical expert about religion, and a practitioner of religion. His work is characterized by both the technical knowledge of the scholar and the techniques of the artist. He is expected to live the faith as a believer, to be an expert in religion, and to practice it with others.

Technical competence and practitioner effectiveness are criteria used to evaluate professionals generally in society, and are indicated by two sets of symbols or titles. Technical competence is symbolized by academic degrees which attest to the professional's intellectual mastery of an area of knowledge that is deemed essential for the practice of a profession. The professional school has the power to grant these degrees. Legitimacy may be indicated by the initials after the professional's name such as M.Div., Ph.D., R.N., or M.Ed. In addition to the academic symbols of competence, professionals are generally required to be certified as practitioners. This certification process may be controlled by a professional society, a government agency or the organization in which the professional functions. The lawyer is admitted to the bar, the teacher obtains a certificate from the state, and the clergyman is ordained by the religious body to which he relates.

The extent to which these aspects of the clergy profession are emphasized is related to the religious tradition in which he has status. One group may stress the clergyman's practitioner service or effectiveness; while another group may stress technical competence as a scholar. Titles of designation and of address reflect this. The term priest in the Catholic tradition, and the term pastor in some Protestant traditions identify primarily the practical function, while the use of doctor as a term of address in some Jewish and Protestant groups would seem to emphasize the technical function.

The distinction between the technical expert function and the service function may also be noticed in the apparel of the clergyman. The Catholic priest and the orthodox rabbi, whose primary functions would seem to be that of spiritual practitioners, have distinctive clothing that is worn consistently. Protestants, especially Lutherans and Episcopalians, wear clothes that have a religious connotation, but these garments are worn as a general rule only when the clergyman is functioning as a clergyman. In other Protestant groups, and in Reformed Judaism, the clergyman is more likely to wear garments such as a business or professional person in society might wear, except that academic robes may be used while conducting religious services.

The role of the clergyman is exceedingly complex. This is related not only to the differing levels of his ministry but also to the specializations in which he engages as he carries out his ministry. On the one hand the terms minister, priest, and rabbi are generalized, and distinguish the clergyman from other professionals. On the other hand, the term rector is specific. It describes the Episcopal priest in his role as the business manager of the parish. The term evangelist may describe a specialized type of minister, or it may refer to a specific type of purpose a parish clergyman may be trying to accomplish.

In order to function, each parish clergyman needs to know who he is, what his status is, and how he is going to play the roles that his professional position requires. In short, he needs to have an image of himself which consists of ideas and opinions that describe and explain his status and role in the church and in the other social systems in society. This is the minister's view of his own personality and what he believes about himself as a professional religious leader and as a person with family, community, and societal relations.

In a study of the self as related to formal participation, Brown (1953) theorizes that "individuals accept for themselves a certain status position and participate in accordance with that self-judgment. The conception of the self would include a feeling either of being expected to, or not expected to, participate in organizations." In support of this theory he reported: "Business and professional men generally had a self-image of being expected to belong to civic organizations such as the Lions Club. They felt expected to spearhead fund-raising drives, to do the planning for the community, and to supervise parades and celebrations. The wives of these business and professional people perceived themselves in a status similar to that of their husbands and felt expected to play leadership roles and to participate actively in the formal organizations." Brown's study tends to show that "individuals have self-images which motivate them to behave accordingly. They have a fairly definite judgment of the role behavior expected with regard to formal participation."

An understanding of the minister's role is crucial to the effective functioning of the system. There are many sources of the image that a local church has of the minister. According to Gustafson (1954) each lay actor in the religious system, regardless of his or her degree of personal involvement, has an image of ministers. The minister of a parish in the performance of his role is a primary contributor to the image. Church officers and other parishioners, adherents of other religious systems, and those who are not active participants in the religious life of a community look at the minister from their own perspective, and therefore have certain pictures of him. Other clergy, seminary professors and functionaries in the denomination also have an image of the clergyman.

In the local church some perceptive parishioners and the minister will be aware that his predecessors have left their own imprint on the image of the clergy which is held by that congregation. Members of the congregation will show deference for some predecessors, sympathy or pity for others, and perhaps hostility or disdain toward a few. In a parish served by the writer, the members held up as a model a minister who had been their leader three decades earlier. There was much hostility expressed toward a more recent predecessor who was rejected by parishioners as a role model. In a church with multiple-clergy staff some members may differ in their acceptance or rejection of individual ministers. The young assistant may find that his more mature clergy associate is a role model from the point of view of some parishioners, who expect that he will be emulated. Parishioners also derive their image to some extent from clergy serving other churches in the community, especially if it involves status identification.

Images are also shaped and reinforced by the concepts which the public have of the Catholic priest, the Jewish rabbi, or the Protestant minister in the community and society. Within each of these three religious traditions, relatively distinct groups of clergy may be identified according to the sub-tradition to which they belong such as the diocesan priest or the priest who belongs to an order; the orthodox, conservative or reformed rabbi; and the ministers of the various Protestant denominational groups (Donovan, 1951; Sklare, 1955; May, 1934).

The portrayal of the clergyman on radio and television provides still another source of image. Among others, Fulton J. Sheen, Billy Graham, Oral Roberts, and Norman Vincent Peale have created, shaped, and maintained an image of the clergyman in our culture through their appearances in the mass media. Images of the clergy are portrayed more generally in literature, novels and plays. (Southard, 1959; Davies, 1959)

The problem of the Protestant minister in a local church is to develop an image of himself adequate to his functions, and to relate himself effectively to the personnel in the social system. The general image that people have of the clergy in our culture and the socialization that they have toward the clergy through previous social interaction is a part of the context of the parish into which a minister must fit. The minister's own self-image is a major factor in this situation; and his problem is to bring all of these images, his own and those of others, into sharp and acceptable focus.

This research is focused on the image that parish ministers have of themselves and not on the images of the minister held by other actors in the system. It assumes that as he performs various roles, the minister is influenced in his behavior by the image that he believes the public holds of him as well as by the picture that he holds of himself. If Parsons and Shils (1954:147) are right that "there must be a fundamental correspondence between the actor's own self-categorization of 'self-image' and the place he occupies in the category system of the society of which he is a part," then, in the absence of systematic knowledge about the image of the clergy held by other actors, it may be hypothesized that there is "a fundamental correspondence" between the minister's self-image and the image other actors in the system have of him. Ambiguities exist, however, which may raise questions about fundamental correspondence, and may hinder (but also necessitate) thorough self-examination.

Self-image of the Protestant Parish Minister

The development of a realistic self-image begins with self-understanding. A Texas clergyman wrote:*

"I receive the most enjoyment from my pastoral work. That is, helping those who need help and counseling those who need it. I love people; so I want to help them, sometimes too much."

A clergyman from New Mexico reported that:

"The problem of professionalism is one of the greatest temptations with which I have to deal. One has to guard against doing those things which will always bring the satisfaction of personal pride or praise, when there will be cases where strict adherence to the principles of Christianity may force one to take the stand which will not bring personal praise. We are all human."

Another thoughtful minister in a process of self-examination mentions:

"The problem of me. The great struggle to overcome perfectionist patterns that arise out of inner-compulsions trick me into discontent with what I am and have, so that time is lost in negative moods of inferiority, etc. I have some understanding of these things, but overcoming comes hard, so that I am free to love people completely, with no strings attached."

When does the structure of the minister's personality interfere with his ministry? When do the firmness or strictness with which he expects people to accept the same theological norms that he believes are essential, and that he feels are operative in his own life, blur his idea of what the function of the minister is to be.

Self-understanding is also related to the minister's personal goals and his professional orientation. Does the clergyman wish to be successful, or does he choose to be effective. Is his self-picture focused on his personal ambitions and self-fulfillment, or is he obsessed with a desire to do things effectively for and with members of the parish? Should he be professionally proficient, even though he does not have a sense of self-involvement; or should he be personally committed at the risk of not being technically competent? In writing about the characteristics of ministers that seem to lead to *effective*

---

*Unless otherwise noted, the material quoted here, and throughout the manuscript, is from clergy participants in this research; and as such, the authors will not be identified by name.

parish work, a Missourian mentioned that "a knowledge of one's own frailty and mixed motives is the secret of understanding the action and motives of others." An Ohio minister expressed concern about *success* goals when he wrote as follows:

"I feel that there are a good many ministers who feel rather lost. I'm among them. We simply cannot see where we are going in the church. Our churches are successful. We gain more members, we have more at church, we have bigger budgets, we have more activities, we have better Sunday school materials, and so on. But we can't see that we are making much of a difference in our communities or in the lives of the individual members of our communities. This disturbs me."

Parish ministers express bewilderment regarding the conflicting views between the local church and the national church bureaucracy. What attitude can a parish minister afford to show toward the denominational leader whose expectations of the local ministerial leader may not be shared in a local church? How is a parish minister to find a clarification of his denominational and interdenominational responsibilities? Sensitivity to the strictures of this ambiguity is reflected by the parish minister who mentions:

"The 'tyranny' of interdenominational activities whereby a minister is sometimes forced by various pressures, within and without his congregation, to participate in functions not pleasing to his own personal taste or opinion. Sometimes these affairs actually interfere with his more important duties."

The church and the clergy are faced with the problems of the professional in a complex organization. As Vollmer and Mills (1966:264) observe: "Even though the clergy have usually been employed by some kind of church organization, there are indications that sizable aspects of the Christian church are becoming more bureaucratic in character—a trend that may be supported further by the mergers occurring as a part of the ecumenical movement." Parish ministers to some extent are independent professionals. It is common for a clergyman to desire "a church of my own." More typically, clergymen are salaried professionals in a large bureaucratized organization (denomination). As such, they are likely to resist bureaucratic rules, standards and supervision, and to resent the loyalty expected of them by denominational leaders.

Regardless of the theological orientation that is held, the realities of these ambiguities must be faced to see what the Protestant seminary and the denomination can give the prospective or practicing minister. On the one hand, ministers are changing the ways in which they function in response to the demands being made upon them by the American community; and this would suggest "fundamental correspondence." This is expected of those who are to be practitioners of religion. On the other hand, the minister, through religious scholarship, has a heritage of theological understandings and traditions. Can a minister remain a minister if he responds to the pressures that seem to create ambiguities? To the extent that the Protestant minister faces these pressures realistically, self-understanding will be achieved, and role expectancies on the part of the parishioners will be fulfilled. Our primary concern is *not to describe* the ambiguities that now exist in the role of minister, or between the minister and other actors in the system; rather it is to *seek a clarification* of his roles so that he may face ambiguities without admitting defeat, and without being unrealistic in the degree of effectiveness which he may expect of himself.

Roles

The clergy profession may be analyzed from the perspective of three types of roles: professional, extra-professional, and non-professional. This book is devoted to an analysis of the first of these, the professional roles, to which all of a parish minister's other potentially competing roles adjust or accommodate. Before we proceed to an examination in the succeeding chapters of the minister's professional roles, it may be helpful to describe in some detail his non- and extra-professional roles.

Non-professional roles

The clergyman plays many non-professional roles. He is a citizen, a community resident (unless he is a member of a religious order), he has kinship roles, he may be a family man (unless he is single or has taken a vow of celibacy), and he has a social status role. Since the non-professional roles are in a sense subservient to his professional roles, we may observe certain consequences. He is a citizen, but the minister is not free to act without regard to his being a minister. He may be husband as well as a minister, but he cannot act in his role as husband without also being a minister. The minister and his wife and children are not free to act without considering the implications which their behavior may have for his profession. The traditional community image of the p.k. (preacher's kid) and the social control function of gossip in relation to the minister's wife underline the interlocking nature of the professional role and the subservient non-professional roles.

Extra-professional roles

The minister is expected to do certain things that are not specifically a part of his parish work, but are demanded of him simply because he is a minister. This may be thought of as an extra-professional or citizenship role. Here we may draw a comparison between ministers and lawyers, using Wardwell and Wood (1956) in their analysis of lawyers. For ministers we define the citizenship role as those behavior expectations that ministers will act in certain ways in relation to the community and the wider society, even though this performance is not technically a responsibility nor a part of the function of the minister. This role excludes behavior expected of any citizen *qua* citizen, and includes only those special community role expectations pertaining to the minister, *qua* minister.

Several considerations make it more difficult to distinguish an extra-professional role for the clergyman than, for instance, the lawyer. The lawyer tends to work with a small number of clients usually on an individual basis (Lortie, 1959); but the clergyman, while he also works with parishioners individually, tends to work with a larger number of persons, usually in groups. This may be described as the difference between the person-oriented activity of the lawyer and the collectivity-oriented activity of the minister. Social visibility makes it more difficult to distinguish between professional and extra-professional roles for the clergyman than it does for the lawyer. The clergyman's garments that in varying degree are distinctive, are readily identifiable, and suggest his function to people. The clergyman may use symbols, such as clergy insignia on his automobile, which aid him in carrying out his professional duties. Garments and symbols make his work more public than private, more group- than individual-oriented. This is not true for the lawyer.

Wardell and Wood note that the content of extra-professional role expectations are of two types: social relationships with persons with whom the professional interacts professionally, and the relationships involved in being a citizen.

Several examples may be cited of ways in which the minister has *social relationships*, as distinguished from professional relations with persons with whom he interacts professionally. First, the clergyman has friendly, first-name associations with other clergymen outside of the local church, and with the denominational and inter-denominational bureaucracy. Professional relations with parishioners and relations of friendship are other aspects of this type of extra-professional activity for the clergyman. Many ministers encourage parishioners to call them by their first name. Presumably a professional relationship with a parishioner is characterized by affective neutrality, and is not one of friendship in which the clergyman himself becomes emotionally involved in his parishioner's problems. Here again the line is thin because the clergyman is expected to have emotional warmth as he does such things as conducting a funeral or entering into the spirit of a wedding. In performing certain roles, as in the wedding or death situation, the minister may not be able to effectively render his religious function if his behavior is not affectively neutral.

Second, in his concern for parishioners it is sometimes difficult to distinguish between religious and non-religious problems. Of particular relevance here is the current interest of the clergy in psychiatry. In a counseling situation, where does the role of the minister stop and the role of the psychiatrist begin? When should the minister refer a parishioner to a psychiatrist?

A third group of people with whom the minister deals professionally and with whom he develops extra-professional relationships is the administrative personnel in denominational and interdenominational institutions, boards and agencies. Professional ethics and the government of his denomination define the formal relationships with these persons, but the clergyman develops personal friendships that may modify the professional relationships that are structured by law, tradition or ethics.

What is the content of extra-professional relationships involved in the minister being a citizen, or the citizenship role? First, it is generally expected that he will be a representative of "religion," without sectarian goals, in various community activities. These services are largely ceremonial and ritualistic. For example, he will pronounce the invocation or benediction at governmental ceremonials such as the induction of elected officials into office, and at patriotic occasions such as a Fourth of July celebration. He will provide similar religious services at school ceremonials, convocations, and graduation exercises. He will be a chaplain to the police and fire departments, and will act as a clergyman when religious ministrations are required during a catastrophe, or for accident victims.

Second, the minister is expected to offer various kinds of leadership in relation to philanthropic activities and welfare services. He personifies the concern of the community for the unfortunate, the downtrodden, the outcaste. Along with Jewish and Catholic clergymen he may symbolize the inter-faith or nonsectarian nature of a privately-supported charity. In many communities he is cast in the role of the legitimizer of fund drives which financially underwrite the welfare programs. In effect he says that these are programs which any good community will provide, and that it is the humane thing to do to support them financially.

There is a third content to the clergyman's citizenship role. This is an activity for which the clergy as a whole feel a responsibility, and is often carried out through an interdenominational ministerial association, or a council of churches. It is not an activity in which all clergymen are active participants, but some may feel a personal or perhaps a professional obligation to work at it. This activity is focused on those persons who are institutionalized in prisons, detention homes, county farms and homes for the destitute, hospitals—both general and specialized, and retirement homes which are not religiously controlled or sponsored. The clergy who conduct religious services in such situations are in effect saying that religion is for all, and they often take turns conducting religious services on a voluntary, non-remunerative basis. They may, however, work for the establishment of a chaplaincy in these institutions. Such a staff person may be attached either to the institution or to a council of churches. When this is done the clergy have broadened this service to become a community responsibility.

There is perhaps another content area to the minister's extra-professional role. This has to do with morality in the community, and community issues that have an ethical aspect. Religion and morality are closely related, and culturally the minister is a symbol of both. In fact, religion is thought to be the underpinning of community morality. On occasions the minister is expected to publicly express the guilt of the community about its own moral level, as for example, parental responsibility for juvenile delinquency. At other times he speaks about the community's concern for an injustice that has a moral basis, such as racial and ethnic discrimination.

The material analyzed in this report contributes only indirectly to a greater understanding of the clergyman's extra-professional role. We do not have very much systematic knowledge about the types of extra-professional roles which the clergy are expected to perform; nor do we know very much about the variables that are related to the extent to which clergymen carry out their extra-professional roles. Future research may want to ascertain which of the following variables may be significant in understanding the extra-professional role: age, marital status, level of education, theological orientation, denominational affiliation (especially its relation to the church-sect dichotomy), regional location, metropolitan or non-metropolitan location, or organizational complexity.

This book is primarily about the self-image the parish minister has of his professional roles, and the extra-professional and non-professional roles of the parish minister are of secondary interest to us. The parish minister's comprehension of his work environment together with his own image of his professional roles in this environment is the criterion variable in this research.

III

CHARACTERISTICS OF THE PROTESTANT PARISH
CLERGYMAN
AND HIS ORGANIZATIONAL SETTING

In Chapter II we stated the need to examine the minister's image of self as related to his or her professional environment. Completed questionnaires were received from 1,111 ministers, the responses depicting varying aspects of self-image.* These materials will be treated as *dependent* variables.

Since our interest in the professional role is both analytic and descriptive, in this chapter we wish to identify and describe two series of factors that may be related to this variability in self-image, namely, characteristics of the minister and of his or her environment. In each of the succeeding chapters, then, these characteristics will be analyzed as *independent* variables in relation to the variability occurring in the dependent variables.

Clergy variables include personal characteristics such as age, marital status, and number of children; personality factors such as authoritarian tendencies, degree of emotional maturity, and openness to change; status, mentor, and support referrents; professional experience such as date of ordination, type of ministerial career, professional mobility and tenure in present parish assignment; and criteria of professional effectiveness and success.

The second series of independent variables are related to characteristics of organization, the parish, which the minister serves: denominational affiliation; regional location; type of community; the organizational complexity of the parish, such as number of congregations in the parish, number of members, number of students and staff in the church school, total number of staff personnel and number of clergy on the staff(s); economics of the parish, such as annual parish or local expenditures, annual extra-parish or benevolence expenditures, and annual per capita expenditures.

Clergy Characteristics

Personal characteristics

A thumbnail sketch of the 1,111 parish ministers who participated in this research will orient the reader. Their ages ranged from 26 to 71 years, the average being 42.6 years. Nineteen out of 20 were married and the average number of children per household was 2.26. The ministers were not asked to give their sex and race; therefore the actual number of persons included by sex and race is not known. However, it is known that there

---

*Open-end questions requiring content analysis were prescribed by the advisory committee; thus inferences were drawn from responses, not formalized by fixed-category response. See Appendix E for questionnaire used in data collection.

were both clergymen* and clergywomen in the sample, and that the Caucasian, Negro and Oriental races were represented.

Personality factors

The human factor is crucial in a minister's performance of his roles. Baker (1949:9-15) has reported the experiences of two ministers who were almost exactly the same age and who were graduated from the same seminary class. Their intellectual achievement varied by not more than ten percent, and their college preparation was essentially of the same order. In seminary they had the same courses of study and came under the influence of the same teachers and the same religious atmosphere. Moreover, they were subject in their development to similar cultural situations and entered upon their professional careers at a time when the nation was waging a war. Yet in their subsequent ministries they differed in the level of their professional usefulness, as determined by the extent to which their own emotional needs were permitted to interfere, and the kind of adaptive responses each made to his life situation. In the world of business Henry (1949) reports a similar finding: "Many business executives have found that persons of unquestioned high intelligence often turn out to be ineffective when placed in positions of increased responsibility. The reason for their failure lies in their social relationships."

Professional practice would seem to be related to the ability to get along easily with people. The minister must be proficient and sophisticated in the theoretical phases of his profession, but the measure of his practice will also be in terms of his ability to meet and work with people at their level of need. Three personality measures were obtained for the clergy informants: a measure of authoritarian behavior, a measure of emotional maturity, and openness to change.

Burchard (1954) proposed the hypothesis that a career in the military chaplaincy appeals strongly to those possessing the characteristics of the "authoritarian" personality. Although he did not have information on the personality characteristics of chaplains in his study, he felt that the replies to some of the items in his interview schedule suggested the existence of basic personality differences between those clergymen who chose the military chaplaincy as a career and those who did not. Burchard's insight about the personality of chaplains was generated in relation to role conflict resolution. It seems prudent to explore his hypothesis as it might relate to parish ministers and role conflict.

Frenkel-Brunswik and others (1947) have defined *authoritarianism* as "the conceptions of an individual whose thought about man and society form a pattern which is properly described as anti-democratic and which springs from his deepest emotional tendencies." The research on authoritarianism indicates the existence of relatively stable syndromes which operate at most levels and in most spheres of social activity. This is something like having a potential personality pattern which might include such attitudes as authoritarian aggression and submission, rigidity and conformity. It is a measure of personality trends which seems to express a predisposition to anti-democratic thought and action. The F-scale, as developed by Adorno, Frenkel-

---

*The words clergyman and associated pronouns are used throughout as generic terms, and are not meant to distinguish the gender of the respondents.

Brunswik, Levinson and Sanford, was used as a measure of authoritarianism.* (Adorno, 1950; Gough, 1951)

The open-end type of questions used in our study produced a large yield of documentary material about the way in which the minister himself faced his daily situation. One observer described the questionnaire as a "depth interview" conducted by mail rather than by a face-to-face interview. The series of questions inquiring into present and past parish (professional) problems were analyzed from the perspective of latent aspects of the personality of the person who gets involved in conflict situations. A minister who had "trouble" in one church might find that the pattern was repeated in another church to which he ministered. In addition to the substantive analysis of documentary material it was also possible by inference to classify the emotional tone of the material. Hence a measure of the *emotional maturity* of the informant was possible.

A series of criteria was used to construct an emotional maturity score, and a scoring system devised to measure the emotional quality rather than the substantive content of the responses of each informant. Four criteria were judged to indicate emotional maturity and were scored as positive (+); four criteria were judged to indicate lack of emotional maturity, or rather immaturity, and were scored as negative (-). The positive criteria were: evidence of an attempt at self-appraisal; demonstration of ability to "wrestle" with ministerial problems; genuine interest in persons in the church and community. The negative criteria were: show of anxiety in exploring ministerial problems; projection of ministerial problems on lay persons; evidence of scathing criticism of other ministers; hostile attitude toward the seminary where the minister received his training. Hence the presence of a criterion in a given series of questions added a plus or a minus one (1) to the emotional maturity score of the informant, depending on whether the criterion was positive or negative. The well-adjusted person, emotionally, would receive a positive score, the ambivalent person a score of zero, and the poorly adjusted person, emotionally, would receive a negative score.

An emotional maturity score was derived for each minister. The distribution of scores is shown in Table 1. The mean score was -0.45. It had been assumed that zero (0) would be the theoretical mid-point on the continuum.

TABLE 1
EMOTIONAL MATURITY CONTINUUM

Score	Immaturity									Maturity	
	-5	-4	-3	-2	-1	0	+ 1	+ 2	+ 3	+ 4	+ 5
Percentage of ministers	*	2%	8	20	20	24	13	9	3	1	*

* = less than 0.05 percent.

*This scale consists of 30 items drawn from the "E" (ethnocentrism) and "F" (implicit anti-democratic trends) scales of a public opinion study. The work of Siegel (1954) suggested the possibility of a fruitful use of this scale in the present study. The reliability and validity of the scale were widely examined in previous studies, and have been accepted by social scientists. The internal consistency of the F-scale in its application to the clergy informants included in the present study has been analyzed by Shimada (1958). All the items were found to discriminate satisfactorily when the Likert method was used (Likert, 1932; Murphy and Likert, 1938).

A third personality factor is the degree to which a minister feels he is *aware of change desired* in the program of the church. It was assumed that members and non-members of a parish are not completely agreed on the program that is available. A realistic appraisal of any organization would assume that there are some members who hold dissident opinions about its structure, leadership and program. The minister who is sensitive to the variety of opinions held by members would appear to be more adjustable than a minister who is not. The same assumption may be made about non-members, except that we would expect a greater proportion to have dissenting opinions. The index used to measure a minister's attitude toward change was derived from the frame of reference the clergyman used, rather than the substantive response he gave, in response to the following two questions: "Are you aware of any way in which members of your parish desire to change the program of the church?" "Are you aware of any way in which non-members of your church who live in the community think that the program of your church should be changed?" A five-point scale was developed. At one extreme were those who stated that they were aware of changes desired by members and non-members; at the other were those who were not aware of changes desired. The distribution of the clergy on this scale is shown in Table 2.

TABLE 2
PERCENTAGE OF CLERGYMEN AWARE OF CHANGES
DESIRED IN CHURCH'S PROGRAM

Awareness of desired change	Percent (N = 1,111)
Aware	27
Somewhat aware	9
Ambivalent	39
Somewhat unaware	8
Not aware	17

Reference groups

The reference groups of the clergyman signify the body of persons toward which his behavior is oriented. A minister may assess his own performance by the model which a referent offers. Reference group theory (Merton, 1950:41-42) centers on "the processes through which men relate themselves to groups and refer their behavior to the values of these groups." We are interested in the degree to which variability in the parish minister's self-image is related to his reference persons or groups. Three types of clergy referents are available for this analysis: status, mentor, and support.

The analysis of *status referents* of the parish minister was derived from responses to the question: "What types of persons (identify by their occupation or some other social factor) do you seek to know?" Content analysis of the essay answers to this question focused on four types of status referents: ideological, equalitarian, occupational, and religious.

The ideological referents are those whom the clergyman believes have a certain social and political orientation. These referents are identified by the following phrases:

"liberals politically and socially, social reform leaders, persons who have a passion for social justice, people who are alive to the realities of our time and who are making a significant contribution to any realm of human endeavor."

More than one-eighth of the clergy informants seek to know this type of person.
The minister whose status referent is equalitarian is illustrated by the respondent who reported:

"I do not seek to know any particular type of people. Every person is equal in my sight—at least, I try to keep it that way."

Or he may state that he seeks to know "all types of people," to show "no preference," to "never make a distinction," and to "mingle with the crowd." The clergyman who identifies his status referents in this manner is being consistent with the broad admonitions to achieve brotherhood that are implicit in much biblical and theological thought. In a sense, a clergyman could not be himself if he did not have this type of referent, and in fact more than half of the clergymen responded in this fashion.

The occupational referent is the most pervasive for the clergyman. Specific occupational groups were identified as status referents by three-fifths of the clergymen, and professional and business persons were mentioned much more frequently than were industrial or labor leaders.

Within the religious system in the community, one-fifth mentioned other clergy or lay persons in the church as status referents.

To discover the *mentor referent* of the informant he was asked: "Please name any person whom you admire as a leader or who has greatly influenced the ways you think and act as a minister." The responses were analyzed according to the station in life the mentor held, and the reason given by the clergyman for the mentor relationship.

When the mentor's station in life is considered, the clergymen admired or were influenced to a greater extent by religious mentors than by secular mentors or friends and relatives.

Among religious mentors, seminary professors were mentioned most frequently, and well-known churchmen or authors next. Fellow ministers were held as mentors by two-fifths of the parish ministers in the study.

To probe into the reason why informants had certain persons as mentor referents, they were asked, "Why do you admire him (them), or how have you been influenced?" Clergymen most frequently selected mentors whose personality they admired; then because their practice of the ministry was admired; and third, mentors were selected because of their scholar image—they were intellectually attractive. Twenty-eight percent of the ministers selected mentors who represented a father-counselor image.

The *support referent* of the minister was identified from responses to the question: "As you have worked out your ways of being the minister of a church . . . what types of persons have you found most helpful when you wished to talk over problems?" Persons identified as support referents may be classified into five general types.* Lay colleagues (the formal and informal leaders of the congregation) were identified as referents by more than half of the clergy. Clergy colleagues were identified as referents by half of the clergy. This is in contrast with the choosing of bureaucratic (denominational) leaders as support referents by only one-fourteenth of the clergy. The professional type includes

---

*Ministers could report a referent in more than one category. Therefore, percentages equalled more than 100.

school teachers, social workers, lawyers, doctors, nurses, and other professional leaders in the community, who are consulted about problems by 42 percent of the informants. The minister's spouse, relatives and friends provided an emotional type of referent for one-third of the clergymen.

Professional experience

The professional experience of the parish minister is initiated by *ordination*, a rite of passage, in which his clergy status and denomination is recognized and appropriately affirmed. The clergy in this study were ordained between 1924 and 1954; with the median years of ordination being between 1940 and 1944.

Almost one-seventh of the ministers were in their initial parish, while one percent of them were in their seventh assignment. The average number of assignments was 2.14.

Although all the ministers in this study were serving a parish, one-fifth had had some non-parochial work experience. The *careers* of four-fifths of the clergymen had been limited to parish assignments. Theoretically, those having had non-parochial assignments will differ in their self-image from those having had only parochial experience. If the non-parochial work experience was another clergy career such as missionary, chaplain or denominational executive, their self-image would reflect a broader religious perspective than would the self-images of those having had only parish experience. However, if the non-parochial work was in a secular organization, a self-image would reflect two occupations.

Professional mobility was defined as inter-parish (or other professional assignment such as a tour of duty as military chaplain) migration. The professional mobility of the clergy involves the number of assignments and the duration of these assignments. The score computed was essentially the number of years per assignment, an index of the mobility of clergymen. The professional mobility scores were then grouped by classes (Table 3).

TABLE 3
PROFESSIONAL MOBILITY OF MINISTERS

Score	Percent (N = 1,111)
High Mobility—Fewer than 4 years per assignment	33
Medium High Mobility—4.00 to 6.99 years	32
Medium Low Mobility—7.00 to 9.99 years	15
Low Mobility—10 years or more	13
No score	7

The *tenure* of the ministers in their current parish (at the time of this study) ranged from two months to 37 years. The mean was 5.3 years and the median was 3.2 years. Almost all had the status of minister rather than associate or assistant minister.

In American culture most professions have evaluative symbols that describe their *criteria of effectiveness and success*. The clergyman shares in this aspect of our culture. He evolves an understanding of the expectations for effectiveness and success in his profession through the interaction he has with parishioners, through his experience as a religious functionary in the church, by the career pattern he is able to follow in the denomination, and in response to the supervision and guidance he receives from denominational boards and officials. His understandings may also be affected by comparisons with the expectations of other professions, the memberships he has in secular groups and associations, and the social status he is accorded in the community.

To secure the minister's picture of those things that make for *effective* parish work, each informant was asked to name those personality traits or characteristics of ministers that seem to lead to effective parish work. It was expected that they would report characteristics that were associated with effectiveness in their own ministry to people, and in so doing would express the self-image by which they sought to relate themselves to people. For analysis, responses were grouped into two foci: personality characteristics and practitioner skills (Table 4).

TABLE 4
MINISTERIAL CRITERIA FOR
EFFECTIVE AND SUCCESSFUL PARISH WORK

Foci	Effectiveness			Success	
	Percent* (N = 1,111)	Criteria		Criteria	Percent* (N = 1,111)
Personality Characteristics	62	Character		Aggressive-enthusiastic personality	25
	58	Out-going personality		Willingness to serve, hard worker	23
	35	Spiritual maturity		Good character	19
	27	Self-understanding		Spiritual life	15
	15	Intellectual ability		Intellectual ability	7
Practitioner Skills	56	Counselor-counselee relations		Ability to perform ministerial roles	44
	22	Good organizer		Administrative skills	8
	18	Maturity in performing roles		Good church program	4
	9	Preaching, teaching, priestly skills		Good public relations	3
	5	Administrative skills			
Denominational Relations	—	—		Cooperation in denominational programs	25
				Politics in denominational office-seeking	10
				Getting along with denominational executives	8

*Categories not mutually exclusive

Character was mentioned most frequently as a personality characteristic of the effective parish minister. This was seen as involving inner direction. Specifically this category included such characteristics as purity, sincerity, sense of responsibility, and trust worthiness.

Respondents felt almost as frequently that the effective parish minister needed to have an out-going personality, or be an "other-directed person." Other terms fitting this category were friendly or radiant personality, and warmth.

Spiritual maturity and self-understanding were mentioned by one-third and one-fourth of the respondents respectively. Spiritual maturity was expressed in such terms as deeply spiritual, true piety, commitment, sense of mission or direction, and sense of inner conviction. Self-understanding included objectivity toward self, self adjustment, and honesty in facing own limitations. A fifth characteristic, intellectual ability, was mentioned by nearly one-sixth.

Counselor-counselee relations in which the counselor is approachable, a good listener, empathetic, and has a love for people was mentioned most frequently as a practitioner skill that leads to effective parish work.

Some informants felt that effectiveness required one to be a good organizer. Specifically they suggested working with people, able to delegate authority, and ability to enlist others. Others decided that maturity in performing the roles of the minister was a prerequisite for effective parish work. Preaching, teaching and priestly abilities and administrative skill were mentioned by some.

A generalized expression of effectiveness is:

"A minister must be an acceptable preacher (not necessarily a great one), be aggressive, have personality (both public and private), organizational ability, administrative or promotional ability, an interest in people which shows itself in personal contacts, calls, etc., and receptiveness to new ideas."

The minister's *criteria of success* is another self-evaluation of his professional fulfillment. In the pretest, ministers resisted using the word success with reference to themselves. Therefore an indirect question was devised to aid the informant in describing his success criteria: "What are the ways that ministers conduct themselves that seem to assure their success in your denomination?" Response was more readily given to a projective question focused on other ministers, and on the denomination rather than the local parish. For analysis the responses were grouped into three foci: personality characteristics, practitioner skills, and denominational relations.

Five personality characteristics were mentioned: one-fourth felt that an aggressive, enthusiastic personality was needed for success. The willingness to serve, or the hard-worker approach to success was mentioned almost as frequently. Good character was cited by nearly one-fifth. The spiritual life of the minister, and intellectual ability were also thought to be important for success (Refer to Table 4). In comparison, Henry (1949) in his research on business executives found that "the successful business executives . . . had many personality characteristics in common. Acquisitiveness and achievement, self-directedness and independence of thought were counterbalanced with uncertainty, constant activity, continual fear of losing ground, and the inability to be introspectively casual. The "absence of these characteristics was coincident with failure within the organization." He viewed the personality constellation associated with success as the minimal requirement for the business system and as the psychodynamic motivation of business executives. He reported: "Individual uniqueness in personality was clearly present; but, despite these unique aspects, all executives had in common this personality pattern.''

The practitioner skill mentioned most frequently was general ability to perform the roles of the minister. Administrative ability, good church program, and good public relations were also mentioned.

Cooperation in denominational programs, getting along with denominational executives, and politics in denominational office-seeking were all thought to be necessary to assure success.

In the analysis that follows, all categories in each of the three foci (personality characteristics, practitioner skills, and denominational relations) are ranked for effectiveness and success as they were mentioned by the respondents from most frequently mentioned to least mentioned (Table 5).

TABLE 5
CRITERIA OF EFFECTIVENESS AND SUCCESS
RANKED BY PARISH MINISTERS

Rank	Percent* (N = 1,111)	Effectiveness Criteria	Success Criteria	Percent* (N = 1,111)	Rank
1	62	Character	Ability to perform ministerial roles	44	1
2	58	Out-going personality	Aggressive, enthusiastic personality	25	2
3	56	Counselor-Counselee Rel.	Cooperation in denominational programs	25	3
4	35	Spiritual Maturity	Willingness to serve, hard worker	23	4
5	27	Self-understanding	Good character	19	5
6	22	Good organizer	Spiritual life	15	6
7	18	Maturity in performing roles	Politics in denominational office-seeking	10	7
8	15	Intellectual ability	Administrative skills	8	8
9	9	Preaching, teaching, priestly skills	Getting along with denominational executives	8	9
10	5	Administrative skills	Intellectual ability	7	10
11	—	—	Good church program	4	11
12	—	—	Good public relations	3	12

*Categories are not mutually exclusive. Ministers reported more than one avenue to effectiveness or success.

The differences in the rank of specific categories highlight the conflict of criteria to which a clergyman is subject. Character is given the highest rank for effectiveness, whereas ability in performing the practitioner roles is ranked first for success. Character was mentioned more than three times as frequently in effectiveness criteria as it was for success criteria. Spiritual life was given a middle rank in both criteria. Intellectual ability was given a low rank in both the effectiveness and success dimensions. Cooperation in denominational programs was mentioned about as often as a success criterion as the clergymen's own self-understanding was mentioned as an effectiveness criterion. Administrative ability is ranked low for both criteria. Self-understanding was not mentioned for success but it was ranked fifth for effectiveness. A service orientation was ranked fourth for success, but was not cited for effectiveness. The preacher, priest-liturgist, teacher roles are cited under effectiveness only. Denominational relations were not mentioned in response to the effectiveness question, perhaps because the wording of the question was not exactly comparable with the success question at this point. Three categories were mentioned in responses to the success questions: cooperation with denominational programs, politics in denominational office-seeking, and getting along with denominational executives and other ministers.

The effectiveness and success criteria give insight about how the minister thinks he is evaluated. The contract between the top-ranking criteria of each is illuminating. For effectiveness, the three top ratings are: character, an out-going personality, and skill as a counselor. For success, general ability in the ministerial roles, an out-going personality, and cooperation in denominational programs are rated first, second and third, respectively. Criteria with non-theological rather than theological overtones appear to be the more dominant, especially for success.

Organizational Context Variables

Denominational affiliation

The dominant reference group for the parish minister is the Protestant denomination in which he holds ordination. This is the group that gives him legitimacy and status as a clergyman. This is the group that, by means appropriate to its system, assigns the clergyman to a place of employment as parish minister, educator, missionary, administrator, or chaplain. Ministers, more than any other professional group with the possible exception of lawyers, are oriented to an ideology or set of beliefs that is essential to the role they play in society. Ministers who serve the differing Protestant denominations subscribe to certain creeds and publicly represent the view of religion held by their church. By church affiliation, by public recognition, and by personal commitment the minister is a man with an ideology. If the minister deviates in his beliefs or professional behavior the denomination, through a jurisdictional agency, may discipline him, and in serious deviations, defrock him. The denomination, therefore, as a reference group for the minister has strong sanctions.

The parishes which ministers in this study served were affiliated with 22 different Protestant denominations: American Baptist, National Baptist, Church of the Brethren, Christian (Disciples of Christ), Congregational-Christian, Evangelical and Reformed, Evangelical United Brethren, Church of God, American Lutheran, Augustana Lutheran, Evangelical Lutheran, Lutheran-Missouri Synod, United Evangelical Lutheran, United Lutheran, Methodist, Moravian, Cumberland Presbyterian, Presbyterian, U.S.A., Presbyterian U.S., United Presbyterian, Reformed Church in America, Protestant Episcopal. In 1954 the 132,265 churches in these denominations had approximately 36,052,076 members. Grouping these churches into eight denominational families shows about one-fourth of the clergymen in this study to be Presbyterians, about one-fourth to be Methodist, one-sixth Episcopalians and one-seventh United Church of Christ. The rest were Baptist-Disciples, Brethren, Lutheran and other denominations (Table 6).

TABLE 6
DENOMINATIONAL AFFILIATIONS

Denominational Group	Percent of respondents (N = 1,111)
Baptist-Disciples	8
Brethren	6
United Church of Christ	14
Lutheran	7
Methodist	23
Presbyterian	24
Episcopal	16
Other denominations	2

Regional Location

The churches these 1,111 ministers served were formed in each of the continental forty-eight states and the District of Columbia. Alaska and Hawaii were not included in the survey. Regionally the greatest proportion of churches were in the North Central area (44 percent), while the West had the lowest proportion (12 percent). Twenty-six percent of the clergymen were from the South. Data are limited, however, on the role expectations of clergy from that area often identified as the Bible Belt. Representation was not available from the Southern Baptist convention and other denominations frequently associated with this part of the South. The Northeast held 21 percent of the ministers.

Type of community

American communities share in the general culture of the society, and there is variability in the expression of this culture within communities. Metropolitanness, urbanness and ruralness are ways in which the variability in community culture may be described. Using the U.S. Census categories (metropolitan-urban, metropolitan-rural, non-metropolitan-urban, non-metropolitan-rural), the parishes were classified by type of community. The greatest representation (39 percent) was metropolitan-urban, followed by non-metropolitan-rural (32 percent). Non-metropolitan-urban accounted for 24 percent, and metropolitan-rural for 5 percent.

Organizational structure

Churches may have relatively simple organizational structures or they may have complex structures. They may have a minimum program of preaching and religious education, or they may have a broad and inclusive program and many organizations within the congregation. The self-image of the minister would seem to be related to the relative complexity of the organization within which he is working.

The *number of parishes* served by clergymen ranged from several congregations ministered to by one clergyman, to one congregation served by several clergymen. Four out of five parishes included only one congregation. A very few parishes (fewer than 0.5 percent) were each served by five clergymen, and only a few churches had four full-time ministers on the staff.

Parish memberships ranged from 40 to 5,250. The average (mean) parish in our study had 572 members. Although the statistic is not exactly comparable, the average (mean) number of members per congregation in the 22 denominations represented in this research was 272. *Church school memberships* ranged from 1 to 2,800 and the average school has 274 members.

The employed personnel in the parish was classified as clergy, other professionals (as religious educators, musicians, social workers, etc.), office workers, and maintenance workers. (The staff of some parishes included seminarians who were not ordained, but who did perform clergy roles. For purpose of staff personnel analysis, the seminarians were functionally classified as clergy.) The average (mean) total staff was 3.207 and the median 1.967. This is expressed in full-time equivalents. Hence considering that some of the personnel were part-time, the actual number of persons employed would be greater than the mean seems to indicate. The largest parish in the study had a staff which consisted of the equivalent of 21 full-time persons.

The average (mean) number of ministers on a church staff was 1.2. One-half of the churches had a part-time lay professional worker (religious educator, choir director, or church visitor) who received remuneration. There was no lay professional staff worker in one-fourth of the parishes. Fifty percent had no stenographic staff member who received compensation. Twenty percent had a part-time secretary. Thirty percent had two or more full-time secretaries. The typical parish staff had a part-time janitor. One-fifth had one full-time janitor, and nine percent had two or more full-time janitors.

Economics of the Parish (1954)

The *local budgets* ranged up to $200,000. However, the average (mean) was $21,033 and the median was $13,294. The top extra-parochial or *benevolence budget* was also $200,000, with the average (mean) being $5,765 and the median $2,111. On a per capita basis parochial and extra-parochial annual expenditures combined averaged $47.33. (Per capita annual expenditures were calculated by totaling the local expenditures and the benevolence expenditures, and dividing that total by the number of church members.) The median was $42.31.

Summary

To summarize, the typical parish served by ministers in this study might have been located in California, New York, Illinois, Ohio or Pennsylvania. Regionally the parishes were especially located in the north central states. The type of community was most likely to be metropolitan-urban or non-metropolitan-rural. The minister served only one congregation. He did all the ministerial work himself (77 percent) and had a part-time lay professional worker (52 percent). He had no secretary (50 percent), and there was a part-time janitor (52 percent). In addition to the reporting minister, the staff included 2.207 man-year equivalent workers who were remuneratively employed. He ministered to 571 church members and was responsible for a church school of 273 persons. The annual (mean) parochial budget was $21,033. On the average there was an additional $5,765 for extra-parochial expenditures. Annual per member expenditures for all purposes was less than $50.00.

IV

THE MASTER ROLE

The analysis of the professional roles of the Protestant parish minister begins with the master role, a concept adapted from the work of Ida Harper Simpson (1956) on the student nurse. A master role identifies the distinctive aspects of an occupation; it distinguishes between the plumber and the policeman, the psychologist and the psychiatrist, the truck driver and the airline pilot. The master role of the minister defines the minister *qua* minister and distinguishes the occupational role of the minister from the occupational roles of other persons. It is the most inclusive concept we will use in describing the minister.

In addition to the master role, other types of clergy roles that may be analyzed from the perspective of self-image are integrative and practitioner roles. The integrative role orientation makes it possible for the clergyman as evangelist, educator, father-shepherd, community problem solver, etc., to focus his master role on specific goals, ends, or objectives. The practitioner roles (preacher, teacher, priest, organizer, administrator, pastor) are means, or professional skills, that he may use to attain the goals of his ministry. This chapter is confined to the minister's self-image of his master role. Integrative and practitioner roles will be discussed in later chapters.

Master role for the minister is closely related to what Donovan (1951) and Brooks (1960:50), describe as total status for the Catholic priest. According to Brooks, this includes both the professional and the personal roles of the priest. "He is ever the priest, whether functioning officially at the altar or relaxing in an informal circle of clergymen. He must always enact his role as total status. This does not mean that he must inject the whole of his personality into every relationship, but it does mean that he must involve his total status in every relationship." Also, the rabbi in an orthodox congregation may be thought of as having a total status (Poll, 1962). It is doubtful that the master role of the Protestant minister is as pervasive as that of the Catholic priest, as described by Donovan or Brooks, but this is a difference of degree rather than kind. The Protestant minister's status as a professional religious leader is probably as pervasive as that of the Catholic priest. However, his extra-professional role and his non-professional roles are not as completely within his clergy status as are those of the priest. "One of the hallmarks of the full professions (e.g., law or medicine) . . . is that the occupational role is institutionalized as the dominant role in the sense that, in conflicts between the role expectations of the occupation and those of some other social role, the occupational demands are given precedence. For example, a doctor would be expected to leave a family gathering to attend to an emergency case" (Mason, et al., 1959). Burchard (1954), suggests that the role which provides the individual with his primary identification takes first place in his hierarchy of role obligations, e.g., the role of military officer provides the primary identification for a chaplain. If this is true, those who follow different clergy careers would find that their master role definition as minister was affected by their primary role or organizational identification. The organizational identification of those serving a local church, an educational institution, a hospital, a church board, or a missionary organization would differ in accordance with the particular organization. To the extent that this is true, parish ministers will structure their roles differently from clergy in other organizational contexts.

Campbell and Pettigrew (1959) distinguish "three systems as relevant to [the clergy-man's] behavior: the self-reference system (SRS), the professional reference system (PRS), and the membership reference system (MRS). The SRS consists of the actor's demands, expectations, and images regarding himself. The PRS consists of several sources mutually related to his occupational role yet independent of his congregation: national and regional church bodies, the local ecclesiastical hierarchy (if any), the local ministerial association, personal contacts and friendships with fellow ministers, and probably, an image of 'my church' . . . The MRS consists simply of the minister's congregation." Perhaps our concept of master role would be similar to a self-reference system (SRS).

Data for the master role analysis were secured by asking each parish minister respondent a situational question: "When you are explaining the work of a minister to people . . . what is the major picture, image, or conception that you seek to give them?" It was an assumption of the question that the minister is influenced in his behavior by the beliefs he holds about himself, and by the image that the public holds of his role as a professional leader. Hence it was expected that he would respond in a way that reflected not only his socialization in the profession, but the length of that socialization. His answer would be structured by both his theological training and his experience as a practicing minister. Had the question been asked in a more formal, academic way in an examination conducted by seminary professors, his answers might have conformed more closely to traditional, formal creedal statements and systematic doctrines about the minister. It may be assumed that a young minister who is just graduating from a seminary and who has not had professional experience has a clear, perhaps academic, orientation to the ideological or theological aspects of his role. When he seeks ordination by a Bishop or Presbytery prior to actual parish work, he tends to be formal and technical in answering theological questions. In that situation he is being examined by his prospective eccle-siastical superior or his professional peers. It may be assumed, however, that in theologi-cal conversations with lay people in the church the mature, ordained parish minister with professional experience would be more informal and less technical in answering ques-tions about himself and his work. When a minister is dealing with people he may find that technical terms are ineffective, and he may seek to present an image of himself in terms that lay persons understand.

An analysis of the documentary answers was made to determine the minister's frame of reference, or definition of the situation, as he explained his work to people. The categories used in this analysis of the minister's master role were constructed induc-tively on the basis of replies received from the parish minister informants. Content analysis techniques were used to group answers having a common theme; and the names used to designate the orientations and concepts were selected for identification purposes after, rather than before, the data were collected.*

The clergy informants had two major frames of reference to their master role; an ideological (theological) orientation and a functional orientation. The former is structured by an articulation of the ideology of his church, and the latter by a series of appropriate and expected ways of behaving in fulfilling his function as a religious practitioner.

An *ideological orientation* consists of ideas and opinions stated by a person to explain his position in the social milieu. The ideology signifies the status and role of the person

---

*Methodological appendices and coding instructions used in the analysis for all parts of the study have been placed among the Blizzard papers at Speer Library, Princeton Theological Seminary, Princeton, New Jersey.

holding it and serves to rationalize his position in the social system in which he functions. The ideology about the ministry would serve to justify the person's identification with, or indoctrination into, the profession. Ideological indoctrination therefore would develop and reinforce his self-concept. As Parsons and Shils (1954) note, "What the individual believes about himself . . . becomes constitutive of his personality itself."

The ideological orientation of the minister to his master role is a part of the total ideology of the church. The minister is an articulator of this ideology. To the lay public he personifies religion. The theological beliefs that he has about himself are only a part of the total ideology that he accepts, and is committed by vocation to persuade others to accept. This lends added importance to those aspects of the ideology that constitute a doctrine of the ministry. Ideology about the ministry would serve to justify the clergyman's identification with the church as a social system and his integration into it as a professional leader.

Not only is the minister an ideological leader in the church, he is also a functionary in the church. As a practitioner of religion he develops a *functional orientation* to his master role. Through this frame of reference he attempts to describe himself to people in terms that will define his purpose and that will permit him to fulfill his purpose as a minister in relation to them. It reflects the day-to-day functioning of the minister in his master role. The functional orientation is an operational definition of the practice of the ministry, whereas the ideological or theological orientation is an operational definition of the theory of the ministry.

Each of these orientations to the master role were expressed through several themes (see Table 7). For example, the ideological or theological orientation about the ministry was expressed in two themes: the minister as a mediator between God and man, and as the servant of God. The functional orientation about the ministry was expressed in three

TABLE 7
MASTER ROLE ORIENTATION

Orientation and Theme	Percent (N = 1,111)*
Ideological (theological) orientation	
Mediator between God and man	34
Servant of God	22
Functional orientation	
Service theme	33
Inspirational theme	22
Pragmatic theme	3
No discernable orientation	28

*Categories were not mutually exclusive. Multiple answers were possible.

themes: the minister as the servant of the people, the inspirational leader, and the pragmatist. Since the question permitted the minister to select his own frame of reference, not all informants introduced the theological or functional orientations in discussing their master role. In fact, 28 percent of the ministers failed to do so. Since multiple answers were possible, a minister informant could be classified in each category and include both concepts of the theological dimension in his response.

Theological themes

Typical quotations from informants expressing a *mediator* theme are:

"An agent by which the heritage of the Christian faith is brought to these times, and through which the dynamic eternal truths of the faith are put into contextual relationship to contemporary problems."
"As Christ was the mediator between God and man, so (the minister) represents God to man and man to God, through Christ."
"(The minister) is a reconciler of men to themselves, to each other, and to God. He is the bearer of the Gospel of reconciliation which helps other men to become reconcilers too."
"(The minister) is called to be the friend of God and the friend of man. He is not an intermediary but he is a reconciler of man to God and man to man."
"A minister must be a channel through which the spirit of God moves into the lives of people and into the community. He is to bring God to the people and the people to God."
The minister is "an active worker in the great constructive enterprises of bringing God and people together (theologically, the work of redemption)."
"The minister is an interpreter helping people to understand God, themselves, and their fellow-men."
"The minister is an ambassador for and a fellow laborer with God in Christ."
"A minister forms a connecting link between Christ and people."

The ministers who were theologically oriented to their master role also used the *servant of God* (or the servant of Christ) theme. A profile of this group may be found in quotations from their responses:

"(The minister) is a servant of our Lord Jesus Christ in the midst of his fellow man. Complete and increasing devotion to Christ and His Church and a faithful work to that end."
"The minister is here to serve, even as Christ came to serve in many ways."
"A picture of one who gives himself unreservedly into the services of Christ, endeavoring to live according to His commandments."
"God's man, anything related to that is my job."
"I try to paint the picture of servanthood. The minister's task is that of a servant (slave) for Christ. As Paul's sentiment goes, we are fools for Christ's sake."
"Servant of God, not slave of people."
"The minister is a servant of God. His object is to serve, and has to please only God."
"The minister is a servant of God more than the servant of man, and therefore he seeks to do GOD'S will and not man's."

Functional orientation

The ministers who were functionally oriented to their master role used three concepts to describe themselves as ministers: the service theme, the inspirational theme, and the pragmatic theme. The most frequently articulated theme was that of the *service* concept of the ministry. Typical quotations from this type of informant are:

"We come to minister unto, not to be ministered unto."
The minister is "one who is always available to help people find answers to their deepest needs."
"The minister is what his title implies, namely, seeking to serve his own members and all others with whom he comes into contact."
The minister "is to help, whatever their needs—but he isn't God—he is only a servant."
"The minister is to serve the spiritual needs of the people, especially in time of crisis."
"The minister is the friend and servant of his people in every and all situations."
"I try to portray a servant role, a man not too busy to hear each individual case and to acknowledge God's guidance in my own personal relationships."
The minister "is one who seeks to serve the people, yet is more than a mere slave of the people."

Illustrative quotations from those using the theme of *inspirational leader* are:

"The minister is primarily a leader of leaders; he raises the visions and sets ideals for the people."
The minister is "an example of what one man believes and hopes to be."
"The minister is interested in lifting the morals and spiritual life of people."
"If a man stands on a busy street corner and looks up, those who pass by will also look up, trying to see what he is looking at. So a minister . . . in all things must be a man looking up and causing others to see God revealed in Jesus Christ."
"The minister is their leader to inspire, instruct and guide them in doing the work of the church, not their slave to do their work."
"The minister's . . . major duty is to encourage, inspire, and motivate people to live at their best in which they use all of their potential abilities and energy."
"The minister has but one main object. That is to live as high spiritually as each day permits, and lead others to that goal."
"The minister is one who is voluntarily disciplining himself to do as Christ would do, were He here, in order that folks may catch the same spirit and so live."
The minister is "one who, knowing the reality of personal faith, contagiously seeks to give it to others."

Typical quotations from those using the pragmatic theme are:

The minister's "task is to point out that religion has more than a personal meaning. It makes a difference in how you look at government and one's community."
The minister is "a man who seeks to help by interpreting the basic ideas and human experiences around which life must be organized."
The minister is "a man who is in business and must operate it to get Christian results."
"I'm a salesman, I have a product which has done me a world of good, something I want you to have, something you need."

Ministers were classified into five types on the basis of the ways in which they described their master role (see Table 8): those who were theologically oriented only, those both theologically and functionally oriented, those functionally oriented only, those neither theologically nor functionally oriented to the master role, and a residual group of ministers who gave idiosyncratic descriptions which were not classifiable, or who had no answer to the question.

TABLE 8
MASTER ROLE TYPOLOGY

Type	Orientation	Percent (N = 1,111)
One	Theological only	24
Two	Theological and functional	24
Three	Functional only	24
Four*	Neither theological nor functional	22
Five	Not classifiable	6

*Persons in this group are functionally oriented, but not specifically to a master role. They are analyzed in later chapters.

A comparison of the themes in theological and functional orientations of the master role yields an interesting difference. Analysis of the theological themes used by Type One and Type Two yields no significant difference.* However, a comparison of the functional themes used by Type Two and Type Three does yield a highly significant statistical difference (.001). Those both theologically and functionally oriented tend to express the inspirational theme about the master role, but those who are only functionally oriented tend to express the pragmatic theme to a greater extent. This difference is understandable since the inspirational theme describes the master role in terms more congenial to the implementation of the theological orientation than do the service and pragmatic themes. It would appear that for the clergy having both a theological and functional orientation to their master role, there is an interaction between these two orientations.

The work of the minister as a professional religious leader involves the application of theological insights into the everyday life of his parishioners. This statement seems to be supported by theologians. For example, Herbert H. Farmer (1947:11-70) in writing about Christian beliefs discusses the world of ideas, and the world of persons. Hence we assume that to accomplish his work the minister needs both the theological and functional orientations to his master role. The Type Two minister, having both orientations, may be described as having a more complete understanding of his or her master role. Type One and Type Three persons have less than complete understandings of their

---

*Differences cited in this and following chapters have been tested, using the chi square technique, for level of probability. Probabilities associated with chi square, of .05 or less are called significant.

master role. If he articulates neither the theological nor the functional orientation we assume that the minister has not generalized about his master role, or has an incomplete role. Some of these Type Four ministers were functionally oriented, but not to their master role. Their responses will be analyzed in later chapters.

The master role, as theologically and functionally defined by the parish minister, is the dependent variable in this chapter. Variability in the orientation the minister has toward his master role is operationally defined by using the five types referred to above. The series of independent variables (formulated and described in Chapter III) used to analyze this variability are characteristics of the clergyman, and of the parish organization which he serves.

Clergy Characteristics

Characteristics of the clergyman considered as independent variables were: personal factors, personality structure, referents, professional career, and criteria of effectiveness and success.

Personal factors

The minister's age, his marital status, and the number of children in his familiy were the variables cross-tabulated with the type of orientation he has toward his master role. Of these personal factors, only age was statistically significant (.01). The younger minister (44 years of age or younger) is more likely to be only theologically oriented to his master role, and the older minister is more likely to be only functionally oriented. Two theoretical interpretations of this relationship are possible.

On the one hand, it can be theorized that the younger minister has been instructed in the seminary more recently than has the older man. The seminary is the place where his formal socialization of the master role takes place. An essential part of his seminary training is instruction in the history of doctrine and systematic theology. When he leaves the seminary his theological orientation is most highly developed. The longer a man is out of seminary and in the parish, the greater the tendency for him to think in functional rather than theological terms about his master role. The necessity for the minister to be effective in his service to parishioners operates to increase his functional orientation.

On the other hand, a second theory about the relation between age of the minister and his orientation to his master role has to do with trends in theological thought. Prior to the time of this study, a revival of interest had taken place in theology. This was especially true in seminaries that had been influenced by neo-orthodox theologians from Europe. This theory would suggest that a change has occurred in the theological orientation given to ministers during their seminary career; and that theological concepts about the ministry have changed, as have ideas in other areas of doctrine. However it is not possible to verify either of these theories on the basis of data available in this research.

Personality structure

Participation in any professional role is related to the personality of the actor. According to Henry (1949), the role of a business executive "is the way of behaving and thinking that he knows best, that he finds rewarding, and in which he believes. Thus the role as socially defined has its counterpart in personality structure. To some extent, too, the personality structure is reshaped to be in harmony with the social role. The extent to which such reshaping of the adult personality is possible, however, seems limited. An initial selection process occurs which reduces the amount of time involved in teaching the appropriate behavior. Persons whose personality structure is most readily adaptable to this particular role tend to be selected, whereas those whose personality is not already partially akin are rejected."

Theoretically, we would expect that the ideological and functional orientations a minister has toward his master role would vary with his personality. We would assume that the minister who is democratic, emotionally mature, and open to change would tend to be both theologically and functionally oriented toward his master role. The minister who is authoritarian, emotionally immature or closed to change would tend to be theologically oriented to his master role, or perhaps have no articulate orientation to that role. The theory is to some extent supported. Emotional maturity was significant (at the .02 level of probability) but authoritarianism and openness to change were not significant. Those with high emotional maturity scores tend to be both theologically and functionally oriented to their master role. Those with moderate emotional maturity scores tend to be ideologically oriented.

Clergy referents

Data provided information for three types of referents in this research: status referents, mentor referents, and support (or dependence) referents. Each of these types was cross-tabulated with the five themes which define ideological and theological orientation to the minister's master role.

The *status referents* of the parish clergyman place him in a curious position. It might be assumed that theologically he would be equalitarian in terms of the people he seeks to know. The data show, however, that with almost equal frequency he seeks to know the professional and intellectual leaders of the community. This is in sharp contrast with the degree to which he identifies with industrial and labor leaders.

On the basis of theory it was assumed that the theologically oriented minister would tend to have ideological and equalitarian status referents to a greater degree than would those who are functionally oriented; and that the functionally oriented minister would tend to have occupational and religious status referents. However, when the status referents are related to the types of theological and functional orientations the clergyman has to his master role, no statistically significant differences were found.

On the basis of theory we would expect the theologically oriented minister to have seminary professors, well known churchmen and authors as *mentor referents* to a greater degree than those functionally oriented to their master role. However, clergymen with differing types of orientations to their master role do not differ in their religious mentors. Those who are only functionally oriented appear to select seminary professors as mentors as frequently as do those who are only theologically oriented to their master role. These images of mentor referents do not differ significantly in relation to his master role.

No significant statistical difference was found when the types of *support referents* of those having differing types of theological and functional orientation to their master role were analyzed. They tend to have the same kind of support referents.

Professional Career

We expected that a minister's master role orientation would change as his career developed. Each stage in his career would require a response to the role expectations of those he served. If he had had a career which included non-parochial appointments, his socialization to the master role would differ from those who had had a parish career only. Those ministers who were highly mobile professionally would adapt their master role orientation to the situation; those with low mobility would not. Again there is only partial support for this thesis. Ministers with a short professional career (those recently ordained), tended to be theologically, or theologically and functionally, oriented to the master role. The longer the career, the greater the tendency of the minister to be functional in his master role orientation (.001). A similar relationship was found for the minister's age.

Criteria for effectiveness and success

We theorized that the criteria which a minister has for effective parish work is related to the orientation which he has toward his master role. We assumed that personality characteristics, especially character, spiritual maturity, and intellectual ability, are associated to some degree with the minister's ideology. We also assumed that practitioner skills involved his functional orientation to his master role. It was theorized that the type of ideological and functional orientation a minister has to his master role would vary in relation to his *criteria of effectiveness* in parish work. However, the effectiveness criteria do not differ significantly in relation to the way in which ministers view their master role. Those who are only theologically oriented, and those who are both theologically and functionally oriented, describe their effectiveness criteria in the same way as do those who are only functionally oriented.

It was theorized that the type of ideological and functional orientations a minister had to his master role would vary in relation to his *criteria of success*. Theoretically, ministers oriented only theologically to their master role would include personality characteristics (especially spiritual life and character) in their criteria of success more frequently than would those with other master role orientations. They would be less inclined to include criteria involving denominational relations than would those who were only functionally oriented. Conversely, those who were oriented only functionally would tend to mention spiritual life less frequently than those with other orientations, and would cite criteria regarding denominational relations more frequently. Criteria regarding ministerial skills would be equally regarded by those holding differing orientations to their master role. The data confirm the theory. When the three foci regarding success criteria were tested for significance in relation to the types of orientation to the master role, a significant difference was obtained at the .05 level of probability.

The relationship that effectiveness and success criteria have to ideological and functional orientations to the master role invites comparison. On the one hand effectiveness and success are dimensions of the minister's master role that are both internal and external to the church culture. They reflect the values of the church and they appear to reflect generalized values in American culture. On the other hand, the ideological and functional orientations focus on criteria that are more or less internal to the specific culture of the church. These latter dimensions involve theoretical values and stated norms in the church. The former dimensions involve functional values and working norms. The relationship of effectiveness and success to ideological and functional dimensions is important for the parish minister. The minister's concept of effectiveness and success should be conditioned by the theological and functional dimensions of his master role. If this relationship is formed, then theological understandings become supportive of the functional understandings at the parish and community level. If not, then a basic ambiguity exists in the minister's self-image of his master role.

Organizational Factors

Characteristics of the parish in which the minister serves considered as independent variables were denomination, regional location, type of community, organizational complexity of the parish, and economics of the parish. These characteristics were cross-tabulated with the minister's orientation to his master role. All except regional location, number of church members, and total staff differed significantly.

Denomination

When the five types of orientation toward the master role were cross-tabulated with the eight denominational groupings which were part of this study (Baptist-Disciples, Brethren, United Church of Christ, Lutheran, Methodist, Presbyterian, Protestant Episcopal, all other), the denomination to which a parish belonged, and in which the minister was ordained, was highly significant (.001) as a variable in relation to the minister's orientation to his master role. Lutheran and Protestant Episcopal parish clergy tend to be Type One; they are typically oriented only theologically to their master role. Presbyterians are typically Type Two, both theologically and functionally oriented to their master role. Baptist-Disciples and Brethren ministers tend to be Type Three, only functionally oriented. However, Methodist clergymen are more strongly Type Three in their orientation than are those of any other denomination. The United Church of Christ minister is ambivalent in his orientation to the master role.

The themes within the two orientations were analyzed by denomination. Considering the theological themes, the servant of God theme was stressed especially by the Presbyterians, but also by the Baptist-Disciples, Lutherans and Brethren. The remaining four denominational groupings, especially the Episcopalians, stressed the theme of mediator between God and man. Considering the functional themes, service was stressed by Presbyterians, Baptist-Disciples, Brethren, and especially by the Lutherans. The inspirational theme was especially stressed by the "other" denominations, but also by the Brethren and Methodists. The pragmatic theme was especially stressed by United Church of Christ ministers and by Episcopalians and Methodists.

The relationship between specific theological and functional themes presents an interesting denominational profile. The Presbyterians, Lutherans and Baptist-Disciples couple the servant of God and service themes. The "other" denominations couple the mediator and inspirational themes. The United Church of Christ ministers couple the mediator and the pragmatic themes. The Brethren, Episcopalians, and Methodists are somewhat ambivalent. Some Brethren ministers couple the servant of God theme with the service theme and others with the inspirational theme. Some Episcopalians couple the mediator with the service theme, others do so with pragmatic themes. The Methodists couple the mediator theme with the inspirational theme or with the pragmatic themes.

The denominational variability in the minister's orientation to his master role is consistent with theoretical expectations. The denominations, especially as grouped, represented different theological traditions, and have unique aspects to their practice of the ministry. The fact that certain denominations stress the theological orientation to the ministry and others stress the functional orientation is also consistent with the emphases in the various traditions.

Regional location

In theory the orientation of the minister to his master role would vary from region to region. It would be expected that ministers in the southern region would tend toward the theological orientation to a greater degree than those in other regions; however, this theory is not sustained by our data. The type of theological and functional orientation the minister has toward his master role is not significantly different on the basis of region.

Type of Community

By reputation, non-metropolitan communities (especially rural) are more conservative in religion, and metropolitan areas are more liberal. We would expect ministers in metropolitan areas to have a functional orientation to their master role and ministers in non-metropolitan rural areas to be ideologically oriented. There is a significant difference (.05) in the master role orientation on the basis of type of community, but not as theorized. Rather, non-metropolitan and rural ministers seemed to be articulate about their master role orientation, while metropolitan urban ministers tended to be inarticulate about it.

Organizational complexity of the parish

Three measures of organizational complexity were statistically significant with respect to ideological/functional orientations: number of congregations in the parish (at the .05 level), number of persons in the church school (.05), and number of clergymen on the staff (.02). However, number of church members, and total number of employed staff members (including clergy, other professionals, office workers, and maintenance workers) were not significant. Clergymen who were both theologically and functionally oriented to their master role tended to be in parishes that had more than one congregation, and to be the only minister serving the parish staff. The smaller the church school, the more likely that the minister was theologically oriented to his master role; conversely, the larger the church school, the greater the tendency for the clergyman to be functionally oriented.

Economics of the parish

Each of the three measures of the economics of the parish (amount of annual local expenditures, amount of annual benevolence expenditures, and per capita expenditures) were significant at the .05 level. The lower the gross budget for local and benevolent expenditures, and the lower the per capita expenditures, the greater the tendency for the minister to be theologically and functionally oriented or only functionally oriented to his master role. Conversely, clergymen who were only theologically oriented to their master role tended to be in high per capita cost and high gross budget parishes.

The frequency with which the themes in the theological orientation were expressed by the minister differed significantly when the economic status of the parish was considered. Ministers serving in high cost churches, as measured by per capita program expenditures, tended to stress the mediator theme, whereas those in low-cost churches stressed the service theme.

The relationship between the minister's orientation toward his master role and the per capita cost of the parish program is not easily interpreted, especially since the number of members in the parish is not significant. When these two measures, number of church members and per capita cost, are cross-tabulated the nature of the relationship becomes apparent. Small churches, those having fewer than 200 members, tended to have a high per capita program cost. These are also the churches whose clergymen tended to be theologically oriented to their master role. The larger churches were more efficient economically and were served by clergymen who tended to view their master role functionally.

Summary

This chapter has probed the minister's self-image about his master role with a view to developing greater understanding of it and of the role-ambiguities that are apparently faced by Protestant parish clergymen. The master role (the minister *qua* minister) is seen as dominant in the total role or status. It is partial rather than total in Protestantism, as contrasted with the total role or status of the Catholic priest. Even though the ministerial role is only partial, it is nonetheless a master role in relation to a clergyman's other roles.

Variability in the minister's concept of his master role has been defined operationally according to the major picture, image, or conception which the minister seeks to give people about the work of a minister. The parish minister is seen as having a dual orientation to his master role, an ideological and/or a functional orientation. The former is basically theoretical, and the latter is practical. Five types were delineated using the possible combinations of the theological and functional orientations. Essentially these types ranged from the most theological to the least theological; and conversely, from the least functional to the most functional.

The dependent variable in this chapter has been the five types of theological and functional orientations which the minister has toward his master role. Two series of independent variables were examined in relation to the variability of master role orientation, clergy and organizational.

In theory it had been expected that the clergy variables (personal factors, professional experience, and evaluative criteria) would be less significant than the organizational variables. This theory seems to be confirmed. Of the clergy variables, only the minister's age and his criteria of success were found to be significantly related to variability in his orientation to the master role. However, the organizational variables (with the exception of regional location and some of the measures of size of parish i.e., number of members and number of staff members) were significant.

The significance of organizational (parish) variables and the seeming lack of significance of the more personal (clergy) variables raises some interesting questions about the socialization of the clergy into their profession. Present knowledge about the social psychology of the clergy is not adequate to permit definitive statements to be made concerning a minister's beliefs about himself in theological or functional terms. The research reported in this chapter is suggestive and exploratory but inconclusive on this point. It does indicate a need for a serious study in depth of the doctrine of the ministry as it is related to a minister's personality structure; his professional experience as a practitioner of religion; his status, mentor, and dependent referents; and his own evaluative criteria for the profession. It would appear from the analysis of the minister's concept of his master role presented in this chapter that clergymen share a common socialization to their profession to a greater degree than present-day popular folklore about the ministry would suggest. A need for restructuring the concept of the minister's work in our society may be implied in this discussion about the master role. Such areas as selective factors in the recruitment of the clergy, the concept of his vocation, and the professional training of the clergy need further research in order to test this implication.

The strength of the organizational variables raises questions about the relationship between clergy in different denominations. The importance of economic differentials would appear to have implications worthy of further research on the relations between the clergy and their parishioners. Furthermore, size of parish as a factor raises questions about the relationship between the minister's orientation to his work and organizational developments within Protestantism. These are only a few of the research questions raised by the strength of environmental factors in relation to the minister's orientation to his master role.

V

THE INTEGRATING ROLES

Ministers have different orientations to their master role. In their professional relations with people and groups they may differ according to the goals toward which their behavior is directed. In this research the minister's goal orientation in relation to his professional work is called the integrative role. It is what he is trying to accomplish with people in his professional practice of religion. It is the end toward which he is working in his professional relationship with parishioners, church associations, community groups, and the general public.

The minister may, or may not, be consciously aware of his integrative roles and the goal orientation that they give to his professional behavior. He may never have been analytic about his behavior from the perspective of an integrative role. If he is aware of his integrative roles he may be either covert or overt in his behavior regarding them. In the present study we are dealing with his overt behavior.

The relationship between the master role and the integrative roles is a matter of the level of generalization. Master role analysis involves a relatively high level of generalization about the parish minister's professional work. Practitioner role analysis, which is discussed in chapters VI and VII, involves a relatively low level of generalization. Integrative role analysis is between the master and practitioner roles. Integrative roles are less general and more specific than is the master role; they are also less universal and more particular. Practitioner roles are the most particular and the most specific in this analysis.

Clergymen may be identified by the differing ways in which their goal orientation is structured. In this analysis thirteen integrative role categories were derived by a content analysis of the themes used by the ministers to describe their work; and were then grouped under three general headings. Five of the thirteen integrative roles have a long history within Protestantism and have substantial religious meaning. We refer to them as the *traditional* integrative roles: believer-saint, scholar, evangelist, sacramentalist, and father-shepherd. Seven of the integrative role categories appear to have a somewhat secular orientation. A specific or unique religious orientation may be associated with these integrative roles, but is not inherent in the role. They are designated as *contemporary* integrative roles: the interpersonal-relations specialist, the parish promoter, the social actionist or social problem solver, the educator, the subcultural specialist, the community religious leader or the representative of the church-at-large, and the churchman or denominational politician. The *general practitioner* has no identifiable integrative role.

Ministers differed in the strength of their integrative roles, and in the number of goals toward which their practitioner role behavior was directed. If a minister had only one integrative role, it was designated as primary. If he had two integrative roles, the stronger or more dominant was designated as primary and the other as secondary. If he had three or more goals he was classified in this analysis as being a general practitioner. He was also classified as a general practitioner if he did not articulate an integrative role (see Table 9).

TABLE 9
INTEGRATIVE ROLE DISTRIBUTION

Integrative Roles	Primary Integrative Role (Percent)	Secondary Integrative Role (Percent)
Traditional roles		
Believer-saint	8	6
Scholar	1	2
Evangelist	9	2
Sacramentalist	1	1
Father-shepherd	20	5
	39	16
Contemporary roles		
Interpersonal-relations specialist	18	5
Parish promoter	13	9
Social actionist	12	3
Educator	4	1
Sub-cultural specialist	2	1
Community religious leader	2	0.5
Churchman	1	2
	52	21
General practitioner (no identifiable integrative role: or 3 or more such roles	9	
No secondary integrative role		63
	100%	100%

Goal Orientation

Traditional integrative roles

The *believer-saint* role has been a traditional one for the clergyman. The minister who has this integrative role lives his life in a way that commands the respect of his parishioners and others in the community. He conceives himself primarily to be a "man of faith" who is humbly seeking God's will for his life. He thinks that personal piety adds a quality to everyday living that is highly desirable and practical. He seeks to be an exemplar for others to follow because he is dependent upon God and he expects that his behavior will inspire emulation from members of his congregation and those whom he seeks to serve. His goal is to live so that others will want to be religious in their lives, as he is in his. The believer-saint was a primary integrative role orientation for 8 percent of the informants, and a secondary role for 6 percent.

The believer-saint tends to depend on the quality of his own spiritual life. Quotations from informants illustrate the several behavioral qualities that are associated with this integrative role:

The believer-saint stresses the *importance of the devotional life*, "personal devotions (not a job, but a ministry)"; "the practice of the presence in prayer."

He seeks to "maintain a growing experience of God," and is concerned with the "deepening of (his) devotional life."

He expresses anxiety about the "problem of growing stale spiritually"; he is interested in "the great devotional classics," and "the study of more devotional literature" in theological education.

He is concerned with his own *sincerity, earnestness* and *personal morality*. One minister noted that in his first parish he learned that he had "to keep (himself) at a high level of moral and spiritual life."

Another felt it a problem in his present parish "to keep (himself) unspotted from the world."

Still another stated that to be successful in the ministry it was necessary to have "a transparent personal and public life which is above reproach."

The believer-saint states that the ministry "is a labor of love, devotion and *conviction* . . . It is too great to be anything but humble about . . ."

He represents himself as "a humble follower of Jesus Christ."

Speaking about effectiveness in the ministry, he states that "most important is likeness to Christ, an imitation of His humility."

Humility is closely related to the strength of the minister's conviction. "Humility . . . is founded upon a faith or assurance . . ."

The minister is expected "to be willing to hold firm to (his) convictions."

Coupled with these qualities is a *personal warmth*. The minister is effective as he has a "warm heart of love for Christ."

It is important that he maintain a "spiritual glow" and that he represent himself as being "a Christian and highly glad of it."

The minister's own life is the focus of the believer-saint integrative role. He is living his religion. He stresses the importance of his own life.

One informant, for whom believer-saint was a primary integrative role, wrote of his "own personal life of prayer and study—this is obviously a separate category from [preacher, pastor, priest, teacher, administrator, etc.] but basic to it."

Another states: "I try to show them that I am so convinced within that I live what I believe to be the work of the minister."

Others articulate the same theme in different words. "The minister is God's man . . . His first responsibility is to God. If he is true to that responsibility, he is thereby bound to be true to his responsibility to his parishioners and fellow men. He is to be a living example of God's will for mankind."

"A minister can only be a minister as he shares God with his people. A minister cannot lead his congregation further in these spiritual things than he himself has gone."

"... We, as ministers, cannot hope to transmit a vibrant, challenging faith in God which will utterly change the lives of men unless we have that faith ourselves." The believer-saint writes of a mentor relationship as follows: "Dr. _____ has challenged me as a very . . . humble, devoted servant of God. He is very spiritual (some people question what that means, he demonstrates it), very humble, very inspiring, understandable, and has a love for people and for his Master."

"I admire the Rev. _____ because of the infectious quality of his life and his ability to relate people to God. It was through my first contacts with him . . . that I was led to study for the ministry. A Christ-centered man."

Other ideas associated with a mentor are: "Schweitzer—for his humility and selflessness"; A professor—"his love for the Scriptures and his contagious spirit"; A seminary instructor—"In him I could see God"; A Bishop—"his spiritual depth."

Similar ideas are expressed about clergy peer referents:

"His deep devotion to our Lord";

"I appreciate his joy in Christ";

"His spiritual power and humility."

One informant wrote about his admiration for a fellow clergyman because he had "a great faith in prayer and in what God can do with an ordinary congregation if completely surrendered."

Other informants report they seek peer relationships with "the genuinely pious" and with those "who are progressing with explorations in the area of prayer."

Traditionally the ministry has been one of the learned professions. In many Protestant denominations the robe of office is an academic rather than an ecclesiastical garment. The clergyman's office is called a study. The minister's life is characterized by a patient examination of the Scriptures, a perspective on church history, and a technical knowledge of the doctrine of the church and its interpretation. He is primarily a student of sacred, as contrasted with secular, learning. The minister is supposed to go beyond mere acceptance of Christianity into a full understanding of its teachings. Regardless of the educational requirements of his particular denomination, the minister is expected to know the technical facts about religion. The layman depends on him to answer questions and to explain as fully as possible about what the faith is. The *scholar* type goes beyond this. He is not only interested in religious knowledge and theological subjects, but he is also interested in a general study of religion in relation to society and culture.

The minister whose primary integrative role is that of scholar sees it as an end in itself. His scholarly interest may lead him into areas of intellectual activity that are peripheral for many clergymen. He goes beyond the clergyman who sees scholarship as a spiritual discipline or as a means to a more effective performance of the practitioner roles. Very few (one percent) of the clergy in this research had scholar as a primary integrative role. It was a secondary role for two percent.

The minister whose integrative role is that of the scholar may have an image of the minister as "a man of profound learning." He may rate "study" as first in importance in his work and state that he has "become increasingly convinced of the importance of study." Or he may "find a great deal of pleasure in studies" and "strive to keep up (his) studies faithfully." The scholar stresses that he "writes" his sermons. As a peer referent he may admire a neighboring minister who has a "keen mind." He may admire a mentor "for his life and careful, thorough thinking," or for his "thorough competency of scholarship."

The scholar may focus his ministry in his own parish or he may have much interest in a ministry beyond the bounds of his own parish.

Typical of the former is the minister who states: "I consider myself a missionary to the intellectuals who feel that church and religion is not for them . . . We have 48 Ph.D.'s in our congregation, 26 doctors, teachers, lawyers, professional men. Our program must be geared to them."

Or the parish minister, who in referring to a mentor relates: "helped me see what a man of real intellectual stature can do in the parish . . . After I met him, I was unable to spend a lifetime with only Plato, Aristotle, Kant and Hegel."

The clergyman who has an interest in a ministry beyond the bounds of his own parish may be illustrated by the man who spends much time as a writer of articles, denominational materials, and books while he carries on his parish ministry at the same time, or the parish minister who is called upon to conduct college and university missions and to lecture at colleges and universities.

The evangelist is dedicated to a "call" to proclaim the Word of God. His faith is like a rock; it is unshakeable. He knows what he believes. He feels compelled to preach the Word with a view to saving souls. Those who are ready to believe are led into a "saving knowledge" of Jesus Christ. Those who are not receptive to his message are confronted with the Wisdom of God and the foolishness of men. The evangelist's behavior assumes that the Gospel is normative for human life. In his effort to make this clear he often deals in "blacks and whites," feeling that shades of gray would compromise his position. Hence this role pattern may harbor in some a type of authoritarianism. For nine percent of the clergy in this study, evangelist is the primary integrative role; for two percent it is a secondary role.

The evangelist feels that "the only program (his) church has is the salvation of souls." Or he may offer this key statement: "There is no substitute in the parish ministry of telling people through your actions and words about Jesus Christ."

"My parish demands a dynamic . . . and evangelistic strategy."

"In my ministry I am concerned about the problem of conversion, how to present the church to the people in it and to others seeking admission."

"We are God's agents called upon to preach the saving Gospel of Christ."

As peer or mentor referents, those who have this integrative role may cite either fellow clergy who have conducted evangelistic meetings for them, or a nationally known big-name evangelist.

The *sacramentalist* seeks to lead a person to see the value of the liturgy as a religious way of life. He seeks to develop on the believer's part a commitment to the sacramental view of life. This integrative role pattern has as its goal the use of a specific and concrete ritual as a part of the many phases of the daily life of the parishioner. One percent of the ministers in this research are sacramentalists from the point of view of a primary integrative role. An additional one percent have sacramentalist as a secondary integrative role.

The minister whose integrative role is that of sacramentalist stresses "the relation of the Holy Eucharist to all work, and . . . (applies) the insights of the modern liturgical movement in Europe and England to (his) ministry."

He thinks that "the ministers must represent a Holy Fellowship centered in the corporate worship of Almighty God and working as a reconciling element in the community, reconciling men to God and men to each other."

He emphasizes "that the corporate approach to liturgical worship has much to say about our problems of living and working together." He thinks that "the sacramental life is a synthesis of matter and spirit," a relationship which is "particularly important in a society which has reduced Christianity to a system of morals and ethics."

He feels that "as the parish (minister) goes about his daily life, it is Christ who acts in him baptizing, consecrating bread and wine, ministering to and healing the sick, and re-creating the society in which the church lives and moves." The liturgy and the sacraments are more than a ritual, they "express the life of the church."

Twenty percent of the clergy in this study have as a primary integrative role the *father-shepherd* pattern. It was a secondary role for five percent. This minister feels he is like a comforting father to his children. As a shepherd of the flock he understands and protects them. He is a strong figure. Implicit in the father-shepherd role is the fact that the minister is a man of unshakeable faith; in his presence God is near to man. The specifics in church work do not have to be accounted for by the father-shepherd. Without doing any specific duty he performs an adequate service to his church in his own mind and in the minds of his parishioners if he is himself and is near when needed. People accept the minister for what he represents to them and for the meaning that his presence puts into the routine as well as the crises of their lives. Thus the routine pastoral calling, cheering the sick and being with the dying, visiting the mother with her new-born child and the aged in his congregation all are part of a good day's work.

The father-shepherd speaks of his mentor as "a wise pastor and a great churchman," and as "a man of prayer, patience and poise."

When he describes a ministry oriented to this integrative role he may suggest: "He can break the bread of life for men and feed them . . . He can stand by a family facing disgrace and know what it means to be God's man for them. He can sometimes say a quiet word to the sick and feel the very current of God's power flowing through him. He can sit with anxious parents waiting the outcome of an operation on a child, and finding them gaining calm because he is there."

Contemporary integrative roles

The *interpersonal-relations specialist* and the father-shepherd integrative roles are similar in that both focus on person-to-person relations with parishioners. However, certain differences are apparent. The father-shepherd appears to be oriented to traditional theological values more often than does the interpersonal-relations specialist, who tends toward contemporary theological values. The father-shepherd is universalistic in his relations with parishioners. While he is interested in persons, he deals rather diffusely with the flock. The interpersonal-relations specialist is particularistic in his work with parishioners. He works with individuals. The father-shepherd tends to take the initiative in calling on parishioners, whereas the interpersonal-relations specialist tends to respond to parishioner's needs through counseling. The former may be the more directive, and steeped in the traditional pastoral arts, while the latter is somewhat nondirective and is committed to the contemporary arts of clinical psychology and the personality sciences.

The integrative role of the minister as interpersonal-relations specialist seems to have increased in popularity among both the clergy and the laity. In part this is related to developments that have taken place in modern mass society. Some ministers are disturbed because they feel that they, as ministers, reflect the cultural norms of society in their work. For example, a trend toward larger organizational units which is evident in society is also evident in the church. Ministers are troubled because they feel that bigness and organizational conformity have become ends rather than goals. As a result they have anxieties about their ministry.

Another factor related to the popularity of the interpersonal-relations specialist role is the increased importance of the psychiatric profession. The psychiatrist seems to be interested in cooperative professional relations with the clergy; and the clergy appear to enjoy supportive identity in their relations with psychiatrists. Furthermore, clinical training as a part of theological education has increased the clergyman's appreciation for and understanding of the techniques of the therapeutic professions.

Many ministers, frustrated in their ministry, have looked for and found increased self-understanding. In this search, they have sought help in various types of therapeutic situations from informal counseling, from clinical training and from psychiatric treatment. As they achieve intrapersonal and interpersonal competence they seek to use the insights and experience gained to increase their own effectiveness as clergymen. In so doing they tend to adopt the interpersonal-relations specialist role as an integrative one. The interpersonal-relations specialist approach is taken by almost one-fifth of the informants. There were five percent for whom it was a secondary role.

As a peer referent one minister reported: "The most helpful person has been a psychology professor who is one of our members . . . I have spent an hour a week for four months with (him) . . . As a result, I am less compulsive and more effective, both personally and professionally."

Key statements that identify this integrative role are: "Increasingly my ministry becomes a series of conferences with people who have crucial problems." "I feel the need personally to understand human personality (my own and others) better to relate the various functions of a church to this understanding in a creative way."

The *parish promoter* is a primary integrative role for every eighth informant, and is the most frequent secondary integrative role. Those who have this orientation apply the skills of the secular organizer and promoter to the local church system. The successful business man who organizes his personnel and promotes his program is the role model of this type of ministerial respondent. This minister seeks to run a smooth organization that measures its effectiveness by statistical standards of attendance, e.g., new members, budget, variety of organizational structures, and recognition by national headquarters for cooperativeness in a denominationally recommended program. The mentor of the parish promoter is seen in this admission: "Some of my best guidance comes from hard-headed business men." In identifying his peer referents another informant stated: "I like to 'pick' the mind of other clergy especially. 'Have you done this or met this problem?' "

Some key statements that portray the parish promoter are: "There are . . . some cliques in this church that have been prevented from dominating the entire life of the church. A pastor of a church of this nature needs to be adroit at knowing when to yield and when to give ground, but if he gives too much ground he will be on the run. How on earth do you develop leaders and still keep them in their place?"

"In most areas I am the spearhead. (Parishioners) wait for me to begin any movement."

"The minister is primarily a leader of leaders in the organizational life of the church . . . he must recruit them, define their job, get them trained and give them a deep consecration for their task."

The *social actionist* or social problem solver focuses on issues prevalent in the local or international communities. This integrative role is somewhat akin to the interpersonal-relations specialist in that both have a role in changing a situation—one a social and the other a personal situation. However, the social actionist works with groups, institutions, and committees, while the interpersonal-relations specialist largely works with individuals. The social actionist is likely to be more aggressive and directive, and the interpersonal-relations specialist is likely to be non-aggressive and non-directive. The social actionist may conceive his role as somewhat akin to the Israelite prophets of the Old Testament times, or he may identify himself with modern crusaders who wish to rectify an injustice or to make some aspect of our life more humane. He may identify himself closely with the interests of economic, political, educational, or health and welfare groups. He may espouse in the name of the Gospel the cause of labor or management, one particular political party, public or private education, and social or individual medicine. This is a primary integrative role for more than twelve percent, and a secondary role for three percent of the clergy in this survey.

The social actionist may admire a mentor referent because he has "strong Christian convictions on social issues which (he is) not afraid to express." He may identify community leaders in social and civic work as peers. A key statement made by a minister with this type of integrative role orientation reported: "The crying need is that the church be more than a social club of middle class, successful people. It must find some ways to strike harder at social problems (crime, alcoholism, delinquency, war, secularism, immorality, neuroticism)."

The *educator* integrative role represents the primary goal orientation of four percent and a secondary orientation for one percent of the clergy respondents. The role of educator is seen by those in this pattern as the most valid expression of the ministry. Religious education is viewed as the major program of the church; plans are to be made, leaders to be recruited and trained, and groups to be supervised. The educator must understand the basic philosophy of education, know the needs and abilities of children and young people, and possess certain special skills associated with an educational program. Minister-educators may range in theological position from conservative to liberal, but it is important that they be committed to the basic goal of religious education, i.e., that faith be communicated appropriately and comprehensively at every age level. To implement this goal a full program involving all resources of the church is in order.

The educator is an integrative role for two general types of parish clergyman: those who are the only minister on the staff and for whom directing the educational program is a central emphasis in their work; and those who are on a multiple clergy staff and specialize in administering the educational program while other clergy colleagues specialize in other aspects of the program.

Typical of the former is the minister who reported: "from experience (in a former parish) I learned that the minister must ever teach."

Such a minister may feel that "the ministry in the local church is essentially a teaching ministry."

Or he may state: "I am more and more convinced that it is extremely important for the (minister) to do effective teaching of the Word of God at every opportunity."

Another minister expressed a similar idea when he stated: "Christian education in the church school is more and more a necessity and ministers need better training in understanding the problem and in fact all youth problems and activities."

One minister stated: "A great deal of a (minister's) work is done in the classroom and much that he does otherwise is teaching too." Another reported: "The minister has the job to teach people about God, whether preaching, teaching, visiting, counseling, etc."

The latter type, the parish minister who specializes in education, may have made his decision as related by one informant: "The decision to specialize in the position of minister of Christian education came more out of the actual experience of the parish, the vision of the need, and the opportunity to take my present work." He described the educational program he administers for a church of 1,600 members as follows: "Planning the Christian education program; enlisting church school teachers, and all phases of the personal relationships involved; administering weekday religious education program; ordering supplies and attending to details of educational program; and planning a new religious education building, consulting with architect."

The *sub-cultural specialist* is a primary integrative role for two percent of the respondents and a secondary role for one percent. This role helps the minister see his work from the perspective of whatever group he chooses for his ministry. It may be a ministry for the inner city, the suburbs or the rural areas. He may consider himself a specialist in ministering to laboring men or to the managerial class, or to a racial or an ethnic group.

Part of the appeal of the sub-cultural specialist role is that the group or area to which the clergyman ministers is characterized by well-publicized problems. These problems are usually symptomatic or indicative of the changing structure of society, and are often the foci of denominational programs designed to support clergy who have this integrative role.

Ministers may be aware of this type of integrative role because of the writings by or about a clergyman who has been, or is, a sub-cultural specialist. John Frederic Oberlin is a prototype of the rural cultural specialist (Beard, 1946). Edmund B. Chaffee (1933) through his work at Labor Temple in New York City, symbolized a ministry to the industrial worker. Father Myers has attracted attention through his work in the deteriorating areas of New York City (Myers, 1957).

The sub-cultural specialist will have strong motivation. Being a minister to a cultural group will be a specific calling for him. He states his call in these terms:

"My call is to the rural ministry—it is not a sacrifice, it is a privilege!"
"The rural ministry has been my chosen field."
He tends to think that his group or area has unique problems that distinguish it from others. "Rural churches do not present the same problem as do city churches."
"I believe my work in the city church is most effective . . . I would not want another type of ministry."

The sub-cultural specialist attempts to identify with a way of life, a culture. "I have attempted to understand their problems and way of life and have been sympathetic in attitude." The minister may have been reared on the farm or in the city slums, or he may be the son of a laboring father. If he has not been reared in a family of the class to which he seeks to minister, he may seek specialized training to assist him in developing identity and understanding. Some sub-cultural specialists actually engage economically in the way of life of the people to whom they minister:

"I own and operate a farm and teach agriculture in a Veteran's Farmer Training School. My knowledge and training in agriculture help me to counsel with farmers in my congregation who may need information and advice."

"I serve in a small church in an industrial neighborhood . . . I also work full time as a machine operator in one of the factories in the neighborhood, and at which some of our congregation also work . . . This is aimed at helping overcome gaps between church and working people, and between pastor and his people . . ."

The *community religious leader* carries on his ministry to the community with his church as a base of operations. He is oriented to the community rather than to a local congregation. He feels that this is the real ministry. He thinks of his church as an integrator of the community and of himself as the coordinator of religious activities in the community. He is the representative of the church in community affairs, his participation in community activities is an essential part of his ministry, and his church program and ministry are community-centered. This is an integrative role for two percent of the informants. Fewer then one percent have it as a secondary role.

The community religious leader integrates his ministry around the idea that "the church must reach out into the community with its influence rather than expect all people to come to it for help." He feels that the chief problem is "the inability of the church to integrate itself in the life of the community and become an integral part of it." He charges that ministers are: "inclined to want to bring the community into their church rather than minister to the spiritual needs of the community." Or he may place "an emphasis upon the need for serving the community rather than building the church as an institution to be served." He tries "to make his church a community church, and to integrate the church into community ventures." Also he tries "to bridge the gap between the church and community agencies."

The community religious leader holds that "the church has a vital place in the community, and he tries to identify the church with the needs of the community." He states:

"I believe a pastor should be a real part of the community and make his presence felt."

"Bring the Christian witness . . . to bear on the community life."

"People expect the minister to be interested in all phases of community life."

"A pastor must learn to work in all aspects of community life."

"The church, to be the church, must have a program that will make God's message live in every aspect of community life."

The community religious leaders describe their ministry as follows: "I try to make myself available as a minister to the spiritual needs of the whole community, both churched and unchurched." "I am willing to be all things to all so far as possible."

The minister is "a man of God and servant of the people always ready to be of service to any person, any group, any organization, any time, anywhere."

"I learned that to fulfill my ministry I must be ready to do anything which must be done and which is going to benefit the people of the parish or of the community at large."

"The minister should attach himself to the community and identify himself with their needs and longings. He must be a friend of the community, a revealer of the truth of God and a guide to those who seek his help and to the community."

The community religious leader may admire a fellow minister for "the earnest attention he gives to every person and problem brought to his attention." His mentor may be Toyohiko Kagawa, Albert Schweitzer, or Sam Higgenbottom because each knew "how to make the church open to all." Or he may be somewhat vague and speak of his mentor as a "tried, trusted and accredited friend at large." The community religious leader admires a clergyman whose biography offers him a model. He may report: "I make a particular point of calling most on the outcast and poor in the community, for it is here that the greatest needs, emotional, physical, psychological and spiritual seem to exist, and once you get to know these people, they seem to be the ones who will most readily come to you and ask for help." He may honor a peer who ministers to a fashionable congregation but who insists on ministering to those on the wrong side of the tracks. When describing his own ministry he refers to "my work as being a friend, a fellow traveler—along life's road—together we can learn and grow and pray and sing and find a greater purpose and joy in life."

The *churchman* (or denominational politican) is a primary integrative role for only one percent, and a secondary role for two percent. As an integrative role it is a product of an explicit or implicit faith in an organizational system. This minister feels that his purposes are best forwarded by conformity to the system, and he will stress cooperative work or connectional work. In a sense denominational matters are part of every minister's work, but for some this is integrative. They are committed to the system; their professional creed is: "take care of the system and the system will take care of you."

The minister for whom churchman is a primary integrative role, has as a goal the running of his parish as a local unit of the denomination. He may have had previous occupational experience in business, in the military or in government where he was a manager, leader, or executive of a unit of a larger organization where his unit program was a part of a national program.

He feels the minister needs "a thorough knowledge of the working program of the denomination (its national organizations, boards, and service agencies) so that he can lead the local church to gear into that program."

He believes ministers should cooperate "with the program beyond the local church and the concerted application of the general church program to their own local church," and states: "The program of our denomination works wonders."

He feels that his denomination must be well united on highly controversial issues and tries to be a good minister of his denomination.

He may state that he is "thoroughly in accord with the system" of his denomination.

The churchman considers that committee work for the conference, diocese, presbytery or association is part of his responsibility as a parish minister. He may say: "I like to go to meetings of the church courts."

He admires a peer as "a good churchman." His mentors are regional and national administrators in the denomination. One parish minister admired his bishop as "one of the most democratic leaders I have ever known." A minister in a denomination with a different polity described four national leaders as "genuine Christian statesmen."

General practitioner

The general practitioner does not have a primary integrative role. His goals are relative and his ministry is not dominated by one or two specific integrative roles. He holds three or more integrative roles with the same relative intensity, and does many things for different reasons. The desire and ability of the minister to fit various aspects of a minister's job into a meaningful whole create this role. He makes a conscious effort to include the many aspects of the minister's work in some workable scheme. Nine percent of the respondents are in the general practitioner category.

It had been expected (from relevant literature) that a greater proportion of the parish ministers would be general practitioners. Carr-Saunders (1955) states:

"the tendency for the general practitioner to give way to the specialist within the professions is almost universal. The only prominent exception is the church, where the priest or minister remains a general practitioner. The church . . . has been less influenced by specialization than any other profession. Priests and ministers remain general practitioners. Despite this fact, the standing of the church has declined. Although it formerly was one of the three ancient professions, the church now seems to the public hardly to rank as a profession at all, or at any rate to occupy an isolated position among the professions at large. The explanation for the situation is not that the functions of the church have altered, but that public view of the functions of a profession have changed. Professional men are increasingly regarded by the public as experts in the advancement of material welfare and bodily well-being. The church, on the other hand, demands self-discipline and standards of conduct that are . . . considered out-moded in an age of science."

We have previously noted that nine-tenths of the parish ministry have a primary integrative role. In a strict sense this is not a specialty, but it does suggest that even in the parish, ministers do practice their professions with special emphases. In multiple-clergy parishes, there is frequently a division of labor. One staff person may be the preaching minister, another the minister of administration, counseling, community relations, etc. Large parishes permit specialization which is less acceptable or necessary in small parishes. If one considers the church in a broader organizational context than the local community, specialization is more readily evident. The variety of clergy careers (e.g., missionary, educator-professor, campus clergyman, chaplain) suggests specialization. But specialization among the clergy is not a recent event; it has been evident in the variety of functions fulfilled throughout the history of the ministry.

Fifty-four percent of the parish ministers in this report had only one integrative role, thirty-seven percent had a secondary integrative role associated with their primary role, and the remaining nine percent were general practitioners. Those holding the various integrative roles differed in the degree to which they also had a secondary integrative role. (Table 10). Among the integrative roles held frequently as a primary role, the interpersonal-relations specialist was least likely to have a secondary role (35 %) and the evangelist was most likely to have a secondary role (48 %).

Among the integrative roles held less frequently as primary, the sub-cultural specialist was least likely to be associated with a secondary role (18%); and the community religious leader was most likely a secondary role (83%).

We have noted that parish ministers differ in the ends toward which their ministry is directed. This variability in goals has been designated as integrative role and is the dependent variable in this chapter.

The integrative roles were grouped two ways for testing in relation to the independent variables. First, they were classified on a four point scale from traditional to contemporary. If a clergyman had believer-saint, scholar, evangelist, sacramentalist or father-

TABLE 10
CLERGYMEN WITH SPECIFIC PRIMARY INTEGRATIVE ROLES
WHO HAVE SECONDARY INTEGRATIVE ROLES

Integrative roles held as primary	Percent of clergy having secondary integrative roles
Traditional roles	
Believer-saint	40
Scholar	44
Evangelist	48
Sacramentalist	67
Father-shepherd	38
Contemporary roles	
Interpersonal-relations specialist	35
Parish promoter	40
Social actionist	37
Educator	51
Sub-cultural specialist	18
Community religious leader	83
Churchman	40

shepherd as a primary role (or as both primary and secondary roles) he was classified as traditional. If he had interpersonal-relations specialist, parish promoter, social actionist, educator, sub-cultural specialist, community religious leader, or churchman as a primary role he was classified as contemporary. Those persons who had traditional integrative roles as primary, and contemporary roles as secondary, were classified as partially traditional. Those who had contemporary integrative roles as primary and traditional roles as secondary were classified as partially contemporary. (Table 11). These four categories were viewed as an *integrative role continuum* from most traditional to most contemporary.

Second, the integrative roles which occurred as primary with sufficient frequency were treated separately: believer-saint, evangelist, father-shepherd, interpersonal-relations specialist, parish promoter, and social actionist. Six of those that occurred much less frequently were grouped. The general practitioner was treated as a separate category. In the analysis this classification of the dependent variable is referred to as *specific integrative roles*.

Variability in integrative roles was analyzed in relation to two series of independent variables: clergy characteristics, and parish or organizational factors. These were tested for statistical significance in relation to the minister's integrative role by the chi square technique.

TABLE 11
INTEGRATIVE ROLE CONTINUUM

Integrative role	Percent of respondents (N = 1,111)
Traditional	29
Partially traditional	10
Partially contemporary	9
Contemporary	43
Not classified	9

Clergy Characteristics

The clergy independent variables included personal characteristics, personality structure, referents, career pattern, and effectiveness and success criteria.

Age was statistically significant (.01 level) for the integrative role continuum, but not for the specific integrative roles. The younger clergymen (those 44 years and younger) tended to be more traditional in their integrative role patterns than the older men (those 45 years and older). However, since the specific roles were not significant, it is not possible to specify which of the traditional roles the younger minister tended to adopt.

This finding with respect to age as a variable in relation to the traditional-contemporary integrative role continuum is consistent with the findings regarding age and the master role orientations. It raises a question of interpretation. Do ministers differ in their integrative role because of their professional education at the time they entered the ministry, or do ministers change their goals during their career. It is not possible to resolve this question on the basis of the present data, but we theorize that the stability of the minister's goals may be affected by environmental factors, and therefore may change from time to time during his career.

In theory the traditional and contemporary integrative roles would require appropriate *personality* resources. Ministers who are oriented to the traditional roles would tend to be authoritarian and lacking in awareness of changes desired. They might tend to be emotionally immature. Conversely, ministers oriented to the contemporary integrative roles would be democratic, emotionally mature and open to change. The theory regarding democratic and authoritarian personality is confirmed. The lower the authoritarian personality score (democratic) the greater the tendency of the minister to be oriented to contemporary integrative roles. Ministers with high scores (authoritarian) tend to have traditional integrative roles. Similar significant findings were found for specific integrative roles. The evangelist tends to have moderately high authoritarian personality scores. Ministers who are interpersonal-relations specialists or social actionists have relatively low scores (democratic). Ministers with high scores (authoritarian) tend to have no specific integrative role.

The *referents*, the *career pattern*, and *effectiveness* criteria of the clergyman do not vary in relation to his integrative role.

Success criteria differ significantly (.05 level of probability) in relation to the specific integrative role that is primary for the clergyman, but not in relation to the traditional-contemporary integrative role continuum. Three groups of success criteria were tested: personality structure, practitioner skills, and denominational relations. The father-shepherd tends to emphasize the clergyman's personality in relation to success. The believer-saint and the evangelist cite personality characteristics and practitioner skills. The interpersonal-relations specialist most frequently mentions ability in the practitioner skills as assurance of success. Finally, the parish promoter and the social actionist tend to mention practitioner skills and denominational skills.

Theory would suggest that integrative roles with goals directed to the individual would stress clergy personality characteristics as criteria of success. Conversely integrative roles with goals directed to groups of parishioners would stress relations within the organization. The theory is confirmed by the analysis. The father-shepherd, evangelist, and believer-saint are oriented to the individual and stress the personality characteristics of the clergy. The parish promoter and social actionist are oriented to the group and stress organizational (or denominational) relations. The exception to the theory appears to be the interpersonal relations specialist. It might be expected that the personality of the clergyman would be important for success in this role. However, the interpersonal relations specialist, we assume, is reasonably in control of his own emotions; and his desire to work with the individual in a counseling, therapeutic relationship helps him to evaluate practitioner skills highly rather than to exploit his own personality characteristics or to manipulate the organization.

Organizational Factors

Denomination, regional location, type of community, organizational complexity and parish economics are characteristics considered as independent variables. These characteristics were analyzed for significant differences in relation to the integrative role continuum, and to specific integrative roles.

Denominational affiliation was significant in relation to both the integrative role continuum (.01) and the specific integrative roles (.001). Presbyterian and Episcopalian clergy tend to be traditional or partially traditional, the Methodist and Lutheran ministers are ambivalent, and the Baptists, Disciples, Brethren and United Church of Christ clergy are contemporary. Hence, the ministers in the congregationally-organized denominations tend to be contemporary in their integrative role pattern; and the ministers in denominations with representative or episcopal polity tend to be traditional. The more structured denominations have clergymen who tend to have traditional integrative roles and the less structured denominations have clergy with the contemporary roles. When the specific integrative roles are considered, Presbyterian clergy tend to be evangelists and the Episcopalians father-shepherds. The Baptists, Disciples, and Brethren tend to be interpersonal-relations specialists and social actionists. The Methodists are ambivalent, tending to be either believer-saints and evangelists or social actionists.

The denominational variability with respect to the minister's integrative role is consistent with theoretical expectations. The clergymen in parishes governed by a Presbyterian or Episcopalian polity are influenced to a greater degree in their behavior by parishioners, fellow clergy and denominational officials than are those in denominations governed by congregational polity. In the latter, a greater latitude of conduct is permitted in local parishes. In fact, their congregations are technically autonomous. Hence they may experiment with the more contemporary and less traditional integrative roles for their clergy. The Methodist clergy might be considered non-conforming in relation to the theory, and this may be interpreted organizationally. Methodist ministers function in a denomination having a pyramidal organizational chart in which the bishop has authority and power and the local clergy are subject to his appointment and the direct supervision of the district superintendent. However, clergy roles in Methodism appear to be organizationally defined rather than theologically defined as in denominations tending to have clergy with traditional integrative roles. Theological ambivalence on the part of Methodist informants may be inferred from the fact that they tend to be believer-saints or evangelists (roles with conservative theological overtones) and social actionists (an integrative role with liberal theological overtones). Hence, it appears that theological and organizational role definitions are not coupled in Methodism.

The *regional location* of the parish served by the clergyman was not significantly different in relation to integrative role. Theory would lead us to expect that parishes located in the South would be associated with the traditional role pattern, especially with the believer-saint and evangelist integrative roles. Inspection of the tabulation of integrative roles by region does show a greater frequency of traditional roles in the South than in other regions. And conversely, the contemporary roles do appear less frequently in the South than in other regions. However, no significant difference is found by the chi square technique; hence the theory is rejected.

The *type of community* in which the parish is located, we theorize, is related to the integrative role orientation of the minister. We would expect that ministers serving churches in non-metropolitan rural areas would tend to be traditional in their integrative role, and that those in metropolitan urban communities would have contemporary integrative role orientations. Ministers in rural areas would have believer-saint, evangelist, or father-shepherd integrative roles to a greater extent than metropolitan-urban clergy. The latter would be more likely to be interpersonal-relations specialist, parish promoter, or social actionist. However, the data do not support the theory. Integrative role orientation does not vary by type of community.

Two of the *organizational* variables were significant. The number of congregations in the parish was significant in relation to the integrative role continuum at the .001 level. It was not significant for the specific integrative roles. Clergymen who are either partially traditional or partially contemporary tend to be in parishes which have more than one congregation. Ministers who are serving one-congregation parishes tend to be either completely traditional or completely contemporary in their integrative role patterns.

The size of parish (number of members served by a minister) is significantly related to the specific integrative role that is primary for him. Ministers in large parishes (600-1,000 members) tend to be interpersonal-relations specialists and those in larger parishes (1,000 or more members) tend to be parish promoters. Apparently these are the two integrative roles that the large parish requires of a minister. Ministers in medium or small parishes tend to have as a primary integrative role one of those found less frequently such as sacramentalist, scholar, educator, sub-cultural specialist, representative of the church-at-large, or church politician. However, the number of church members is not significant in relation to the integrative role continuum.

Other measures of size of parish (number in the church school, number of total staff and of clergy staff) do not vary significantly in relation to integrative role.

Theoretically it would be expected that the larger the parish the greater the number of clergymen who have contemporary integrative roles. The opposite would also theoretically be true, namely that ministers having traditional integrative roles would be serving the smaller churches. There is some support for this theory in the data, especially if it is recognized that multi-congregational parishes tend to be small parishes. There appears to be a trend in Protestantism for the size of parish to increase over time. If this trend continues, and if the relationship is sustained, then it may be expected that ministers will increasingly follow the contemporary integrative role approach to their master role. This would be especially so for the parish promoter integrative role.

Parish economic variables do not vary significantly in relation to the clergyman's integrative role.

Summary

This chapter has examined the minister's self-image with a view to developing a frame of reference within which the goals of his ministerial behavior may be analyzed. The integrative role is the end that the minister has in view as he practices his profession. It gives a purposeful focus to his work whether he is conscious of it or not. It is what he is trying to accomplish for people in his relations with them as ministers.

The integrative role concept is midway between the abstractness of the master role and the concreteness of the practitioner roles. It is less abstract than the master role concept and less concrete than the practitioner roles. Because of its abstractness it is difficult of observation. In fact, in this research we are limited to a content analysis of statements made by the clergymen.

Three classes of integrative roles were derived from documentary data furnished by the informants: (1) traditional roles (believer-saint, scholar, evangelist, sacramentalist, and father-shepherd) which were primary for 39 percent of the ministers; (2) contemporary roles (interpersonal relations specialist, parish promoter, social actionist, educator, sub-cultural specialist, and churchman) which were primary for 52 percent of the clergy; and (3) the general practitioner (nine percent). While these data do not permit a conclusion about trends regarding the traditional-contemporary integrative role continuum, the large percentage of clergy in the completely contemporary class may imply the utility of these roles in present day society.

This analysis found that four integrative roles are primary for 63 percent of the parish ministers studied. These role patterns are oriented to the world of people rather than to the world of ideas. The father-shepherd, the interpersonal-relations specialist, the parish promoter, and the social actionist patterns may have varying ideological undertones but essentially they involve inter-personal, intra-group and inter-group relations. Two role patterns are primarily integrative for more than one-sixth of the informants: the believer-saint, and the evangelist. Both of these integrative roles are ideologically oriented.

The remaining seven integrative roles are held primarily by one-fifth of the ministers researched; but aside from the general practitioner, none of these is a primary integrative role for more than one in 25. This is notable since the educator, the subcultural specialist and possibly the sacramentalist are strongly recommended by church executives and theological educators.

The dependent variable in this chapter has been the twelve integrative roles. Two series of independent variables (clergy or personal variables; and parish, organizational, or environmental variables) were tested in relation to the variability of the integrative role patterns.

In theory we would expect that the clergy factors would be significant in relation to integrative role variability. The goals of the clergyman would seem to be related to his personal characteristics, his personality structure, his referents, his career pattern, and his professional criteria. However, only the age, the personality (authoritarian or democratic), and the success criteria of the minister were significant, suggesting that social psychological factors are not as effective in relation to his goals as theorized.

The variability of the minister's success criteria in relation to the integrative role which he holds is suggestive. On one hand, father-shepherd, a role in which individual relations are important, is associated with clergy personality characteristics as success criteria. On the other hand, parish promoter and social actionist, roles which are associated with group relations, are associated with denominational criteria. Those in between, believer-saint, evangelist and interpersonal-relations specialist, have their own unique criteria profile.

In theory we would expect that the organizational factor would be significantly related to variability in the integrative roles. The goals of the organization are in part effectively achieved by the professional services of the clergyman. His integrative role should relate his personal goals to the purposes of the parish program. This theory is in part confirmed since denomination and two measures of size of church were significant. However, the parish variables were less significant for the integrative role than they were for the master role.

Denomination appears to be a consistently significant variable. This would imply that there is diversity among denominations, and uniformity within a denomination. The degree of heterogeneity among the denominations and the homogeneity within the denomination may be related to differing theological orientations. However, the fact that the highly structured denominations tend to have clergy with traditional integrative roles and the less structured denominations tend to have clergy with contemporary roles suggests that several factors may be associated with denomination as a variable.

The relationship of size of parish to integrative role variability is of considerable interest in view of the trend in size of parishes. As parishes increase in size it may be expected that integrative roles in which group relations rather than individual relations are assumed will become increasingly important as models for clergy behavior.

When the significant independent variables are considered it would appear that the association of organizational variables and the integrative role is greater than is the association of the role with clergy factors. A minister's age and his criteria of success both appear to be related to parish factors. One possible interpretation is that age is significant because clergy change their goals as they change parishes, and success criteria in part are related to denominational goals. If so, then in so far as the clergy and organizational factors as operationally defined in this analysis are concerned, the latter is more powerful in relation to differing integrative roles than the former.

VI

THE PRACTITIONER ROLES

We have now identified the master role and the alternative integrative roles the parish minister may select in fulfilling his functions. This chapter is focused on the minister's self-image as a practitioner of religion. The practitioner roles are the means by which the integrative roles are implemented. When compared with the master role which is a relatively high level of generalization, and the integrative role which is an intermediate generalization, the practitioner roles are at a relatively low level of generalization.

The practitioner roles are performed publicly and are what the public thinks the work of the minister to be. The behavior involved in performing these roles is visible, concrete, and specific. Hence, in addition to the goal and means distinction between the integrative and practitioner roles, we may say that the former is covert behavior while the latter is overt behavior.

This theory may be further developed with respect to the way in which the clergyman evaluates the practitioner roles. Since they are means to an end, then the minister may evaluate them in relation to his own norms or to those of his denomination, to his own effectiveness in performing the role, and to his own satisfactions in fulfilling the role.

We further theorize that if the behavior associated with the practitioner roles is visible, concrete and specific, then it is open to evaluation by the minister who is performing the role; by the parishioners who are being served by the minister; and by the executive leadership of the denomination, especially the executives of local judicatories. This type of evaluation is more easily made for the practitioner roles, which involve overt behavior, than for the integrative roles, which involve covert behavior. Furthermore, since covert role behavior is more abstract and less specific than is overt practitioner role behavior, the layman is less able to observe and is not as well informed about the minister's integrative roles as he is about the minister's practitioner roles. In this chapter the practitioner roles will be analyzed from the perspective of the variability in the means the minister employs to reach his ends or goals as a clergyman. We would therefore expect organizational factors, in so far as they reflect the role expectations laymen have of clergymen, to be more important than clergy characteristics in relation to variability in practitioner role behavior.

Data regarding the parish minister's self-image of the practitioner roles were obtained from a series of questions in which the minister first described his work, and then evaluated the types of work from a normative, satisfaction, and performance perspective. By content analysis procedures six practitioner roles were derived from the types of work mentioned by the clergy: administrator, organizer, pastor, preacher, priest, and teacher. These terms for the practitioner roles are used in a functionally specific sense, and are not used as general terms to be equated with the master role of minister or with the integrative role of the clergyman. This would also exclude the use of the terms preacher, priest or pastor as designations for the master role of a professional religious leader.

Practitioner Role Description

The practitioner roles cover the whole gamut of skills performed by the parish minister and are behaviorally homogeneous. They are a cluster, a complex of behaviors. They may be classified as traditional, neo-traditional, or contemporary.

Traditional roles

The roles of *preacher, priest* and *teacher* are those which the Protestant clergyman traditionally has performed. There are Biblical models for these roles. Furthermore, there is a theological rationale associated with the traditional offices, and clearly defined means within church traditions that are accepted behavior for these roles. Role definitions, expectations and ideology are all present; hence the parish minister knows how to fulfill the roles of preacher, priest and teacher with legitimacy.

The preacher role includes the preparation and delivery of sermons for regular and special services in the local church and elsewhere. The priest leads people in worship, administers the sacraments, officiates at weddings, conducts funerals and other rites of the church. The teacher role involves the minister in preparation for teaching, instruction in the church school, the conducting of confirmation classes, and study-group leadership.

The traditional roles are oriented to the world of ideas. Preaching and teaching, and some aspects of the priestly role are activities in which the minister is seeking to communicate ideas through spoken words or symbolic behavior. He converys meaning, a message about Jesus Christ as the self-revelation of God to man. He performs the traditional roles in a social milieu, but the ideological intent of the roles is paramount. The role behaviors are selected on the basis of their efficiency in conveying the message. The minister develops preaching, teaching, and the liturgical practices as an art. The content of the religious ideology is communicated by using many media. In each of the traditional roles the minister is essentially an actor in relation to an audience. To be effective he has to be the central actor and to vary his techniques as the audience responds.

Neo-traditional role

The *pastor* role involves interpersonal relations and is classified here as neo-traditional. It has a Biblical tradition and an ideological definition. However, in the present situation there is considerable ambiguity regarding the way in which it is to be performed. There is less consensus about what constitutes legitimate behavior in performing this role than there is for the three traditional practitioner roles. There is an older or traditional way in which role expectations are defined in the pastor role, and a newer or contemporary way. In the former, the pastor does the visiting among the parishioners and prospective members and ministers to the sick and distressed. The office of confessor is included in the traditional definition of the pastor role, even though in some religious traditions the clergyman is called a priest in the confessional. However, in the contemporary scene the behavior associated with this role is being re-defined within the newer understanding of clinical psychology and pyschiatry. Ministers are now assimilating mental health concepts and techniques to be used for guidance and counseling. This has led to the newer way in which this role is defined, namely, the counseling approach which involves the cure of souls and a therapeutic concern for parishioners. The minister is a counselor to youth, the troubled, the aged, and all who seek his guidance.

Contemporary roles

The contemporary roles are those of administrator and organizer. These roles are newer to church tradition and practice. The scriptural and ideological bases of these offices are not as clearly defined. Most Protestant denominations do not have names for the clergyman that designate the administrator and organizer roles. Rector is the term used by the Episcopalians to designate the administrative role; moderator is a related term used by Presbyterians. There is, also, a lack of consensus about legitimate behavior in the performance of these roles. Men who are recruited for the ministry usually have an image of the minister as preacher, priest, teacher, and pastor. They lack a religiously oriented image of the minister as organizer or administrator. They are more likely to associate these roles with a social worker or a business executive than with an ordained clergyman.

In the *administrator* role the minister is an executive. He is the manager or director of the parish. Institutional continuities are facilitated by administration. At the local church level this includes general church planning, financial administration and promotion, publicity, physical plant supervision, and clerical and stenographic work. Except for official board, staff and committee meetings that involve intra-group relations, most administration involves desk and paper work. Administrative tasks include denominational and inter-denominational assignments as well as local parish work.

There are many organized groups or associations within a parish that are devoted to the specialized needs within the parish. There are also numerous organizations and associations in the community (e.g., civic, political, health, welfare, fraternal, economic) with which the church is associated. At times the minister participates as an actor within these groups; at other times he is involved in the interactions between these organizations. The *organizer* role, the way he performs within a specific group (intra-group) or between specific groups (inter-group), includes his actions as participant; whether he is leader or follower, advisor or director, supporting the present leadership in a group or training new leaders. The organizer role emphasizes task definition as distinguished from the administrative role which focuses on task achievement. (Wallace, 1964:231)

The neo-traditional and the contemporary practitioner roles are those in which the minister is most involved with people. The social interaction of persons in the cultural environment is a more important dimension in these roles than is the communication of ideas. Also, the minister is performing his role as an actor in a group rather than as an actor before an audience. Ideas are communicated, but it is more likely to be a two-way communication in which both parishioners and minister seek to convey meaning rather than the one-way communication that is typical of the actor-to-audience situation. To be effective in the neo-traditional and contemporary roles the minister must be a mature person who is skilled in interpersonal relations and who can function as a group member.

The practitioner roles differ in interaction patterns. Some are primarily person-to-audience relations; others may involve interpersonal or inter-group relations. The following schematic paradigm shows the interaction pattern appropriate to the specific practitioner role:

FIGURE 1
PRACTITIONER ROLE INTERACTION PATTERN

Role	Interaction		
	Person to audience	*Intergroup*	*Interpersonal*
Preacher	X		
Priest	X	X	
Teacher		X	
Organizer		X	
Administrator		X	X
Pastor			X

The differential interaction which the roles of the minister require is confirmed by Kling (1958). A 1956-57 survey of 545 ministers and 520 laymen from 13 denominations distinguished four major role activities for ministers: performance before a group (teacher, discussion leader, preacher, public speaker); interacting with people (planner, group worker, promoter, executive, personnel worker, peacemaker, community worker); working with individuals (counselor, comforter, visitor, developer of fellowship); and activities performed alone (prayer and meditation, study).

Classification of practitioner roles then becomes evaluative, and the roles that are traditional would seem to be more acceptable and perhaps more valuable than the contemporary roles. We expect that the minister has internalized this evaluative scheme, and that it is reflected in his own evaluation of the practitioner roles.

Clergy Evaluations of Practitioner Roles

After the ministers listed their various tasks, they were asked to evaluate them from three perspectives; with normative, satisfaction, and performance ratings. The analysis of materials obtained in this self-judgment procedure is limited in this chapter to the practitioner roles of preacher, priest, teacher, pastor, administrator, and organizer.

Normative evaluation

It was assumed that when a minister rated the tasks in order of their importance he would reveal his normative evaluation to the practitioner roles. The normative implies a standard of behavior that is authorized or recognized as legitimate. It reflects the minister's concept of an ideal ministry as he functions in the parish. It is the way he thinks things should be. It is for the minister a model for practitioner behavior. The level of importance that he assigns to each task is an indicator of the degree to which he has been indoctrinated about his denomination's standards for the practitioner roles. By rating the importance of each job he is stating his own understanding of what the church as an institution expects of his behavior in the practitioner roles. His ratings also reflect his understanding of what his parishioners expect of him, as well as the degree to which he feels that each of the roles is essential to him in fulfilling his integrative roles. Hence his normative evaluation is influenced by denominational standards, by parishioner expectations, and by his own goals.

The practitioner roles were evaluated normatively by 866, or 78 percent of the ministers.* (See Table 12.) Traditional roles were most important for three-fourths of these ministers (especially the preacher role which was cited by nearly two-thirds). The neo-traditional role was noted as most important by more than one-fourth, and the contemporary roles were rated as important by fewer than one in twenty ministers.

TABLE 12
NORMATIVE EVALUATION OF PRACTITIONER ROLES

Role	Most Important Percent (N = 866)		Least Important Percent (N = 866)	
Traditional	74		15	
Preacher		64		8
Priest		8		4
Teacher		2		3
Neo-traditional	22		8	
Pastor		22		8
Contemporary	4		77	
Administrator		3		39
Organizer		1		38

The ranking of the tasks that make up the minister's job permitted a ranking of the least important as well as the most important. Contemporary roles were ranked as least important much more frequently than were other roles. The administrator role was cited as least important most frequently. Of the administrator tasks so evaluated, 53 percent pertained to the parish, 30 percent to the denomination, and 17 percent to inter-denominational matters. The organizer role was cited as least important almost as frequently. Three out of four of the organizer tasks so evaluated pertained to the community rather than to the parish. The minister's evaluation that parish tasks were more important than non-parish tasks in the contemporary roles is consistent with his evaluation of the preacher role. When this traditional role is ranked least important, the minister has reference to preaching to non-parish groups. Hence the fact that a minister considers a role to be important involves not only the nature of the role but its relevance for his parish.

Summarizing the normative view of the six roles as seen by the parish minister informants, the traditional and neo-traditional roles were thought to be more important

---

*The remaining 22 percent referred to their personal and family living (Chapter VII) or to the master role or integrative roles (Chapters IV and V), not to practitioner roles.

than the contemporary roles. Specifically, the order of priority for a *normative* view of the practitioner roles of the parish minister, from most important to least important, is as follows: preacher, pastor, priest, teacher, administrator and organizer.

The significance attached to the traditional roles confirms our theory about the minister's concept of the importance of an ideological message. The communication of ideas seems to be more important for the minister than his relationships with people and groups. The traditional roles are reinforced by Biblical and theological underpinnings, and there is a high degree of consensus regarding their legitimate performance. Their relationship to the communication of ideas is apparent.

Satisfaction evaluation

Informants were asked: "What aspect of the parish ministry gives you the most personal enjoyment?" Their answers were viewed as an indication of the satisfactions they found in the ministry. It was assumed that this evaluation involved the minister's own motivation. While all of the evaluations are based on self-judgments, this is the most personal of the three. We would theorize that factors which are associated with variability in satisfaction evaluation differ from those regarding the normative and performance evaluations. The standards of the denomination and the judgments of parishioners did not seem to determine a minister's satisfaction as did his personality. Practitioner roles that involve interpersonal relations would seem to be evaluated more highly from the perspective of satisfactions than roles which involve audience relations. In particular, the neo-traditional role would seem to present situations in which the interactions of face-to-face relations with parishioners could be highly enjoyable (see Table 13).

TABLE 13
MOST ENJOYED PRACTITIONER ROLE

Role	Percentage of ministers (N = 1,011)	
Traditional	50	
Preacher		37
Priest		6
Teacher		7
Neo-traditional	41	
Pastor		41
Contemporary	9	
Administrator		2
Organizer		7

Summarizing the satisfaction evaluation of the six practitioner roles as expressed by the parish minister informants, the neo-traditional role was most enjoyed, and one traditional role (preaching) was enjoyed almost as much. They enjoyed other roles much less. Specifically, from most to least enjoyed the practitioner roles are as follows: pastor, preacher, teacher, organizer, priest, and administrator.

The minister's satisfaction evaluation confirms the theory regarding his motivation in fulfilling the practitioner roles. The fact that he gains somewhat more enjoyment from a role that involves interpersonal relations rather than audience relations has implications for the motivation of the clergy. The personality structure required for one type of practitioner role may differ from that required for other types. Assuming this to be true, then personality must be considered in recruitment of ministers and in the type of assignment given a clergyman. In a parish requiring the services of one or more clergymen, lay officials may wish to take these findings into account in determining the duties to be performed by each minister. It also has implications for those who supervise the work of clergymen or who counsel with them.

Performance evaluation

In the final stage of the self-analysis procedure, clergymen were asked: "What phases of your work do you think you are most effective in performing?" The intention of the procedure was to secure the minister's own sense of effectiveness in his performance in each of the practitioner roles. Again, as in the normative evaluation, we assumed that he has been influenced in the performance rating by denominational models of effective and/or ineffective role behavior, and by the consensus of parishioners regarding effective behavior.

Considering only the 866 ministers who rated the practitioner roles on the basis of their own effectiveness, nearly three-fifths felt they were most effective in performing the traditional roles, while nearly one-third felt most effective in the neo-traditional role. The contemporary roles were mentioned much less frequently as ones in which the clergymen felt they were effective (see Table 14).

Summarizing the performance evaluation of the six roles as seen by the parish minister informants, one traditional role (preacher) and the neo-traditional role of pastor were seen as their most effective roles. They felt much less effective in the other traditional roles and in the contemporary roles. Specifically, from most effective to least effective the practitioner roles are as follows: preacher, pastor, teacher, administrator, priest, and organizer. This is the order of priority for a performance rating of the practitioner roles of the parish ministry, and it is consistent with theoretical expectations. In the immediate context of the parish it has implications for the day-to-day operation of the religious program he leads. It also has implications for the professional training of the clergyman, both at the seminary and post-seminary level.

Inter-relatedness of all evaluations

The minister's evaluations of the practitioner roles on the basis of norms, satisfaction, and performance may be compared. The relative evaluations are made more apparent in a ranking of practitioner roles by each evaluation than by noting a percentage distribution (see Table 15). A composite of the three evaluations from highest to lowest is as

TABLE 14
MOST EFFECTIVE PRACTITIONER ROLE

Role	Percentage of ministers (N = 866)	
Traditional	57	
Preacher		44
Priest		6
Teacher		7
Neo-traditional	31	
Pastor		31
Contemporary	12	
Administrator		7
Organizer		5

follows: preacher, pastor, teacher, priest, administrator, and organizer. The traditional (especially preaching) and neo-traditional roles are consistently rated high; the contemporary roles, low.

TABLE 15
PRACTITIONER ROLES RANKED BY CLERGY EVALUATIONS

Role	Importance	Enjoyment	Effectiveness	Average Rank
Preacher	1	2	1	1.3
Pastor	2	1	2	1.6
Teacher	4	3	3	3.3
Priest	3	5	5	4.3
Administrator	5	6	3	4.6
Organizer	6	4	6	5.3

On the basis of the ranking it would be possible to theorize that the normative, satisfaction, and performance evaluations are closely related. A complementary configuration is seen whereby the three evaluations tend to be mutually supportive. Protestant parish ministers seem to find enjoyment and feel effective in those practitioner roles which they have rated as most important in their orientation to the ministry. The normative evaluation is supported by the satisfaction and performance evaluation. In theory, if this relationship is sustained, the minister would feel a three-fold motivation while he fulfills the practitioner roles.

This theory is not completely sustained on closer inspection of the data. The rankings cover up the intensity of the evaluations. The preacher role was not evaluated as highly in terms of performance-effectiveness as it was in performance-importance. The satisfaction the minister feels in performing the practitioner roles differs somewhat from his other evaluations. In particular, the neo-traditional role was rated as most enjoyable more frequently than were the traditional and contemporary roles. In this case it exceeds the preacher role, which was mostly highly rated in importance and effectiveness. The fact that the pastor role was more highly evaluated in this respect than the preacher role brings into contrast the relationship of satisfaction evaluations to normative and performance evaluations. The effectiveness ratings tend to support the importance ratings. However, the high satisfaction rating given to pastor means that the minister has less than the highest evaluation for the role he feels to be most important and is most effective in fulfilling.

Comparative data on the normative and satisfaction evaluations of the Protestant ministry are available from a study completed several decades ago (May, 1934). May asked ministers to rank six types of activities according to degree of importance and degree of satisfaction. The results were as follows:

MOST IMPORTANT	MOST SATISFYING
Pastoral	Ministerial
Ministerial	Pastoral
Homiletical	Homiletical
Administrative	Educational
Educational	Administrative
Civic	Civic

His categories differ somewhat from ours, but by his definition ministerial and homiletical seem to cover much of what we included in the Priest and Preacher roles. His educational activities are roughly equivalent to our teacher role; and his civic category is our community organizer role.

The degree to which the practitioner roles were considered important is not equally sustained by the satisfaction and performance evaluations made by the clergymen. A cross-tabulation of the evaluations is helpful in analyzing the interrelationship. Slightly more than one-fourth who evaluate a role as most important also evaluate it highest in terms of enjoyment and effectiveness. However, more than a third feel that their most important role is neither their most enjoyable nor their most effective role. If we add to this group those who feel that their most important role is either not their most enjoyable or their most effective role, then almost three-fourths of the ministers are not supported in terms of a feeling of enjoyment and a sense of effectiveness in fulfilling the practitioner role they think most important (see Table 16).

The contrast between the traditional and neo-traditional roles in this respect is notable. Those who feel that the pastor role is their most important one, tend to feel it to be their most enjoyable and their most effective role to a greater extent than do those who give a high rating to the traditional roles. This contrast is more apparent when the priest and teacher roles are compared with the pastor role than is the case when the preacher role is similarly compared.

The differential relationship between the normative, the satisfaction, and the performance evaluations was further tested by correlation analysis using the rank-order method

TABLE 16
EFFECTIVENESS AND ENJOYABILITY OF MINISTER'S
MOST IMPORTANT PRACTITIONER ROLE

Most Important Role	% Enjoyable and Effective	% Effective but not Enjoyable	% Enjoyable but not Effective	% Neither Enjoyable nor Effective	Total Percent (N = 907)
Traditional	27	19	15	39	100
Preacher	29	18	15	38	100
Priest	14	24	14	48	100
Teacher	25	20	0	55	100
Neo-traditional					
Pastor	34	17	25	24	100
Contemporary	0	47	0	53	100
Administrator	0	60	0	40	100
Organizer	0	0	0	100	100

(Spearman's rho). The satisfaction evaluation is highly correlated with the normative evaluation. The performance evaluation is less highly correlated with normative and satisfaction evaluations (see Table 17). Ministers tend to find the most enjoyment in fulfilling those practitioner roles they think important. However, they are not as adequately reinforced by a sense of *effectiveness* in relation to the roles they consider important.

TABLE 17
INTERCORRELATION (RANK ORDER) AMONG
THE PRACTITIONER ROLE EVALUATIONS

	Normative	Satisfaction	Performance
Normative (Important)	—	.75	.42
Satisfaction	.75	—	.33
Performance (Effective)	.42	.33	—

The theory requires revision regarding the degree to which the minister is sustained in his most important practitioner roles by his feelings of enjoyment and effectiveness. Most ministers do not feel that the role which they rate the highest normatively is also their highest-ranking role when evaluated for both performance and satisfaction. The neo-traditional role of Pastor is sustained to a greater extent than are the other roles. The preacher role is sustained to about the same degree as the average for all roles. The contemporary roles are supported least often, the other traditional roles somewhat more; but the majority of the parish ministers evaluate the roles of Priest, Teacher, Administrator, and organizer as either low in performance or in satisfaction. These findings have implications for the motivation of the minister.

The minister's evaluation of the practitioner roles from the perspective of norms, satisfaction, and performance is the dependent variable in this chapter. Variability was analyzed in relation to two series of independent variables: clergy characteristics and parish characteristics.

Clergy Characteristics

The practitioner roles are performed under circumstances in which the behavior of the clergyman is visible, and is continually reviewed by parishioners and others for whom a service is being rendered. We would expect that clergy factors are not associated with variables in practitioner role evaluation, but that factors in the work environment would be. Hence, we theorize that clergy factors are not associated with variability in a minister's evaluation of the practitioner roles. An exception is made of the criteria of effectiveness and success, because the clergyman's ideas on these matters have probably been internalized from the particular culture of the denomination in which he is ordained, and are pertinent to his career development.

The data support the theory with one exception. The minister's criteria of effectiveness did not vary in relation to his evaluation of the practitioner roles; however his criteria of success did vary in relation to his normative and satisfaction evaluations. Ministers who feel that the traditional roles are most important tend to stress the importance of personality, especially an out-going nature and a willingness to serve. Those who rate the neo-traditional practitioner skills and contemporary roles as most important tend to stress denominational relations.

An interesting note is provided by those who rate the neo-traditional role high on satisfaction. They tend to believe that a person's character is important to a greater extent than do those who feel other practitioner roles are most enjoyable. Those who rate the traditional roles as most enjoyable, stress outgoing personality as a success criteria.

Organizational Factors

The dependent variable, practitioner role evaluation, was also cross tabulated with denomination, region, type of community, size of parish, and parish economics. We theorized that organizational factors are associated with variability in practitioner role evaluation. Parishes having differing characteristics could be expected to differ in their role expectations of the clergyman serving the parish. The minister in turn will articulate different evaluations in response to the role expectations of the organization he seeks to serve. We would expect greater variability in his normative evaluations, and the least variability in his satisfaction evaluation of practitioner roles.

In general the theory is supported by the data. Denomination is highly significant (at the .001 level) for each of the three evaluations of the practitioner roles when all denominations are considered together. (See Table 18.) If the Episcopalians are excluded, however, denomination is not significant at the .05 level for any of the three evaluations. For the Episcopalian clergy, the *normative* evaluation of the practitioner roles differs from that of all the other Protestant ministers. The pastor (neo-traditional) role is most important for them, with the traditional roles of priest, preacher and teacher next in order. This normative relationship is confirmed by the research of Wood (1964:94) in the United States; and by Coxon (1965:520-521) in England. The pastor role also assumes first place for the Episcopalians in terms of both *performance* and *satisfaction*.

TABLE 18
EVALUATION OF PRACTITIONER ROLES BY DENOMINATION

Practitioner Role	Denomination (Percentages)							
	Baptist-Disciples	Brethren	United C. of Christ	Luth.	Meth.	Pres.	Epis.	Total
	Normative Evaluation							
Administrator	4.3	10.0	2.4	1.3	1.0	3.0	3.8	2.8
Organizer	0	0	1.6	0	0	.5	3.0	.8
Pastor	18.8	10.0	21.3	5.3	24.3	19.0	40.9	22.4
Preacher	73.9	67.5	69.3	81.3	70.5	72.0	14.4	63.1
Priest	2.9	10.0	3.1	10.7	3.3	3.0	31.8	8.6
Teacher	0	2.5	2.4	1.3	1.0	2.5	6.1	2.3
TOTAL (with rounding)	99.9	100.0	100.1	99.9	100.1	100.0	100.0	100.0
N	(69)	(40)	(127)	(75)	(210)	(200)	(132)	(853)
	Performance Evaluation							
Administrator	8.3	8.0	6.8	5.5	6.8	6.0	6.0	6.6
Organizer	8.3	0	7.7	5.5	5.3	2.8	3.3	4.6
Pastor	33.3	36.0	23.9	16.4	27.1	29.3	51.0	31.7
Preacher	43.3	48.0	48.7	54.5	53.1	53.5	11.4	44.4
Priest	3.3	6.0	6.8	5.5	5.3	2.3	12.8	6.0
Teacher	3.3	2.0	6.0	12.7	2.4	6.0	15.4	6.8
TOTAL (with rounding)	99.8	100.0	99.9	100.1	100.0	99.9	99.9	100.1
N	(60)	(50)	(117)	(55)	(207)	(215)	(149)	(853)
	Satisfaction Evaluation							
Administrator	1.3	1.8	2.2	2.5	1.7	2.1	1.2	1.8
Organizer	10.4	0	7.3	3.8	8.3	6.2	6.7	6.7
Pastor	39.0	42.1	38.0	31.2	37.3	43.2	52.4	41.2
Preacher	45.5	36.8	40.9	42.5	44.0	41.1	11.6	37.1
Priest	1.3	10.5	6.6	5.0	5.0	2.9	12.2	5.9
Teacher	2.6	8.8	5.1	15.0	3.7	4.6	15.9	7.2
TOTAL (with rounding)	100.0	100.0	100.1	100.0	100.0	100.1	100.0	99.9
N	(77)	(57)	(137)	(80)	(241)	(241)	(164)	(997)

Note: The normative evaluation was based on the order of importance for the tasks of the minister (see Appendix F, "Personal Job Analysis"); the performance evaluation was scored from the question on phases of work in which the minister feels he or she is most effective; and the satisfaction evaluation is based on the responses to the question "What aspect of the parish ministry gives you the most personal enjoyment?"

The differences on practitioner role by denomination are significant at the .001 level, as determined by chi-square. For the impact of denominational differences excluding Episcopalians, refer to the text, pages 93, 94.

While not statistically significant, it may be interesting to examine the remaining six denominational groupings for each evaluation. Looked at *normatively*, the preacher role is held to be most important by all of the six; although they differ somewhat on what is of secondary importance. The Methodist, United Church of Christ, Presbyterian and Baptist-Disciples ministers next assign importance to the pastor role; while the Lutherans believe the priest role to be important, and the Brethren divide their secondary ratings equally between priest, pastor and administrator.

Viewed for *performance*, once again all six groupings believe they are most effective as preachers, followed by effectiveness as pastors.

The preacher role is considered to give the most *satisfaction* to Baptist-Disciples,

Methodists, Lutherans and United Church of Christ clergy, while Presbyterian and Brethren enjoy the pastor role first and the preaching role second. The teaching role gives secondary satisfaction to the Lutherans.

The normative evaluation of the practitioner roles varies significantly at the .05 level by region; however it does not vary for performance and satisfaction evaluations. The ministers serving a parish in the South tend to evaluate the pastor role as most important, and those in the north-central and western regions place the greater normative evaluation on the preacher role.

The type of community in which a clergyman conducts his ministry is not significant in relation to his evaluation of the practitioner roles. A similar finding was reported by Douglass and Brunner (1935): "Urban and rural ministers agree in the order of importance which they attach to the several types of duties and in the degree of difficulty which they ascribe to them."

Two measures of size of parish were significant in relation to the minister's evaluation of the practitioner roles. Ministers serving parishes consisting of only one congregation tend to evaluate the traditional roles more highly from the normative, enjoyment, and performance standpoint. Ministers serving parishes consisting of two or more congregations tended to give the neo-traditional and contemporary practitioner roles a higher normative, satisfaction, and performance rating than they do the traditional roles.

The size of the church school is also significantly related to the minister's evaluation of the practitioner roles. Those serving parishes with small church schools (149 students or fewer) tend to evaluate the teacher role as more important and effective. Those in churches with larger church schools evaluate the preacher role as more important and effective. The satisfaction evaluation was not significant in relation to size of church school.

The amount of the parish budget for local expenditures was significantly (.02) related to the minister's normative evaluation of the practitioner roles, but not to his effectiveness or enjoyment evaluation of them. The larger the parish local budget the greater the tendency for the minister to give a high normative evaluation to preaching. Conversely, ministers serving churches with smaller budgets tended to evaluate the other traditional roles (teacher and priest) more highly.

Summary

This chapter has analyzed the practitioner roles, the means-oriented behavior by which the minister seeks to achieve his goals of evangelizing, of aiding individuals in their adjustments to life, of directing an organized group of believers, or of stimulating social action. The practitioner roles have been classified as traditional (preacher, priest and teacher), neo-traditional (pastor), and contemporary (administrator, organizer). We have examined the consensus, or lack of it, that parish clergymen have about the practitioner roles. Consensus was derived from the normative, satisfaction, and performance self-judgments that ministers make about the six practitioner roles.

The traditional roles are highly rated from a normative point of view, and the contemporary roles low. The performance evaluations closely follow the normative ratings, but the feelings ministers have about their effectiveness in the practitioner roles are not as strong as the importance they attach to the roles. The minister's satisfactions seem to be more strongly related to his normative evaluation of the practitioner roles than to his performance evaluation. Hence, the enjoyment a minister feels in performing a role is supportive of the roles he feels important. However, he does not rate himself as effective in these same roles.

In view of the three evaluations that the minister has made of the practitioner roles, questions may be raised about his own motivations. It is suggested that the type of personality recruited for the ministry should be evaluated carefully. Further, that the minister's sense of effectiveness needs to be reinforced by redesigning professional education and through supervision by denominational and local parish officials. It would also seem probable that the minister's sense of security in his practitioner roles may increase as training and supervision are improved.

Clergy characteristics, with the exception of criteria of success, were not associated with differing evaluations of the practitioner roles. The parish factors, however, were found to be related to variability in the minister's evaluations of the practitioner roles. The implications of these findings are far-reaching. Apparently the minister is oriented to the organization he serves, hence he may perhaps change his evaluation of the practitioner roles as he changes parish assignments.

The data regarding the practitioner roles analyzed in this chapter have focused on the minister's own evaluations. In the next chapter further analysis of the practitioner roles is made on the basis of how a clergyman allocates his work-time to them.

VII

THE PRACTITIONER ROLES: TIME MANAGEMENT

The parish ministry is a profession in which there are a few fixed and regularly occurring appointments. The minister conducts services each Sunday according to a traditional, fixed, and advertised schedule. The preaching and priestly roles on these occasions are performed before relatively large groups of persons; therefore these role activities are open to public scrutiny by participants in the service. However, except for Sunday, there are few stated meetings and there is no schedule that is followed from day to day. Much of his work is unscheduled, or is scheduled on an *ad hoc* basis. Priestly and liturgical ceremonies (such as weddings, funerals, and related rituals) are conducted on occasion, rather than at stated, regularly recurring times. Much of his work in other practitioner roles is done alone, or with individuals or small groups; it is not done under the scrutiny of the public eye, and of necessity some of it is confidential.

As might be expected, the management of time is a major problem in the professional life of the parish minister. When asked the question, "What specific problems in your professional life are you concerned about as you seek to be an effective minister?" Fifty-two percent of the clergy in this study mentioned time as a problem. This included remarks about the management of time as well as lack of time to perform the practitioner roles, and of time for self-maintenance and growth.

The normative, satisfaction and performance evaluative judgments about the practitioner roles were consciously made. The choices a minister makes in the allocation of time to the practitioner roles is the fourth evaluative procedure in which the minister engaged with respect to these roles. The decisions the minister makes in allocating time to a particular role may be made consciously, but it is also likely that such decisions are made unconsciously. That is, few ministers consciously make choices (which reflect his considered judgment) about time allocation to one practitioner role as opposed to another. The time allocation question could be answered on the basis of how a minister feels he should make decisions about his time, or on the basis of what he actually does with his time. Our interest lies in how he spent his time, not how he would like to have spent his time. The decisions the minister makes in allocating time to a particular role permit inferences to be drawn about his evaluation of it. In theory, ministers make choices regarding the use of their time. In so doing they judge one possible activity as more important or necessary than another.

The conscious or unconscious decision a minister makes when he allocates time to a particular practitioner role is an evaluative decision. The choices he makes indicate the importance he assigns to a particular role, but it differs from the normative evaluation. The former is an operational evaluation from which the relative importance of a role may be inferred; the latter is a theoretical evaluation which may represent the minister's intention. There is a difference between his intended decision and his actual decision regarding the use of time.

We are interested in the degree to which ministers differ in their time allocation to the practitioner roles. Time management, or decision-making about time, is the dependent variable. Operationally, the dependent variable is the time allocation of the professional work day, which includes the time devoted to each of the practitioner roles. We are interested in the factors which explain in part why ministers differ in the relative time they allocate to the respective practitioner roles. In addition to the independent variables (clergy and organizational factors), we consider the following situational variables: non-professional time, season of the year, day of the week, and typical or non-typical day.

Source of Time Allocation Data

To study the decisions ministers make regarding the use of their time, a supplementary questionnaire was mailed to each minister who completed the first questionnaire. A diary was requested from each minister of their activities for one particular day (see Appendix G).

The problems of obtaining time-allocation information about ministers are evident. Several precautionary measures were taken in this research. The questionnaire was mailed for systematic coverage of the months of the year and the days of the week. The researcher, not the minister, selected the day to be reported. The minister was asked to give the day, month and year for which he was reporting, and the responses were checked for prompt replies. There was no follow-up. Full rather than selective reporting was encouraged for all personal, family, and professional activities. Ministers were asked to describe each activity, the location where it took place, the persons or groups present, and the amount of time involved; then they were asked to classify the day as typical or non-typical. Their name and address were not requested. Completed questionnaires were screened for words or phrases which implied that estimates of time spent were reported for a usual or customary activity, rather than for actual events. Respondents were compared with non-respondents.

Professional and Non-Professional Activities

All of the minister's activity during a specified day, from the time he awakened in the morning until he retired at night, were included in the diary. The activities during the "waking day" were classified as professional, or non-professional or private. That part of the waking day which was devoted to professional activities was designated the "working day," all the rest was either non-professional or private.

Non-professional or private activities were classified as either personal or family. There were four types of personal activities:

Spiritual growth included prayer, Bible study and meditation, and religious reading that was not to be used immediately in the performance of a practitioner role.

Intellectual development included the reading of newspapers, magazines, and books that were secularly oriented, as well as informative and educational radio and television programs. Such personal activities as spiritual growth and intellectual development might be considered by some to be professional work time, because these activities are essential for the minister to perform his work. The effectiveness of a clergyman could be related to the degree to which he keeps up in his religious and secular reading and other informative activities. However, in this report it is considered as self-maintenance, since it is not directed to the fulfillment of a specific practitioner role.

Physical needs include bathing, shaving, dressing, and eating at home.
Recreation (alone) included entertainment, hobbies and napping.

Family life was divided into four categories:

Spiritual life included all corporate devotional activities.
Fellowship and recreation included conversation with family members, recreational activities, and family travel and trips.
Family care included child care, housekeeping chores, cooking, and transporting children to school.
Business and maintenance for the family included shopping; care of the house, garden and grounds; family accounts and banking; and automobile maintenance.

All professional activities were classified according to the practitioner role being performed. Transportation time was allocated to the role involved. For example, a sick call might involve a fifteen minute hospital visit, but it might require a three-quarter hour trip. The whole hour would then be allocated to the pastoral role. To avoid arbitrary decisions about the length of a sermon and the time a minister devotes to the leadership of worship at a Sunday service, the time devoted to preaching and priestly activities was considered as a unit.

The average (mean) length of the waking day was 16 hours and 7 minutes. The *waking day* was divided into professional (62 percent) and non-professional activities (38 percent). That portion of the waking day devoted to professional activities took 9 hours and 57 minutes, while non-professional activities took 6 hours and 10 minutes. Personal activities were allotted 64 percent of this non-professional time, and family activities 36 percent. For a complete list of these time allocations, see Appendix B.

Time Allocations to the Practitioner Roles

Time allocation for the traditional practitioner roles was less than one-fourth of the work day. The parish minister devoted an average of one hour and 50 minutes to preaching and priestly activities per day. Conducting services in his own church took one hour and 16 minutes. Sermon preparation required 44 minutes per day. There are priestly activities included under preaching because it was difficult to distinguish between the activities associated with the two roles when they were being performed in a public service of worship which included preaching. However, the minister devoted 28 minutes to liturgical duties that could be separately identified. Weddings and funerals required about half of this time (15 minutes) per day.

Teaching and the preparation for teaching occupied 29 minutes a day. Ten of these minutes were devoted to the church school, and the remaining 19 minutes were allocated to other teaching (including confirmation, weekday religious classes, and study and discussion groups).

Pastoral role activities averaged 2 hours and 35 minutes per day. Visiting the sick and distressed, church members and prospective members, as well as chatting with members after meetings and communication by telephone, required two hours and two minutes. Counseling required 19 minutes, and fellowship and recreation with individuals and informal groups required 14 minutes.

Administrative activities required three hours and 53 minutes a day and included four types of activity. *Local church administration* includes general planning, publicity, budget promotion, physical plant supervision, and clerical work as well as official board, staff, committee and lay leader meetings. These activities required an average of two hours and 49 minutes a day. *Denominational administration* includes participation in meetings of diocese and other judicatories and committee work. *Interdenominational administration* includes work for the National Council of Churches and other cooperative agencies as well as participation in ministerial association meetings. Denominational administration averaged 47 minutes a day, a few minutes more than was reported for sermon preparation. Interdenominational administration took 10 minutes. *General non-professional activities* required seven minutes a day and include operation of the church plant (starting the furnace) and taxi service for parishioners (when no practitioner role is performed).

Activities of organization take one hour and 10 minutes per day. Work with church groups and associations averaged 40 minutes. The largest segment of this time (26 minutes) is participating in and attending meetings, and advising and cooperating with group leaders. Time for community organizations averaged one half-hour a day.

When the total professional work day of the parish minister was considered, the order of activity from most to least time-consuming is as follows: administration, 39 percent; pastoral, 26 percent; preaching and liturgical, 18 percent; organizational, 12 percent; and teaching, 5 percent. The parish minister devotes 23 percent of his work day to the traditional roles (preacher, priest, teacher) and 26 percent to the neo-traditional role (pastor). The remaining 51 percent is devoted to the contemporary roles (administrator and organizer). Considered from another perspective, 23 percent of his practitioner time each day is spent on idea-oriented roles (preacher, teacher, priest) and 77 percent of his work day is devoted to roles oriented to people and groups. (See Table 19.)

TABLE 19
TIME ALLOCATION TO PRACTITIONER ROLES

Role	Percent (N = 751)	
Traditional	23	
Preacher & Priest		18
Teacher		5
Neo-Traditional	26	
Pastor		26
Contemporary	51	
Administrator		39
Organizer		12

Comparison of Time Allocation Studies

Material on the length of the minister's work day may be examined by comparing the Russell Sage Survey (1954-55) with that of May (1934), and that of Hartshorne and Froyd (1945:69-74). May reported that rural ministers worked 78 hours and 48 minutes per week. His categories are not exactly comparable to ours, but his report does compare with our finding of 80 hours and 23 minutes of practitioner role work and related personal activities per week. (See Appendix C.)

Hartshorne and Froyd (1945) report the time 152 Northern Baptist ministers allocated to professional work, personal and family activities, and sleep. Their professional work week was 61 hours and 29 minutes when travel time, preparation, and miscellaneous and unaccounted-for time is considered. Personal and family activities were 50 hours and 15 minutes. Sleep was 56 hours and 4 minutes. On a daily basis the working day was 8 hours and 47 minutes, family time was 7 hours and 13 minutes, with 8 hours for sleep.

Comparisons of the Baptist ministers' time allocation to practitioner roles with those of the interdenominational sample (Russell Sage Foundation) show that the waking day is about equal, but in 1944 the ministers devoted more time to personal and family affairs while the interdenominational group in 1954 had the longer work day.

Inspecting the time allocations to specific practitioner roles, we find the preacher-priest allocations are about equal. This is also the case for the pastor and organizer roles. The Baptist ministers committed the greater amount of their time to the teacher role, and the inter-denominational ministers devoted a greater amount of time to administration. (See Appendix D.)

The categories which Hartshorne and Froyd used for the professional work week (preaching, etc., teaching, pastoral, administrative, and service to community) were similar to the practitioner roles used in the present study. A careful comparison of Table 11, Hartshorne and Froyd (1945 p. 69), "How ministers . . . divide their time among 40 types of activity," with the coding of the Russell Sage Practitioner Roles, permits slight adjustments to be made in the components from Hartshorne and Froyd for relative consistency in the definition of the "practitioner roles" for both studies. (See Appendix E.)

A comparison of the May 1934 study with the present 1954-55 study yields one interesting contrast. On the one hand, in 1934 the preacher-priest roles required nearly one-half of the clergyman's professional work week, but 20 years later they were allocated about one-fifth of his work week. On the other hand, the administrator-organizer roles were allocated about one-fifth of the minister's work week in 1934, but two decades later the time allocated to these roles was one-half of the minister's work week. The pastor and teacher roles showed little change. The work week (or the work day) remained relatively constant, even though the time allocated to the several practitioner roles was redistributed. Such findings are consistent with the increased size and complexity of local church organizational structure during the last several decades.

Practitioner role evaluations and time management

A basic problem in the professional practice of clergymen is the relationship between the normative, satisfaction, and performance evaluations of the practitioner roles, and the relative time the minister actually devotes to their performance. Are his time management decisions regarding these roles consistent with, and supportive of, his other evaluations of them? Does he devote most of his time to the important roles and the least time to those roles that are relatively unimportant? Does he devote more time to those roles in which he is least prepared to perform effectively and less to those for which he is least prepared to perform? Is he able to devote more time to those roles that are satisfying to him and less to those that are not?

Time allocation to professional activities did not vary as expected with practitioner role evaluations. The exceptions to this generalization are of theoretical interest. There is a reciprocal relation between time allocated to the neo-traditional and to the contemporary roles. Those who devote more time to the pastor role tend to devote less time to the organizer role, and conversely. The formal and informal aspects of the church system seem to be kept in equilibrium.

We have already noted in Chapter VI that a normative indoctrination about the practitioner roles may furnish the minister with an ideal goal, and his sense of effectiveness and satisfaction in performing these roles may motivate him as he seeks to perform them in a normative manner. However, the normative, satisfaction, and performance evaluations place the practitioner roles in quite a different order of priority from that of the operational requirements of the parish. With the exception of the role of pastor, those roles having high normative, satisfaction, and performance evaluations tend to be rated somewhat lower when judged by time allocation. Roles that are rated low by these evaluations tend to be performed more frequently.

In a sense, then, the practitioner roles a minister performs in American society are basically equivocal. On the one hand, the church has a traditional set of normative evaluations regarding the practitioner roles by which the minister is expected to be guided. Further, there are performance evaluations that are held by the minister and those whom he serves. In addition he has his own evaluations of the relative satisfaction he derives from the various practitioner roles. On the other hand, operationally, the various practitioner roles are evaluated differently when the time management of them is considered. In a sense, the evaluations are contradictory. The minister places the practitioner roles in one rank order when the normative, satisfaction, and performance evaluations are considered; and in quite a different order when they are operationally evaluated, as measured by relative time allocation to them (Table 20).

TABLE 20
A COMPARISON OF THE RANKINGS OF PRACTITIONER ROLE EVALUATIONS

Normative	Satisfaction	Performance	Operational (Time allotted)
Preacher	Pastor	Preacher	Administrator
Pastor	Preacher	Pastor	Pastor
Priest	Teacher	Teacher	Preacher and
Teacher	Organizer	Administrator	Priest
Administrator	Priest	Priest	Organizer
Organizer	Administrator	Organizer	Teacher

Clergy Characteristics

In theory it was expected that there would be greater variability in relation to time allocation to the practitioner roles and clergy characteristics than had been the case when the master, integrative, and practitioner roles were considered. This theoretical expectation is based on the assumption that the allocation of time involves overt behavior whereas subscription to concepts of the master and integrative roles is covert behavior. The evaluation of the practitioner roles was made by the ministers themselves rather than by a supervisor.

Practitioner role time allocation is a measure of what a clergyman puts into his work. This is especially so when the length of the work day or work week is considered. To the extent that clergy vary in the amount of work they do, we may theorize about independent or predictor clergy variables in relation to total work day or time allocations to each practitioner role as a criterion or dependent variable.

Personal factors

Age is related to the development of a clergy career. We would expect that the younger men and women have different and more limited work opportunities than middle aged or older persons. We theorize that the older a clergyman, the longer his total work day will be; and conversely the younger a minister, the shorter his work day.

This theory was, in a limited way, sustained by the empirical analysis. Age was found to be significant in time allocation to the practitioner roles with respect to the total work day (.05 probability level). Clergymen between the ages of 40 and 49 tended to work longer days than did those who were younger, or those who were older. (See Table 21.)

TABLE 21
TIME SPENT IN TOTAL WORK DAY BY AGE

Age	Hours:Minutes
25-29	9:27
30-34	9:50
35-39	9:41
40-44	10:19
45-49	10:32
50-54	9:20
55-59	10:07
60 +	9:43

This would indicate that age in relation to work day is curvilinear, whereas our theory was stated in linear terms. The organizer role was the only practitioner role that was found to be statistically significant in relation to the clergyman's age (.01 probability level).

Ministers who are older spend more time performing the organizer role than do those just initiating their career.

We would theorize that *marital status* and *parental responsibility* would affect the amount of time ministers devote to their professional activities, and that single clergymen would have a greater work input than would married clergy. We would expect married clergy who have no children to work a greater amount of time than those who have children.

The theory was sustained in part. The marital status of the clergyman is not significant when the total work day and time allocation to practitioner roles is considered. However, the number of children he has was significant at the .001 level in relation to time devoted to the teacher role. Clergymen who had no children spent more time teaching than did those who had one or more children.

Personality structure

With respect to the personality structures of ministers, we would theorize that a selection process operates within the profession. Ministers with personality characteristics which are related to effectiveness in the practice of the ministry continue in the profession. Those who are ineffective because of personality characteristics tend to select or move into non-parish clergy assignments, or to take up other occupations. Empirically there is support for our theory. Personality characteristics as measured by the authoritarian scale and the emotional maturity score do not vary in relation to time allocated to professional activities.

Clergy Referents

The three types of referents—status, mentor, and dependent—have not been related to clergy role behavior thus far in the analysis. However, when the referents of the clergyman were cross-tabulated with the time ministers devoted to professional activities some significant results were obtained. To a limited degree the clergyman is influenced in his time allocation by his referents.

The relationship between *status* referent and length of professional work day approached significance. The status referent was not significant for the specific practitioner roles activities. Ministers who have ideologically-oriented persons as status referents, work the longest day (10 hours and 40 minutes) and those who have religiously-oriented persons as status referents work the shortest day (nine hours and 26 minutes). The ideological referent has a social and political philosophy that is attractive to the minister. He is interested in social reform and social justice. The religious referent is a clergyman or layman within the religious system. Hence we may conclude that those clergymen who identify with ideological status referents express their concern for improving the lot of man by working a longer professional day. Likewise, clergymen who have religious status referents seem less interested in change, and work a shorter day.

The *mentor* referent was significant (.05) in relation to the total work day, but was not significant for specific practitioner roles. Those who worked the longest day selected theologically attractive persons, or persons who were crusaders, as mentors. Those who worked the shortest day selected mentors who had a scholar or a father-counselor image.

The *support* referent was not statistically significant in relation to the total time devoted to professional work; and teaching was the only practitioner role approaching significance. Those who spent the greatest amount of time teaching had clergy colleagues or denominational leaders as support referents. Those who spent the least time in the teacher role had lay colleagues as support referents.

The minister who works a long day has a referent who is ideologically and theologically oriented and is a person who is interested in changing the status quo. The minister who works a short professional day is the quiet, scholar type whose referents are largely found within the religious system.

Professional Career

Theory would suggest that the length of the clergy work day is a function of tenure; and that the less mobile a minister is and the longer he has been in one location, the longer his work day would be. However, analysis of the data indicates that occupational mobility was significant, but tenure in present parish was not. Ministers with high mobility worked a shorter day (9 hours and 31 minutes) than those with low mobility (10 hours and 11 minutes). The pastor role was the only one that was significant. The more mobile clergy devoted less time to this role than did the less mobile minister. The fact that there is a relationship between occupational mobility and the work day but that parish tenure is not related to variability in the length of the work day suggests that our theory requires revision. The minister who changes parish assignments frequently, has a minimum work input; the infrequent changer of parish assignments has a maximum work input. Length of work day would seem then to be related to the attitude of the clergyman toward his work rather than the length of tenure in a specific parish.

Criteria for effectiveness and success

Effectiveness criteria did not vary in relation to time allocation to professional activities. Success criteria, however, did approach significance for the total work day. Ministers who worked the longest day tended to regard denominational relations as important for success. Those who favored personality characteristics as a criterion for success tended to work the shorter work day. Success criteria also approached significance for time devoted to the preacher-priest role and to the pastor role. Those who devoted much time to preaching and priestly work tended to regard denominational relations as important for success; but those who devoted less time to preaching and priestly work favored personality characteristics as a factor in success. A large time allocation to the pastor role is associated with personality characteristics; and practitioner skills are associated with a relatively small allocation of time to the pastor role. Success criteria were not significant for the other practitioner roles.

Organizational Factors

Practitioner role time allocation, the dependent variable, was also cross tabulated with organizational factors, the independent variables. These included denomination, regional location, community culture variability, organizational complexity of the parish, and parish economics. Theoretically, these factors would influence the minister's time allocations to the practitioner roles.

Denomination

Denomination has consistently been a significant factor in relation to variability in the minister's image of his master, integrative, and practitioner role evaluation. However, it is not significant when time allocation to practitioner roles is considered. Ministers serving churches in one denomination appear to devote about the same amount of time to practitioner roles as do those serving in another denomination.

Our finding about denomination as a variable in relation to ministerial time allocation is consistent with the results of the May study (1934) as interpreted by Douglass and Brunner (1935:104-135). They state: "from the standpoint of the distribution of time between duties, not much difference appears in the reports of ministers of different denominations. On account of greater stress on the sacraments and the larger number of services traditionally held, Protestant Episcopal ministers and those of other liturgical churches spend somewhat more time on the average in priestly functions. That the difference is not more extreme is another evidence that the minister's task is essentially conventionalized. . . . all kinds of ministers of all denominations do substantially the same things . . ."

Hepple (1958) included a broader spectrum of denominations in the Missouri study which permitted him to use the church-sect typology as an independent variable in relation to the total work week, the dependent variable. He reports that ministers serving church-type religious organizations full time devote a greater amount of time (47.8 hours) to the seven activities he researched than do ministers serving sect-type organizations full time (36.4 hours).

Interpretation of the finding about denomination in the present study as a predictor variable in relation to practitioner role time allocation is difficult. One aspect is the relatively narrow group of denominations included. They would be church-type predominately, rather than sect-type. Another consideration is the difference between the master, integrative, and practitioner role judgments considered in chapters IV, V, and VI, and the time allocation data. The former are all judgments from the ministers about themselves, but the time allocation data report behavior involving other actors in the religious system. This suggests that the differences in role as conceived by ministers of different denominations are not realistic when seen in an interaction context with parishioners.

Regional location

Region and community type variability reflect differences in the structure of the society. Metropolitan areas, or regions which are highly developed industrially, would present different requirements for the church than would the more rural non-metropolitan areas and less developed regions.

The findings support this theory about the response of the church to environmental factors. The regional location of the minister's church is significantly related to the length of the work day, but not to the amount of time devoted to the various practitioner roles.

Ministers in the South work the shortest day (9 hours and 35 minutes), and western ministers the longest (10 hours and 56 minutes).

Community Type

The degree of metropolitan-ness or lack of it and the urban or rural location of the church served by the minister is significantly related to the length of the minister's work day. Urban ministers worked the longest day (10 hours and 31 minutes) and rural ministers the shortest (9 hours and 2 minutes).

The amount of time per day devoted to the traditional practitioner roles is not significantly related to urban or rural location. However, time spent in performing the pastoral role (neo-traditional) is significantly associated with type of community. Ministers located in a metropolitan area give most time to the pastor role and rural ministers give least. In the contemporary roles, non-metropolitan rural ministers devote the least time (3 hours and 18 minutes) to administration and metropolitan-urban the most (an additional hour). Urban clergymen give the most time to organizational work and rural men the least.

Douglass and Brunner, reviewing the May materials, state: "in spite of extraordinary environmental and organizational differences between the churches which they serve, rural and urban ministers show no substantial difference in the distribution of their time between the various classes of duties." While the difference is not substantial as viewed by Douglass and Brunner, it is the same direction as found in the present study.

Organizational Complexity

In addition to the environmental factors just discussed, we would theorize in a similar manner about the relative simplicity or complexity of the church as an organization. The more complex the organization, the greater the work load of the minister. Furthermore, as the organizational complexity of the church increases we would expect the minister to devote more time to the pastor role, the administrative role, and the organizer role.

There is substantial support in the data for this theory. All of the factors measuring organizational complexity, except the benevolence budget, were significant in some respect when time allocation to practitioner roles is a factor. For example, clergymen who ministered to only one church worked a shorter day (nine hours and 17 minutes) than did those who served two or more churches (ten hours and 45 minutes); however the time devoted to the specific practitioner roles is not significantly related to the number of churches in a parish.

Size of church is significantly related to the length of the minister's work day. The more complex the church organization, the longer the minister's work day; those who serve in churches with less complex organizational structures have a shorter work day. In fact, ministers in churches with fewer than 200 members averaged nine hours and 28 minutes a work day whereas those in churches with over a thousand members worked ten hours and 52 minutes a day. As regards the practitioner roles, the larger the church, the less time a minister devoted to teaching. However, the larger the church, the greater the time the clergyman devoted daily to administration. (Three hours and 16 minutes for churches with under 200 members as compared to four hours and 38 minutes in churches of 1,000 or more members.) The ministers in the large churches devoted more administrative time to staff and committee meetings than did those in smaller churches.

Ministers in churches having 400 to 599 members devoted more time to clerical work than did those in smaller or larger churches. Two aspects of the pastoral role (calling on the sick and distressed, and personal counseling) are significantly and positively related to church organization complexity. The remaining practitioner roles (organizer, preacher, priest) are not related when size of church and time devoted to these roles are considered. The Douglass and Brunner study confirms our findings regarding size of church and length of work day.

Another measure of organizational complexity is the *number of students in the church school.* The larger the church school, the longer the minister's work day. The practitioner roles do not vary in time allocation; but the time a minister devoted to teaching outside of the church school did vary significantly. Ministers in smaller churches tended to allocate more time to confirmation classes, leadership training, week-day religious education, and discussion groups.

The *number of staff members* (including staff other than clergy) remuneratively employed by a church is positively and significantly related to the length of the minister's work day. Ministers who were the only employed staff person worked an average of nine hours and 28 minutes a day. When the staff numbered six or more persons, the average work day for the minister was longer by one hour and 13 minutes. The preacher and priestly roles, as traditional practitioner roles, are significant in relation to variability in time allocation and size of employed staff, but the teacher role is not. In churches where there was only one staff person, the minister devoted an average of two hours and two minutes per day to the preacher-priest roles; but when the staff consisted of six or more persons, the allocation per day was one hour and 32 minutes. Time allocation to the pastor role (neo-traditional) increased as the staff size increased. In one-person staff churches, ministers averaged two hours and 20 minutes per day in the pastor role, and three hours, 11 minutes when six or more persons were on the staff. This is statistically significant. The time allocation to the administrative role is also statistically significant. The larger the staff, the greater the time allocation of the minister to administration. In the large-staff church (six or more persons) the minister devoted nearly an hour more than the three hours and 27 minutes devoted to this role by a minister in a church staffed by one person. The other contemporary role (organizer) was not significant. In short, the larger the church staff, the less time the minister gives to preaching and liturgical duties and the more time he devoted to administrative and pastoral activities.

Comparable material is reported by Douglass and Brunner (1935) who found that the job records of ministers of staffed churches showed distinctive differences from those in non-staffed churches. "With ministers with small staffs, homiletical duties, which take more time than any other type with the whole body of ministers, sink to second place; and to third place with ministers with large staffs; while administrative duties correspondingly rise. Of the major types of duties, the pastoral and ministerial are least affected by staff relationships. The minister of the staffed church, however, concentrates on fewer kinds of duties than are engaged in by the minister who works alone; and he gives relatively less time to such minor duties as clerical work, attending meetings for which he is not responsible, and regrettably, to cultural pursuits. On the contrary, he gives more time to civic duties" (pp. 122-123).

When time management is considered in relation to the size of the clergy staff, variability is not as great as it is for total staff size. The length of the total work day was significant. Ministers serving in churches staffed with more than one minister worked a longer day (ten hours and 28 minutes) than did those on a one-clergy staff (nine hours and 47 minutes).

The total work day of the clergy does vary in relation to the *local budget of the church.* The larger the budget, the longer the clergy work day. When the budget was less than $5,000 per year the minister worked an average of eight hours and 59 minutes; but when the budget was $50,000 or more the minister averaged ten hours and 58 minutes. While the local budget was statistically significant, the benevolence budget was not.

The *per capita cost of the local church program* is significantly and positively related to the length of the minister's work day. The greater the cost per member the longer the minister worked in a day. However, the time the minister devoted to the various practitioner roles was not related to per capita cost.

Parishioner Perception of Ministerial
Time Management

The time allocation data reported and analyzed in this chapter is derived from the clergymen. Glock and Roos (1961) theorize (concerning Lutheran ministers) that "the image of a profession among its clientele will largely be informed by what is visible in professional activity." They analyzed time allocation materials obtained in 1956 from 2,229 parishioners in 12 urban Lutheran churches in the East and Middle West. Parishioners ranked seven professional activities from most time to least time having been devoted to them by their ministers as follows: sermon preparation, work for the church-at-large, attending church meetings, office work, giving people advice, visiting non-members, and visiting members. These parishioner judgments hardly compare with the minister's own reported time allocation in the present report. The seven activities classified as components of professional roles in the present report involved an average daily time allocation of four hours and 45 minutes, and ranked from most to least time allocated daily as follows: office work, visiting members, working for church at large, preparing sermons, attending church meetings, giving people advice, and visiting non-church members. (See Table 22.) Glock and Roos also report that parishioners ranked the minister's own recreational activities as involving less time than the seven professional activities. Ministers in the present study devoted 39 minutes a day to personal recreation, about the same time allocation that he devoted to attending church meetings. Parishioner information about clergy time allocations and the actual time allocated to these activities by parish ministers are in sharp contrast. Glock and Roos suggest that "the church and its ministry have perhaps failed to communicate effectively to the membership just what the ministerial role entails in practice." They conclude that "(parishioner) approval is most likely to come where the minister is perceived as devoting considerable time to visiting members and non-members, as not spending much time on office work, and as striking a reasonable balance in the amount of time spent in sermon preparation, work for the church at large, attending church meetings, and giving people advice. If he fails to strike a proper balance in these last four activities, he is (thought to be) better off to emphasize sermon preparation and giving people advice and to de-emphasize working for the church-at-large.

TABLE 22
TIME ALLOCATION FOR
SELECTED PARISH ACTIVITIES

Parishioner judgments about the minister's use of time 1956 data [Glock & Roos (1961)]		Parish minister's actual time allocation Russell Sage Foundation Study - 1954		
Rank	Activity	Rank	Activity	Average time per day minutes
1	Preparing sermons	4	Sermon preparation	44
2	Working for church at large	3	Denominational adminstration	47
3	Attending church meetings	5	Church organizer, excluding planning	38
4	Office work	1	Clerical work	72
5	Giving people advice	6	Counseling	19
6	Visiting non-members	7	Visiting new people	7
7	Visiting members	2	Visiting members	58

Mild approval is given to attending church meetings almost regardless of perception of time spent on it." To Glock and Roos it appears that "parishioners would like ministers to spend more time on visits and less time on sermon preparation." They further suggest on the basis of these results that "the pastoral . . . and preaching functions of the ministerial role are paramount to the parishioner, that he wants his minister to focus his energies on these tasks, and that he is prone to be critical where these expectations are not met." In the Russell Sage study the preacher and pastor roles are normatively evaluated most highly by ministers. If clergymen are guided in time allocation by their normative judgment, it would seem that ministers and laity are not far apart in their preferences.

Situational Variables

Situational factors, in addition to clergy and organizational factors, affect the practitioner role time allocation of the clergyman. Time allocated to non-professional activities during a waking day, time allocations which vary by season of the year, the day of the week, and the degree to which a day is typical or atypical, are all factors which help explain variability in time allocated to professional activities of the minister's work day.

Non-professional activities and clergy characteristics

We theorize that the minister must choose between professional and non-professional allocation of time; these two types of activities would seem to be competitive. The minister's personal desires or his family responsibilities may be powerful factors in affecting his professional behavior.

Personal activities were found to be significant at the .01 level. Ministers who were 50 (or more) years old devoted more time to these activities than did those who were younger. Those who were under 30 years averaged three hours and 59 minutes on personal activities, whereas those who were 60 or more averaged almost an additional hour. Also, there was a tendency for the amount of time allocated to *family* activities to increase as the number of children increased. These two time allocations may be compensatory in that family responsibilities increase as each child enters a home.

The *personality* of the clergyman is not a factor in his non-professional time management. An authoritarian clergyman does not differ significantly in non-professional time allocation when compared with the democratically oriented person. This also is the case when the clergyman's degree of emotional maturity is considered in relation to non-professional time. The *status, mentor,* or *dependent* referents do not vary with differing time allocations to non-professional activities.

The *occupational mobility* of the clergyman does vary with time allocation to non-professional activities. The highly mobile clergyman devoted more time to family life (two hours and 43 minutes per day) than did the less mobile (one hour and 44 minutes).

Time management of non-professional activities does not vary with *criteria of effectiveness* or *success.*

Non-professional activities and organizational factors

We expect organizational factors to have a greater influence on the time management of professional activities than they would for non-professional activities. The clergyman is expected by parishioners and other laymen to give priority to his professional activities. His personal desires and family influences may be less powerful than are persons and groups in the parish.

Denomination is not significant in relation to non-professional time allocation. However, *region* is significantly related to personal activities. In this case western ministers had the least time for personal activities (three hours and 27 minutes), and Southerners the most (four hours and 19 minutes). Family time was not affected by regional location. Urban ministers had the least time for personal activities (three hours and 42 minutes), rural ministers the most (four hours and 15 minutes). Ministers located in metropolitan areas also had the least family time.

Professional time commitment does vary with the degree of *organization complexity* in the parish, but it is much less important for non-professional time allocation. Non-professional time allocation is not related to the number of congregations in the parish, or the number of church members. Those serving parishes with small church schools tended to have more personal time than did those with larger church schools, but the larger the staff the less time per day a minister devoted to family activities. However, the amount of personal time does not vary significantly. Ministers in churches staffed with multiple-clergy devoted less time to family matters (one hour and 55 minutes) than did those in a single-clergy church (two hours and 21 minutes). Non-professional time allocation does not vary in relation to parish *economic factors*.

Three additional situational factors were analyzed in relation to time allocation to professional activities. Season or month of the year, the day of the week, and the typical or non-typical day were cross tabulated to see what influence, if any, they had on practitioner role time allocation.

There is an ethos in our culture regarding the minister's work which provides a strong stereotype of how and when the clergyman should work. For the layman, this stereotype suggests that the minister works only (or mostly) on Sunday. From the clergyman's standpoint a typical day is one that fits the stereotype of the clergyman at work, and the non-typical day deviates from the predominate theme of the ethos as to how the clergyman works. The minister internalizes this ethos about his work through interaction with teachers at the seminary, and in his contacts with laymen.

Season of the year

The season of the year would seem to be an intervening variable in relation to the minister's allocation of time. Summer is a period of vacation, and the other seasons are associated with the school year. Furthermore, seasonal holidays, some of which have religious meaning, seem to influence decisions about the use of time. The day of the week introduces variability also. Sunday (for Christians) is a day for religious services. Week days are work days for parishioners. The seven days of the week have a rhythm of work and leisure which are reflected in the stereotype.

The length of the professional work day varies significantly with the month of the year. September has the shortest work days (7 hours) and December the longest (14 hours and 30 minutes). Time devoted to traditional practitioner roles differs significantly from month to month. Ministers apparently spent the most time on preaching and priestly activities, especially sermon preparation, during the winter when preaching demands are greatest, rather than during the summer as some clergymen are reported to do. Teaching duties are heaviest in the fall. Time spent on the neo-traditional role (pastor) is at a peak in the fall and at a low ebb in the spring. Time for contemporary roles (administration and organizational work) is not significantly different from month to month.

Day of the week

The amount of time allocated to each of the practitioner roles by the parish minister differs significantly by the day of the week. Monday is the heaviest day for administration (4 hours and 58 minutes). Tuesday is characterized as the day when the most time is allocated to pastoral work (3 hours and 14 minutes), particularly visiting church members (one hour and 24 minutes). On Wednesday, Thursday and Friday the practitioner work load is not unique, except that an unusual amount of time is given over to administrative staff and committee meetings on Wednesday; and Thursday seems to be the day for calling on the sick and distressed (one hour and two minutes). Friday is the day when the least time is devoted to teaching. Saturday being the shortest work day, a minimum of time is used in administration, organization, and pastoral work. It is, however, the day when most sermon preparation occurs (2 hours and nine minutes). Time devoted to sermon preparation per day from Monday through Friday varies from 22 to 43 minutes.

On Sunday the greatest amount of time for the week is spent on preaching and liturgies, teaching, and organizing. Sunday is the day when the least time is given to clerical work, administrative staff and committee meetings, pastoral visiting, and calling on the sick and distressed. Over all, the mid-week (Wednesday, Thursday, and Friday) follows a routine that differs strikingly from the weekend and the early days of the week. More than 60 percent of the time allocated to sermon preparation during a week is spent on Friday, Saturday and Sunday.

Typicalness of day being reported

Ministers were asked to state whether they considered the day for which they were reporting to be typical or non-typical. The total work day was significantly related to the typicalness of the day, the work day being longer on a typical day. The time allocated to the traditional roles (preacher, priest, and teacher) is not statistically significant when considered for typicalness. On what the minister considered to be a typical day he devoted more time to the neo-traditional role of pastor (especially visiting, 2 hours and 54 minutes) as compared with 1 hour and 43 minutes for a non-typical day. The contemporary roles also differ significantly when typicalness was a variable. A typical day required more organization work, and a non-typical day more administrative work (especially denominational administration). Considering a typical day for practitioner roles, less time was thought to be devoted to administration, but more time to organizational and pastoral work. On a non-typical day the minister said that he devoted 4 times more time to denominational activities than on a typical day. However, on a typical day he spent more time in meetings with his church staff and administrative committees. A significantly greater time is devoted to sermon preparation, pastoral calling on the sick and distressed and visiting church members in the parish on days thought to be typical.

Summary

Chapters VI and VII both focus on the practitioner roles. They are separated to give emphasis to the minister's evaluation of the practitioner roles in one, and the minister's decisions to allocate time to the performance of these roles in the other. They also differ in that one chapter analyzes the conscious judgments of the minister, and the other analyzes the less conscious decisions about time management.

The parish minister is in large part the manager of his own time. Some of his appointments are scheduled by tradition, but he is at liberty to arrange most of his professional activities at such convenient times as he and those he serves may wish or require.

About two-thirds of a minister's waking day is devoted to professional activities, and less than one-fourth of this working day is devoted to traditional practitioner roles. A slightly higher proportion of time is allocated to the neo-traditional role of pastor. More than half of the work day is given over to the contemporary roles, especially administration. Hence about three-fourths of the minister's work day is directed toward people-oriented roles and the remaining one fourth to idea-oriented roles. His evaluation of the idea- and people-oriented roles is not consistent with the time he allocates to them.

For the Protestant parish minister the relationships between normative, satisfaction, and performance evaluations reflect the various influences and pressures created by those who guide him and those who seek his professional services. The normative orientation apparently reflects the way in which he is theologically oriented, and the theological norms of the denomination. The satisfaction evaluation reflects his personal commitment and involvement in the profession. The performance evaluation reflects expectations of denominational administrators and parishioners. The operational evaluation reflects the day-to-day decisions he makes as he seeks to perform the practitioner roles within the parishioner's expectations and the community's definition. It also reflects the extent to which the local parish minister adopts programs promoted by national and regional denominational headquarters.

Clergy characteristics, in relation to variability in time allocation, tended to be significant less frequently than did organizational factors. Time allocations vary in relation to the clergyman's age and occupational mobility. A peak work load is carried by those in their late forties. The less mobile a minister is, the greater his work input. The clergyman is also influenced in time allocation to practitioner roles by his mentor referent. Those working the longest day are influenced by mentors they consider to be theologically attractive, or by crusaders. For those who work the shortest day a mentor is likely to have a scholar image or a father counselor image.

The regional location of the church served by the minister is a variable factor in the length of the work day; ministers in the West work the longest day, and those in the South, the shortest. Urban ministers work the longest day and rural ministers the shortest. All of the measures of organization size and complexity, except benevolent or extra-parish budget, vary in relation to practitioner role time allocation. A theoretical implication of these findings is the relationship between ecological factors and organizational complexity. Relative simplicity of organizational structure is characteristic of certain ecological areas, while a relatively complex organizational structure is characteristic of other areas.

In making time management decisions, the minister is required to take into account the season of the year, the day of the week and the degree to which the day is typical. The professional work day is shortest in September and longest in December. Monday is dominated by administrative tasks, Tuesday tends to require a heavy time investment to the pastoral role. Friday, Saturday, and Sunday are primarily devoted to sermon preparation. Wednesday, Thursday, and Friday are not unique in role demands. A typical work day is shorter than an atypical day. Denominational activities are thought to be atypical, while typical days feature staff work, administrative committees and calling on those who are sick.

There are several dilemmas which the parish minister faces as he performs the practitioner roles. These arise out of basic ambiguities which confront him. (A related set of dilemmas regarding the institutionalization of religion has been analyzed by Thomas F. O'Dea, 1961.)

The first dilemma focuses on the parish clergyman who has a high normative view of a practitioner role. How is he to secure motivation through a sense of enjoyment and effectiveness that will aid him in meeting the expectations of that role held by the parishioners he serves, as well as by denominational administrators and seminary professors who articulate theological norms?

Another dilemma focuses on the traditional roles in contrast to the neo-traditional and contemporary roles. Protestant churches now reflect changes in our society. The social structure of society is becoming more complex, and the organizational functions are accordingly becoming more centralized. The number of members in each local church is increasing and the organizational structure of the local church is becoming more specialized. An aggressive evangelistic policy and mergers are resulting in larger denominational bodies. Both of these changes, nationally and locally, have placed greater importance on contemporary practitioner roles for the development and management of the formal structure of churches and denominations, and on the neo-traditional roles for the maintenance of the informal structures of churches and denominations. At the same time organizational complexity requirements have tended to over-shadow those functions fulfilled by the minister in the traditional roles. Have the idea-oriented traditional roles been restructured to the same extent and as appropriately as the people-oriented, neo-traditional and contemporary roles?

A third dilemma focuses on the balance between professional time and personal and family activities. During a waking day professional and non-professional activities compete for the allocation of time. If the minister has a long work day, there is less time for personal and/or family affairs. If he has heavy time commitments to personal or family activities, there is less time for professional activity.

Several factors are related to variability in non-professional time commitments. The older the minister or the greater the number of children, the greater the amount of time allocated to family activities. Ministers in the South devote the greatest amount of time to personal affairs and those in the West the least. Metropolitan-urban ministers have least time for personal activities and non-metropolitan rural the greatest. As for family time, ministers located in the metropolitan area have the least and non-metropolitan ministers have the most. In small parishes ministers have more time for personal activities and those in large parishes have less time. Ministers serving churches with large staffs have the least amount of non-professional time available to them. All of these factors limit the options open to the minister as he seeks to act responsibly in the management of time for professional, personal, and family activities.

A fourth dilemma focuses on the work schedule of the parish minister. It is complex and flexible, rather than simple and rigid. Hence, it is difficult of management, a fact we reported as being repressed by the parish minister. There is no routine answer to give the clergyman as a steward of his time.

VIII
ROLE CONFLICT

The minister performs his roles in a social milieu. He is the central actor in a theologically-oriented social system, and interacts with various persons within and outside the system. The expectations of actors in these situations have been conceptualized for analysis as involving several role types for the minister. He has the role of a professional person, his master role, which involves goals (integrative roles) and means (practitioner roles); and these roles may be either traditional or contemporary in their orientation. The practitioner roles are in one order of priority when evaluated by the minister on the basis of norms, satisfaction and performance; and in another order of priority when the time allocated to their performance is considered. In addition he has private, or non-professional, roles such as family man, citizen, and participant in the church as an adherent or a believer.

The problems of the minister as a professional person have been introduced where appropriate in the foregoing chapters and the possibility of problematic situations has been deduced from the data as analyzed; but the emphasis has been on the eufunctional aspects of the roles of the minister. A conscious effort was made to include dysfunctional aspects of the clergyman's role in the analysis, however this possibility has been latent in the discussion. Role conflict would seem to be implicit in the structuring of these roles. This is especially evident when clergy characteristics are compared to parish organizational factors in our role analysis.

Role Conflict Theory

Role conflict as used in this analysis follows Sarbin (1954) and Gross, et al. (1958:244-250). Any situation in which a person is in a status in which he is confronted with incompatible expectations is described as having a role conflict. The incompatible expectations may result from the actor occupying a single status or more than one status. Gross terms the former intra-role conflicts and the latter inter-role conflicts. The minister, for example, may have a role conflict because of two incompatible roles as minister and family man. Conflict may also result from situations in which incompatibility is related to differing degrees of legitimacy associated with role expectations; e.g., in the ministry the practitioner roles differ in legitimacy. For example, there is greater legitimacy for the preacher role than for the administrator role.

Two major factors may in theory be related to variability in role conflict, personal expectations and organizational factors. No role is defined the same way for each actor. It is possible for a variety of actors to fill the same role provided only that they possess the required technical competence. The crucial differences in behavior are a function of the interaction between the different personal expectations and the role expectations. The extent to which conflict is felt is also a function of differences in personality structure (Ackerman, 1951; Getzels and Guba, 1954; Stouffer and Toby, 1951).

Other highly relevant variables are the social norms that exist in any group organization or institution. "Roles in organizations, as contrasted with many other roles that individuals fill, tend to be highly elaborated, relatively stable, and defined to a considerable extent in explicit and even written terms" (March and Simon, 1958:4). When norms are explicitly and clearly articulated in an organization, actors in the system will tend to conform to role expectations. According to Stouffer (1949), if the norms are clear and unambiguous the individual actor has no choice but to conform or take the consequences of group resentment. If, however, an actor has roles in two or more groups and simultaneous conformity to the norms of each of the groups is incompatible, he is faced with a role conflict situation. Stouffer found with a pencil and paper test administered to college students, that considerable variability exists in the social norms. He notes that it is common in sociological writing to think of a social norm as a point, or at least a very narrow band on either side of a point. He feels that a more realistic view would be to recognize the ranges of permissible behavior. The variability of social behavioral norms may result in differing concepts of role expectations for the actor.

The importance of organizational environment for the definition of a person's role may be seen in the role conflicts which are related to a dual organizational status. Getzels and Guba (1954) studied the role conflicts of teachers at the Air University. They found that there was a major conflict between the officer role and the teacher role. This was especially so for those who, although presently officers, had received a major part of their training as civilian professionals in such schools as business or law. In short, in addition to their role as officer, they had also internalized and become accustomed to the role expectations of the civilian professional status they occupied.

A related role conflict problem is that of the military chaplain. The chaplain's conflicts are interesting because potentially they arise out of the fact that he is a functionary in both an ecclesiastical and a military organization. Burchard (1954) has reported on a small inter-faith sample (71) of chaplains and ex-chaplains in the San Francisco area.

The military chaplaincy is a clergy career in which the possibility of role conflict is endemic. The chaplain's role-set and his status-set involve two major institutional structures. The goals of the religious and military institutions are in some respect mutually exclusive. Chaplains not only share the dilemma of the Christian regarding war, they also function as officers in both ecclesiastical and military organizations. As officers they are responsible in part for the achievement of the ends specified. To become chaplains they need the endorsement of the religious body in which they are ordained; and to be chaplains they also must contribute to the attainment of the goals and objectives of the military in which they have rank, regardless of the uniqueness of their rank and position in the table of organization. The military chaplain has, therefore, two basic ambiguities in the ways in which his role is defined, one ideological, the other organizational.

Burchard assumed that there are five major items in Christian ideology which contribute to role conflict for the clergyman in the military. These doctrines of love, universal brotherhood, peace, non-resistance to evil, and the commandment "You shall not kill" are manifestly incompatible with the goals of military defense or war as a national policy. The ideological is confounded by conflicting church and state relations, which becomes a question of loyalty.

Two of the hypotheses tested by Burchard are of interest in the present discussion. First, the position of the chaplain does lead to a conflict in roles for the incumbent of that office. This hypothesis is supported in two ways: by a philosophical analysis of the two social roles of clergyman and military officer and by the responses to questions dealing with rank and those dealing with relations between religion and war.

The second hypothesis, that the chaplain serves as interpreter of the values of the military organization, that he helps resolve value-dilemmas for individual servicemen and helps promote smooth operation of the military organization, is less strongly supported. Such data as were available indicate that the hypothesis is tenable. If a serviceman were in doubt about the morality of military activity, a majority of the chaplains would endeavor to assure him that his relationship with God would not suffer thereby. All chaplains' welfare activities are designed to help the serviceman adjust more smoothly to the military situation.

A related role conflict problem occurs when a professional person is responsible to two levels in an organization. Wilson (1959) notes in a study of an English pentecostal sect, that the minister is "in many ways merely an agent of the (sect's) headquarters." Churches are organized in this sect after a revival campaign. A crucial phase in the transition from a revival compaign to an established church is the choice of the ministerial leadership. Policy in the sect is to bring in a new minister at the time of establishing a church, rather than to allow any of the revivalists who directed the campaign to continue in the role of minister. The minister must be acceptable to the members of the congregation even though they did not choose him initially. Thus there is a conflict between the minister's commitment to national headquarters and his responsibility to his own church members. (See also Falk, 1962; and Foley, 1955.)

Campbell and Pettigrew (1959) treat self-expectations as an independent variable. They point out that "the standard model of role conflict treats ego as forced to decide between the incompatible norms of groups that can impose sanctions for non-conformity . . . the actor is important analytically only because he is caught between contradictory *external* expectations." These cross pressures and the associated sanctions for nonconformity are external to the actor. Campbell and Pettigrew argue that the cross-pressures model "skirts the issue of whether ego imposes expectations on itself and punishes deviations." This model, they state, "tends to be historical in the sense that a finite number of cross-pressuring groups are used to predict the actor's behavior." The question hinges on whether or not it is assumed that the actor can develop "from periods of prior socialization any normative expectations for his behavior which would have an independent existence." It is the contention of Campbell and Pettigrew that the actor can, and that "this system seems especially significant where personal action is contrary to the pressure of known and significant groups."

Articles in popular magazines and religious journals have long suggested that conflict is implicit in the various definitions of the minister's role. F. K. Stamm (1935), for example, wrote a forthright article forty years ago on this theme. Two decades later Wesley Shrader (1956) wrote an article which was discussed vigorously in religious journals. These and other articles (Berckman, 1956; Hudnut, 1956; Pearson, 1956; Sittler, 1959; Williams, 1956; Oates, 1961; Duncan, 1932; Moore, 1957; Mills, 1966; Judd, et al., 1970; Whitman, 1968) called attention to the tension under which ministers felt they were working, and why some were leaving the ministry. Such articles, by calling attention to the lack of role consensus, the differing role expectations for the clergyman, or the tendency for clergymen to withdraw from the profession, underline the importance of role conflict analysis.

The importance of role conflict for the ministry cannot be treated lightly. Leadership involves skill in the solution of role conflicts. Chester I. Bernard (1938) has observed that skill in handling role conflicts is a *sine qua non* at the highest executive levels. Skill in managing role conflict situations would appear to be no less important for the clergyman. However, the purpose in this chapter is to analyze the clergy role conflicts, not to resolve them. For those interested in the problem, each of the following authors has explored aspects of the problem of role conflict resolution: R. P. Abelson (1959); Waldo W. Burchard (1954); J. W. Getzels and E. C. Guba (1954); John T. Gullahorn and Jeanne E. Gullahorn (1963); Kozaburo Shimada (1958); Samuel A. Stouffer (1949); Samuel A. Stouffer and Jackson Toby (1951); J. P. Sutcliffe and M. Haberman (1956); and Jackson Toby (1952).

Role Conflict Model

The role conflict model developed for this analysis is based on two assumptions. First, it is possible to classify the roles of a minister into occupational or professional roles, and personal or non-professional roles. Second, it is possible for a clergyman to fulfill his private and professional roles in both traditional and contemporary styles. These assumptions permit a set of four role constellation categories to be identified which permit the analysis of possibly conflicting intra-role and inter-role expectations.

The four role constellations identified in the model are (A) traditional-personal roles; (B) contemporary-personal roles; (C) traditional-occupational roles; and (D) contemporary-occupational roles. The role conflict model has two axes, the personal (or non-occupational) and the occupational role axis; and the traditional and contemporary value axis. (See Chart 1.) The traditional-occupational and non-occupational roles are those that have greater legitimacy for the ministry as evidenced by biblical definition, theological foundation and church traditions. The contemporary-occupational roles are those that have less legitimacy. Since they have more recently emerged in the ministry, there is a lack of biblical definition, theological rationale, and institutional patterning. (See Chart 1.)

The traditional-personal role constellation (A) is somewhat unique in relation to the other constellations. It involves roles that both parishioners and clergyman share. Minister and parishioners are believers and students of the doctrine, traditions and practices of the church. However, they do differ in the degree to which they are expected to fulfill the role. The minister's pre-ordination experiences as a church member include acceptance of and training in the belief system of the church. His decision to enter the ministry and his subsequent professional education tend to distinguish him from the rank and file church members. As a clergyman his status in the religious system is elevated. His commitment as a believer and his technical understanding are expected to increase appreciably. The traditional-personal role orientation is a prerequisite for the clergyman. However, he is expected to play the role without publicly calling attention to his fulfillment of it. He represents an ideal type with which the church member identifies, even though the layman does not hold the same status in the religious social system. This role constellation is oriented to personal contemplation and study to a greater degree than are the other three constellations, which are more action-oriented. Furthermore, this role pattern is performed in private to a greater extent than are the others, which are more likely to be performed in public.

The contemporary-personal role constellation (B) identifies those roles that the minister shares with others in the society in which he lives. The minister may consider himself as a professional man and personally identify with lawyers, physicians, teachers and other professional persons. As such he is a community leader with other professional and business people. His residence may be on church property and be called a parsonage, manse, or rectory; but he and his family function as community members as do other residents. He may be a member of a service (luncheon) club, go to P.T.A. meetings

CHART 1
ROLE CONFLICT MODEL

	Traditional	Contemporary
Personal	**A** Believer Scholar - Technical Theologian	**B** Family man - Husband Father Citizen - Community member Professional person
Occupational	**C** Believer Saint Scholar Evangelist Sacramentalist Father Shepherd	**D** Interpersonal Relations Specialist Parish Promoter Social Actionist Educator Sub-cultural Specialist Community Religious Leader Churchman
	Preacher Priest Teacher Pastor	Organizer Administrator

as a father, vote in elections as a citizen, and contribute to community welfare drives. He is like any other member of the community, an ordinary man who has relatives, who relaxes as he desires, and who is a citizen with concerns about education and politics.

The traditional-occupational roles (C) are those which have legitimate patterns of behavior in church tradition, biblical definition and theological foundation. The minister's sense of vocation and his professional education in the divinity school support these role constellations. Ministers are aware of the expectations, ideology, and definition of these roles. In performing these roles the minister is in the position of being an actor before an audience in inter-personal relations with parishioners.

The contemporary-occupational roles (D) are those which have more recently emerged in the ministry, therefore there is a lack of biblical definition and theological rationale for them; also they are not uniformly patterned institutionally. These roles are somewhat removed from the traditionally sanctioned authority of the minister. This constellation includes roles that are either derived from, or are an adjustment to, the structure and dynamics of contemporary society; and have been developed to sustain the church as a social system in a complex social order. The fulfillment of these roles places the minister as an actor in inter-personal and intra- and inter-group relations, but does not require him to be an actor in relation to an audience.

It is conceptualized that an individual minister could have a role conflict between any two of the four role constellations. Personal and occupational roles may be in conflict as well as the traditional and contemporary orientations. Chart 2 below illustrates the six interaction patterns where conflict may occur. The model assumes that the four role constellations each have unique orientations that may conflict. These are coded AB, AC, AD, BC, BD, and CD. However, the letter may be reversed to indicate inter-action in both directions.

CHART 2
ROLE INTERACTION PATTERNS

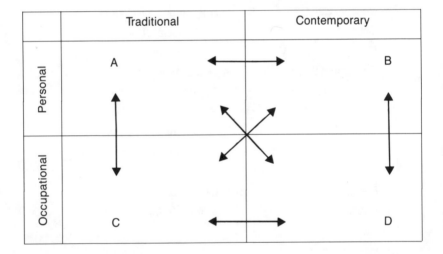

The role conflict model used in this analysis is not completely satisfactory from a theoretical point of view. It seems reasonable to assume that the clergyman has one set of statuses and roles that may be called personal in the same sense as every person in a society does. He also has a set of statuses and roles that have specific reference to his occupation, his master role. It then seems reasonable to assume that there are traditional and contemporary aspects to these statuses and roles. However, it would appear that the fourfold classification fails to take into account the fact that the traditional-personal role pattern (A) also has contemporary aspects. Furthermore, this role pattern is relatively unique to the ministry. It also fails to take into account the fact that the contemporary-personal role pattern (B) has both traditional and contemporary aspects. There are also some ways in which the community member-citizen role might be considered as occupational rather than personal. In short, the types are not always mutually exclusive in reality. They are, however, useful for analysis.

Analysis of Role Conflicts

The identification of possible conflict situations was made possible by a content analysis of the responses which were made by the respondents to 21 questions. Examples of these questions are: "What aspects of your work seem to be the most irritating to you personally?" and "What problems seemed to be most urgent in previous ministries? These may have been personal, church, community, denominational, or other problems."

Evident role conflict

The analysis that follows is based on the frequency with which the ministers mention each of the six role conflicts in the model. Some measure of the intensity of role conflict for these informants may be inferred from the number of role conflicts that individual clergymen articulate. (See Table 23.) One-third mentioned no role conflicts, nearly one-half mentioned only one, and about one-fifth mentioned two or more role conflicts.

TABLE 23
NUMBER OF EVIDENT ROLE CONFLICTS HELD BY MINISTERS

Number of articulated role conflicts	Percentage of ministers (N = 1,111)
None	33
One	45
Two	17
Three	5
Four or more	0.5

The six evident role conflict types are: traditional-personal vs. traditional-occupational (AC); traditional-personal vs. contemporary-personal (AB); traditional-personal vs. contemporary-occupational (AD); contemporary personal vs. traditional-occupational (BC); contemporary personal vs. contemporary-occupational (BD); and traditional-occupational vs. contemporary-occupational (CD). The frequency with which clergy informants identified each role conflict for themselves is found in Table 24.

TABLE 24
DISTRIBUTION OF ROLE CONFLICT TYPES

Role conflict	Percentage of ministers* (N = 1,111)
AC	9
AB	14
AD	28
CB	14
CD	24
BD	2
None articulated	33

*Categories not mutually exclusive. Informants could have more than one role conflict.

The evident role conflict model includes two axes, the personal-occupational and the traditional-contemporary. Four of the role conflict types involve a conflict on only one of these axes. Those involving a conflict on the traditional-contemporary axis are the traditional-personal and the contemporary-personal roles (AB), and the traditional-occupational role and the contemporary-occupational role (CD). Those involving a conflict on the personal-occupational axis are traditional-personal vs. the traditional-occupational (AC) and the contemporary-personal vs. the contemporary-occupational (BD). Two of the role conflict types involve a conflict on both axes: the traditional-personal vs. the contemporary-occupational role (AD) and the contemporary personal role vs. the traditional-occupational role (BC). (Refer to Chart 2.)

The *traditional-personal* role vs. the *traditional-occupational* role conflict (AC) occurs within one context, the traditional. The basic question for the minister is how to allocate his resources in relation to his personal and occupational roles. It involves the choice of means within the traditional context. Within this orientation he cannot resolve the personal and occupational role conflict. If he is a believer and scholar as he may wish to be, he may not be the pastor who spends much time calling on parishioners. He has a unified approach to his person and job, but he is not up to the demands of both roles. Nearly one-tenth are categorized in this evident role conflict type.

This conflict is expressed in many ways. Examples are:

"I have no time for personal devotions and my pastoral work";
"I have to discipline myself to regular study";
"The dogmatists and the fundamentalists have specifics which I cannot give my people in my pastoral role. I often have not been able to answer their questions."

The *traditional-personal* role vs. the *contemporary-personal* role (AB) is an intra-personal conflict, although it may be seen in his family and other inter-personal non-occupational relationships. About one-seventh were aware of this role conflict in their work. The minister is "a man of faith"; he is "called by God." This means that he is separated or set apart from other people. Yet his parishioners want a "good mixer" who will not be very different from themselves and will be able to understand them. There are other ways in which his traditional-personal role conflicts with his contemporary-personal role. He has a family and wants to spend time with them. He also wants to fulfill his roles as a private citizen. This may involve affiliation with educational, fraternal, political and recreational groups and participation in these and other types of activities. He may feel that these associations are not consistent with his call to the ministry. Or he may be sensitive about comments made by parishioners about these activities.

The traditional-personal vs. the contemporary-personal role conflict is illustrated in the following statements from informants:

"I need to decide how a minister should fit into the community—how can he enter into the responsibilities of the community and yet command self-respect."
"People just don't want us (ministers) to be a 'stuffed shirt.' "
"I am trying to decide now whether I (a minister) should join a community lodge."

The traditional-personal vs. the contemporary-personal role conflict may be one that may be unique or peculiar to the religious functionary. Although the lawyer, especially one on the bench, may face a similar conflict, his administration of justice may require that his personal moral code be consistent with the expectations of his profession. For the clergyman there may be a clash between the image of being "a man of faith" and "a man of God," or of being "a good Joe" and "a regular guy." This conflict arises out of the tradition that clergy are set apart from other persons.

The *traditional-personal* role vs. the *contemporary-occupational* role (AD) cuts across both axes in the role conflict model. Ministers are inclined to perceive it as a clash between the spiritual qualities in a minister's life and mundane approach to his work. As they see it, the believer and the scholar are forced to deal with the less spiritual aspects of the ministry. Or the specialist in matters of interpersonal and intergroup relations is critical of the pious expectations that are made of the minister. Considerable belligerence may be expressed, and rash or extreme statements may be made, revealing this type of role conflict. More than one-fourth of the informants were consciously aware that they had this conflict.

The minister who has an evident role conflict of this type may feel that he has "no time for reading and study because of small details of administrative work."
Or he may feel that "the denomination cares more for statistics and is unaware or unconcerned about the real worth of ministers."
He may report "I've seen good men held down in the ministry while salesmen and merchants move in."

The *contemporary-personal* role vs. the *traditional-occupational* role (CB) is another conflict that involves the two axes (traditional-contemporary and personal-occupational). Contrary to expectations, it was an evident role conflict for only one-seventh of the parish ministers included in this research. Here the contemporary concept of personality comes into conflict with the more traditional concept of the ministry. The minister feels that he is on the edge of a conflict arising out of tension between his attempts to be himself and to enjoy his family and the community, and his attempts to fulfill his tasks in the church as traditionally defined. This role conflict brings the family man (husband and father) and the citizen into tense situations.

One informant speaks of "adjusting to the sometimes dormant and sometimes active hostility of my wife to demands made upon me because I am a minister . . . when to heed my wife and when to heed the parish demands."

Another mentions "the conflict of my work and my family, each demanding and deserving more time than I can give either one."

Another minister reports: "the intelligent minister knows that it pays to take time out for recreation and relaxation, even though the 'Lord's work' has to be delayed."

The *traditional-occupational* vs. the *contemporary-occupational* role conflict type (CD) is the second strongest among the types. Nearly one-fourth described this as an evident role conflict for themselves. This role conflict type offers strong evidence of the changing concept of the minister's role in the church and in society. It is evidence of the clash of values in religious culture. The minister is torn between two value systems that affect his occupation, the traditional and the contemporary. It reflects a secular trend in our culture and implies a change in our values. It is a change to which it is not easy for the minister to adjust because he may feel that it undermines the traditional ideologies about the ministry. Or he may want to move to a more secularized orientation to his occupation, but feels pressure within the church to conform to the more traditional orientation.

The traditional-occupational vs. the contemporary-occupational role conflict is evidenced by many familiar and repeated complaints that ministers make.

"How can we find time to minister to our congregations and deal with the burning issues of our community!"

"I carry on a running battle with educators who would like to use every resource for Sunday school, making worship a poor second."

There is "no time to cover all areas of church leadership and be a pastoral minister."

"Building program is absorbing most of my time, robbing other pastoral duties."

"It is my policy to listen to comments (traditional pastoral approach) . . . then since the responsibility is mine (as an administrator) I try to make a fair adjustment and follow it."

The *contemporary-personal* vs. *contemporary-occupational* role is an evident role conflict for fewer than two percent—the smallest group of informants. Its infrequent occurrence suggests that it may only theoretically be a role conflict category. Since the minister is operating within the contemporary sphere in both the personal and occupational role, the conflicts are not severe. The minister who organizes his job on a contemporary basis can presumably find time to be a community citizen, take care of his family, and be a "human being."

The problems of the parish minister in a changing cultural situation are more sharply focused when the role conflict types are arranged in rank order by frequency of occurrence. The traditional-personal role vs. the contemporary-occupational role (AD) is the most frequent conflict. Here the traditional image of the minister as a person is threatened by the contemporary concepts of the minister's integrative and practitioner roles. The second most frequent conflict type is the traditional vs. the contemporary concept of the occupational role (CD). Here again the conflict involves a threat to the traditional concept of the minister. The next most frequent role conflicts involved the contemporary-personal role in conflict with the traditional-personal role (AB) and the traditional-occupational role (CB). The conflict between the traditional-personal role and the traditional-occupational role is next most frequent (9 percent). It is the conflict between the person who is believer, saint, "called-one," or theologian, and the traditional practitioner. The least conflict is found between the contemporary-personal role and the contemporary-occupational role. (Refer to Table 24.)

The role conflicts of the minister involve the traditional-contemporary axis much more frequently than they do the personal-occupational axis. This suggests that these conflicts are a reflection of the changing concept of the ministry, of the more legitimate versus the less legitimate ways of functioning as a minister.

Apparent role conflict

One-third of the ministers were not aware of any role conflict. It may be more accurate to say that they were not articulate with respect to role conflict in their documentary responses. This lack of information raised a question of interpretation. If the respondents did not specify a role conflict, is it possible that they had role conflicts but did not identify them? Is it possible to infer role conflicts by analysis of the written materials they furnished?

To probe more deeply into the situation, and to seek answers to these questions a distinction was made between evident role conflict and apparent role conflict. Evident role conflict refers to conflict that was identified as such by the clergyman. Apparent role conflict was not identified by the informant as a conflict, but was inferred by the research analyst from incongruous material written by the informant. It is implicit within the total framework of the questionnaire responses.

The apparent role conflict involves the tendency for a minister unconsciously to identify himself with one role constellation as opposed to another; for example, with the traditional role constellation rather than the contemporary role constellation, or vice versa; and with the personal role constellation rather than the occupational role constellation, or vice versa. Some ministers may be more oriented to traditional roles and make them their own frame of reference, but others may be more oriented to contemporary roles. The apparent role conflict score is a measure of the minister's identification with, or propensity for, a particular constellation of roles. It permits a localization of conflict. It is a measure of high discrepancy between patterns, indicating a possibly rigid adherence to one role pattern or an overly strong compulsion to perform in one role pattern at the expense of others. It is not a measure of the presence or absence of a particular role conflict, like evident role conflict. It may be inferred that the minister who has a strong identification with or a propensity for one role pattern alternative will have an incipient role conflict against the opposing role constellation. This measure is a reflection of the high frequency of reference to one role constellation as opposed to another in the answers he gave to various questions. He revealed a frame of reference toward the role constellations by the high or low frequency with which he introduced them into the material he reported. It is assumed that all four constellations involve roles that are expected of the Protestant parish clergy in contemporary American society. This assumption then permits an inference about apparent role conflict if a minister has a frame of reference to the role constellation that excludes one pattern, or gives it minimal status.

The distribution of apparent role conflict scores is diagramatically expressed in Chart 3. The mean scores for the apparent role conflict model are 0.85 for the traditional-contemporary axis and 4.25 for the personal-occupational axis. These are the actual scales, not theoretical scales. Theoretically the intersection of the axes would have been at point 0.

CHART 3
APPARENT ROLE CONFLICT MODEL

	Traditional	Contemporary
Personal	A +10 +8 +6 +4 +2 Mean = 0.85	– 10 – 8 – 6 – 4 – 2 B – 2 – 4 – 6 – 8 – 10
Occupational	C	+ 2 + 4 Mean = 4.25 D + 6 + 8 + 10

The apparent role conflict scores were cross-tabulated with evident role conflict, and the means of the apparent role conflict indices were calculated for each evident role conflict, as AB, AC, etc. Analysis of variance was used to test the significance of the means. The scores on the personal-occupational index were significant at the .01 level of probability, but the traditional-contemporary index scores were not significant. Ministers with high personal-occupational index scores tended to have traditional-personal vs. traditional-occupational (AC) and contemporary-personal vs. traditional-occupational (BC) evident role conflicts. Those with contemporary-personal vs. contemporary-occupational (BD) evident role conflicts, or no evident role conflicts, tended to have low index scores on the personal-occupational axis of the apparent role conflict. The personal aspects of the minister's role appear to be in conflict with the traditional and contemporary aspects of his occupational role. This is the inference that may be drawn from the apparent role conflict analysis. This is in contrast to the findings in the evident role conflict analysis where the greater conflict was between the traditional-occupational and contemporary-occupational roles (CD) and the traditional-personal roles (AC). The minister, it would appear, has role conflicts involving his personal life that he does not readily identify or openly articulate. Since those who identify no evident role conflict have low apparent role conflict index scores, we find additional support for the notion that these ministers do not have role conflicts to the degree that others do. The low apparent role conflict score for those having the BD evident role conflict is by definition expected, since their conflict involves only the traditional-contemporary axis with respect to occupational rather than personal roles.

Evident role conflict, or conflict identified and articulated by the minister, is the dependent variable in this chapter. Variability in relation to clergy characteristics and organizational factors are independent variables.

Clergy Characteristics

We expected the characteristics of the clergyman to be related to role conflict. The age of the minister in part reflects his maturity in the profession. Younger ministers would tend to have the greater number of role conflicts and to be concerned about personal factors. Older ministers would tend to have fewer role conflicts and to be concerned primarily with contemporary role conflicts.

Role conflict is both intra-personal and inter-personal. We would expect measures of the clergyman's personality to be related to role conflict. Clergymen who are democratic, emotionally immature and open to change might be expected to articulate role conflicts. Clergymen who are authoritarian, emotionally mature, and closed to change might articulate relatively few role conflicts. We expected the clergymen's referents to be related to role conflict.

Role conflict may be associated with career variables. Parish ministers who had been recently ordained could be concerned with role conflicts involving personal roles and traditional-professional roles. Those who had had much professional experience could be concerned with conflict involving contemporary roles, or perhaps tend to articulate no role conflicts. Ministers whose career had been in the parish might have different role conflicts from those who had had other types of professional experience. The more mobile clergyman would have more role conflicts than the less mobile ones. The clergyman's criteria of effectiveness and success would be associated with role conflicts; the latter would be so because of the relationship of these criteria to the organizational expectations of the minister.

The data support the theory in part. The age of the clergyman was statistically significant (at the .001 level of probability). However, such personal characteristics as marital status and number of children were not significant. Younger ministers (less than 35 years old) tended to articulate the traditional-personal vs. the traditional-occupational conflict (AC). Those who were somewhat older experienced the contemporary-personal vs. the traditional-occupational (BC) and the traditional-occupational vs. the contemporary-occupational conflict (CD) to a greater extent than other ministers. Ministers in the middle age group articulated the traditional-personal vs. the contemporary-personal (AB) conflict, and the traditional-personal vs. the contemporary-occupational conflict (AD). The ministers who identify no one role conflict more frequently than any other were in the older age groups (45 years or more). It would appear that there are role conflicts that are relatively unique to each group in the ministry, and that role conflict declines with age.

The intra-personal nature of role conflicts places special relevance on clergy personality characteristics as an independent variable in relation to the type of role conflict the clergyman experiences. The type of role conflict identified by the clergyman as a problem was cross-tabulated with his score on the authoritarian scale. When the distribution of scores by quartiles and role conflict type was tested by the chi square it was found to be significant at the .01 probability level. The highest scores on authoritarianism were received by those who identified no evident role conflicts. Those having a traditional-personal vs. contemporary-personal conflict (AB) were most likely to have medium high scores. The medium low scores were most typically those having a traditional-personal vs. contemporary-occupational conflict (AD). The lowest scores were obtained by those with contemporary-personal vs. traditional-occupational (BC) or a traditional-occupational vs. a contemporary-occupational (CD) conflict. Those with a traditional-personal vs. a traditional-occupational (AC) or a contemporary-personal vs. a contemporary-occupational (BD) conflict received scores that were distributed relatively evenly from low to high. The role conflict types as experienced by an authoritarian person are arrayed from most likely to least likely as follows: none, AB, AD, BC, CD. The highest scores go to those ministers who display the greatest authoritarian tendencies and are inarticulate about role conflict. The next highest scores involve the traditional-personal role in relation to the contemporary roles. The lowest scores involve the traditional-occupational role in relation to the contemporary roles.

The variability in evident role conflict was also probed in relation to the emotional maturity of the minister. Are those who articulate role conflicts more mature or less mature emotionally than those who do not articulate conflicts? Are those who articulate one type of role conflict more mature, or less mature emotionally than those who articulate another type of role conflict?

The theory is that there is a degree of emotional maturity and stability (or the absence of these) that may tend to prevent a minister from becoming involved in a role conflict, or conversely may tend to promote his involvement in role conflict situations. Some ministers appear to so order their problems that role conflict does not result regardless of the situation; or where it does occur, they are able to manage it within a healthy tolerance. Other ministers are not able to do this. The approach they take to themselves and to others enhances the possibilities of role conflict. They seem to have a proneness to role conflict even before it confronts them in a specific situation. They have a "low boiling point." Their level of emotional maturity is productive of conflict.

The emotional maturity scores were cross-tabulated with evident role conflict. The hypothesis was that ministers who did not evidence role conflict would be most mature, and those who evidence contemporary-oriented role conflict (BD, CD, BC, BA) would be least mature. Those that had traditionally oriented role conflicts (AC, AD) would fall in between. The distribution was statistically significant at the .01 level of probability. The evident role conflicts of a contemporary nature were experienced by those with the lower emotional maturity scores. However, those not identifying role conflicts and those identifying traditionally oriented role conflicts both tended to have the higher emotional maturity scores.

Interpretation of this finding would seem to be consistent with overall theory about the roles of the clergyman. The traditional roles are more clearly defined. They have an articulated biblical and theological rationale, and there are traditional behaviors available for performing the roles. Hence those who are oriented to these roles have a greater possibility of developing an emotional structure that is consistent with the role expectations. The contemporary roles, on the other hand, do not have these supportive biblical and theological ideas. They are ambiguously defined, and have divergent behaviors that are followed in their performance. Those who are oriented to these roles have less possibility of developing a mature and stable emotional structure.

Length of professional experience and type of ministerial career were related to role conflicts (.001 probability level). However, occupational mobility and tenure in present parish were not. Clergymen who had been ordained for two decades or more tended to articulate fewer role conflicts than did those who had been ordained a shorter time than twenty years. However, those with more professional experience were not concerned with conflicts involving contemporary roles as predicted. Ministers with ten to twenty years professional experience were concerned with traditional-personal vs.

contemporary-occupational (AD) role conflicts to a greater extent than other ministers. Parish ministers with less than ten years professional experience tended to articulate contemporary-personal vs. traditional-occupational (CB) role conflict to a greater degree than did those with more than ten years of professional experience.

Parish ministers who had had experience as assistant or associate ministers, and those who had had non-parochial as well as parochial experience, tended to articulate role conflict less often than those in other career types. Ministers in these career lines, as well as those who are in their first parish tended to articulate traditional-personal vs. contemporary-occupational (AD) role conflicts, whereas those whose whole careers had been as senior ministers or as the only clergyman in a parish, tended to be conscious of traditional-occupational vs. contemporary-occupational (CD) role conflicts.

The criteria a clergyman has for success are significantly related to evident role conflicts at the .05 level. Those who identified no role conflict tended to feel that personality characteristics were important as success criteria to a greater extent than did other clergy. Those identifying role conflicts AB and AC were most likely to evaluate denominational relations highly as success criteria. Those having AD, BD, and CD role conflicts were inclined to feel that success criteria involved a combination of ministerial skills and denominational relations.

Organizational Factors

On the basis of the literature on role conflict we have developed the theory that variability in evident role conflict is associated with parish (or organizational) factors. Denomination, region, type of community, size of parish, and parish economics are independent variables that help explain the type of role conflict a minister articulates as being a problem.

We would expect that a clergyman serving a parish that is congregational in government or whose polity is based on local autonomy or democracy would be less likely to experience role conflict than would clergymen in a more highly structured titular polity; and that the type of role conflict he identifies would vary in relation to the denomination with which his church is associated. We would in theory develop the hypothesis that ministers serving parishes in one region of the country will have different role conflicts from those in other regions. To be specific, we would expect that clergy serving churches in the South would be less likely to identify role conflicts than others. Relating our theory about types of community and variability in role conflict to regional location, we would expect that clergymen serving churches in non-metropolitan communities, especially rural as contrasted with urban, would be less likely to identify role conflicts than those serving churches in metropolitan communities. With respect to size of parish, we would expect that ministers serving the small parishes would be involved in personal and traditional role conflicts, and that those in larger parishes would be involved in conflicts oriented to contemporary role definitions. This hypothesis assumes that larger churches are more complex organizations, and therefore involve the minister in conflicts arising from diffuseness of his role. A related hypothesis would state that as the size of the parish increases, the more frequently the role conflicts of the clergyman would be oriented to contemporary definitions of his role.

The hypothesis regarding denomination is sustained by the data, but those concerning region and type of community are not sustained. The denomination to which the parish belongs was significantly related to variability in role conflicts (.001 level of probability as tested by chi square). In congregationally-oriented denominations clergymen either identified no role conflicts, or they articulated role conflicts involving the traditional-personal role vs. the contemporary-personal (AB) or the traditional-occupational (AC) roles. This was true for the Baptist-Disciples, Lutheran, United Church of Christ, and Brethren denominational groups. In the episcopally-oriented denominations, clergymen tended to identify role conflicts involving other patterns such as AD, CB, and CD. The Presbyterians whose collegial governmental structure is in between the titular, highly structured Episcopal system and the relatively loose local autonomy structure of the congregational system, were also in between with respect to role conflicts (AB, AC, BD).

Two measures of parish size were significant: number of congregations in the parish (.001) and number of members in the parish (.02). Clergymen having parishes which serve more than one church tended to have conflicts focusing on the contemporary-personal roles AB, CB, BD, whereas those serving a one-church parish experienced role conflicts involving mainly the traditional roles AC, AD, CD. In a similar pattern, those in the smaller parishes tended to identify their role conflicts as AB and AC, and those in larger churches as BC, CD, and AD. The former are concerned with conflicts that are person-oriented and the latter with those that are occupation-oriented.

The amount of the local budget is the only measure of the economics of the parish that was significant (.05). Ministers in churches with small budgets had role conflicts oriented to personal roles, while those in churches with large budgets had conflicts oriented to occupational roles, especially the contemporary-occupational role pattern.

Summary

This chapter focuses on the dysfunctional aspects of the parish minister's role and status as contrasted with the eufunctional aspects of his role and status which were the primary focus of four previous chapters. Role conflict analysis tends to emphasize the problems of the profession, the strain and stress that accompanies involvement in and performance of the roles of the minister.

Role conflict is implicit if the definition of role is a set of complementary expectations regarding the clergyman as he interacts with parishioners and others in the church. Since there is a multiplicity of actors and roles, consensus and dissensus about role expectations set the stage for possible role conflict. Consensus about the role of the minister, the central actor in the church social system, would seem to be more critical than consensus about the role of the layman in the system. Laymen are permitted greater latitude and freedom in role performance than are clergymen. An added factor is that the status of the minister involves him more completely in the system; whereas the status of the layman involves him less completely in the system.

The work environment of the minister has many incongruities which set the stage for role conflict. The minister may be a member of a minority group, and as such finds that his statuses and roles as a clergyman and a minority group member are in conflict. Some parish ministers have conflicts in which aspects of their private life (such as marital tensions, or avocational interests of which laymen disapprove) impinge on their professional responsibilities. However, the more frequently articulated conflicts relate to traditional as contrasted with contemporary roles, both of which the minister is expected to play.

The analysis of the dysfunctional aspects of clergy role behavior uses a role conflict model. The role constellations in the model distinguish between professional and private roles, and between traditional and contemporary expectations in these roles. The model makes it possible to analyze inter-role conflict but not intra-role conflict. Inter-personal relations are included in the model, but intra-personal relations are not. We assume that emotional health factors are selective with respect to the minister, hence personality factors are treated as independent variables.

One limitation of the analysis is its dependence on self-reported data. Role conflicts included in the model were identified by analysis of documentary materials in which the minister mentions or implies conflict. Some ministers did not report evident role conflicts. The possibility of unconscious omissions in reporting was probed by an analysis of apparent role conflicts. This concept as operationalized seeks to measure conflict discrepancy of which the minister may not be consciously aware. It was found that those who identify no evident role conflict have low apparent role conflict index scores. A further difficulty is the possibility that laymen may view role conflict from a different perspective than do clergymen. This suggests the need for further research.

Role conflict decreases as the age of the minister increases. It would also appear that there are role conflicts that are relatively unique to each age group in the ministry.

The findings regarding authoritative personality and role conflict tend to be similar to those for age. The role conflicts of ministers who had low authoritarian scores tended to be the same as the conflicts reported among the younger ministers. No role conflicts were reported by those with a high authoritarian score, and older ministers also tended to report no role conflict.

Emotional maturity was found to be a significant independent variable in relation to role conflict. Those who had contemporary-focused role conflicts tended to have low emotional maturity scores. Those who had no role conflicts or who had traditionally oriented role conflicts tended to have higher emotional maturity scores.

The longer a minister has been in professional practice, the less likely he is to have evident role conflicts. Those with the longer experience tend to have traditional-personal vs. contemporary-occupational (AD) role conflicts, and those with a shorter period of professional practice tend to have contemporary-personal vs. traditional-occupational (BC) role conflicts. Professional experience as a clergy staff member or in a non-parochial post is associated with fewer role conflicts. Role conflicts typical of ministers who are in their first parish post tend to be traditional-personal vs. contemporary-occupational (AD). The traditional-occupational vs. the contemporary-occupational role conflict is more typical of senior ministers, or the minister who is the only clergyman on the parish staff.

Success criteria, a frequently significant variable, was also related to role conflict. Those reporting no role conflicts felt that personality characteristics were important success criteria. Those who felt denominational relations and ministerial skills were important success criteria had role conflicts that focused largely on their professional roles. Those with role conflicts involving private (or personal) roles were concerned about denominational relations.

The denominational affiliation of the clergyman was a significant independent variable in relation to role conflict. If those in locally autonomous denominations had a role conflict, it tended to be person-oriented. If those in a titular system had a role conflict, it tended to be profession-oriented. Ministers in collegial denominations tended to have role conflicts more like those in locally autonomous systems than those in a titular system.

With respect to parish size, ministers serving one congregation with a large membership and a high local budget, tended to have role conflicts involving professional roles. Those serving two or more congregations with a small membership and a low local budget tended to have person-oriented role conflicts.

Role conflict analysis naturally raises questions about how the clergy resolve the conflict. Unfortunately, the discussion in this chapter has sought only to conceptualize, identify, and classify the conflict; and to test the relationship between selected clergy and organization variables and role conflict. Resolution of conflict for ministers was not possible with our data, except by inference.

IX
THE MINISTER'S CONCEPT OF THE CHURCH

The minister is recognized as the professional leader of a theologically oriented social system (the church) which includes views about God, man, redemption, the church and society.

It is a basic assumption that theology is normative in the life of the church, and that behavioral expressions about beliefs, ethics and the practice of religion are derived from this theology. Thus the church expects that that minister's image of the church will reflect his assent to its theology, and assumes that as a central actor in the local church system he will perform his roles in the parish in a way that is consistent with its ideology. In short, the minister is influenced in his behavior in and his relationship to the church by the theology of that church. The church affirms through ordination—a rite of passage—that the minister's socialization in the church is adequate for him to function as a clergyman. A sociological theory about theological norms held by the church would seek to explain the degree to which a minister conforms to or deviates from these norms in the practice of his vocation.

The ideology of the church is a statement of purpose and is a resource for the guidance of professional functionaries in the system. The importance of this ideology for an understanding of the clergyman's master role has been discussed in Chapter IV. In fact, we theorize that his ideological view of himself and of the church is but part of a larger body of his ideological views regarding God, man, and society.

The analysis in this chapter focuses on only one aspect of these theological norms, the minister's image of the church, which would seem to be basic to an understanding of the way he functions in relation to the parish. This image consists of ideas and opinions that describe and explain his concept of the church as a social system of interacting persons committed to a set of beliefs, practices, and values, and it becomes a statement of behavioral intent on the part of the clergyman. It is what he conceives the local parish to be, but it is also what he conceives the function of the church to be.

Since Protestant denominations differ in the doctrine of the church which they hold, it would be expected that their clergy would also differ in the theological definitions or dimensions which they have of the church. If theology is normative for the minister and the parish church, it would be expected that ministers having differing theological images of the church would in consequence hold structural and functional images of the church that varied in relation to their theological images. The dependent variable in this chapter is the differing views of the church held by the clergy.

This chapter is informed by clergy views of the church. However, it is assumed that parishioners have their own images of the church. To the extent that the minister's view conforms to that of the parishioners and vice versa, a common ideology exists. However, to the extent that they do not have common views, the minister and his parishioners are in conflict.

There appear to be some expectations on the part of ministers that parishioners will be Biblically and theologically illiterate. This is apparent in their response to the question: "What specific problems are you concerned about in the area of the lives of your parishioners as you seek to be an effective parish minister?" The most frequent response concerned the clergyman's personal problem of doubting his own effectiveness. However, the most frequent problem that ministers saw in the lives of their parishioners was theological; and other problems in the lives of parishioners are seen in this context:

"theological and biblical illiteracy,"
"tendency to cling to childhood religious phantasies,"
"religion isn't too important as long as you behave."
"the proneness of many to embrace and believe popular beliefs not in the mainstream of Christianity, and to follow sensational religious leaders."
"irregular religious habits,"
"compartmentalizing religion,"
"surface living in comfortable community," and
"lack of desire for religious study and investigation."

The Church: An Operational Definition

Doctrine, as recorded in creeds and affirmations, is a formalized expression of what the church is thought to be. The minister through his socialization as a professional leader in the church has internalized these aspects of religious culture. The way in which the minister expresses or uses doctrine will depend in part on the actors with whom he is interacting, within or outside the system. When he discusses doctrine with other clergy he may use technical language to a greater degree than he does in conversation with laymen. When he is preaching he may explain doctrine with more formality and precision than he would when he is performing his role as pastor. In the day-to-day operation of the parish he would express doctrine in a different way than he would in conversation with a professor of theology. In this chapter we are interested in the doctrine of the church as the minister expresses it in the parish.

Data for the analysis of the minister's concept of the church were secured by asking each informant the following question: "When you are explaining the church to people . . . what are the major ideas you seek to have them understand?" It was expected that in responding, ministers would describe their day-to-day operation of the church rather than make a systematic statement of doctrine.

A content analysis of the documentary answers was made to determine the frame of reference and basic concepts the minister used in explaining the church to people. To be systematic in the content analysis, instructions were prepared for the coders in the same way as was done regarding the master role in order to assume a consistent set of homogeneous categories. Three frames of reference, or orientations, of the minister's concept of the church were identified: the ideological or theological, the functional, and the structural. Each of these orientations was expressed through several themes. (Table 25) Ministers' responses provide illustrations of each of these themes.

Theological frame of reference

God's instrument. The church is

"an instrument of God's grace"
"the mediator of the Biblical revelation"
"a divine institution through which, in the means of Grace, God (The Holy Spirit) seeks to rule in the hearts of men. It is the agency through which God administers his redemptive grace to the salvation of men."

TABLE 25
CHURCH ORIENTATION THEMES

Frame of reference	Theme	Percentage of ministers* (N = 1,111)
Theological	God's Instrument	31
	Body of Christ	24
	The Evangel	9
	Individualistic or Personal	38
	Fellowship or Community	34
Functional	Pragmatic or Relevance	26
	Social Critic	6
	Social Action	16
	Values	7
Structural	Denominational	12
	Interdenominational	
	Ecumenical	8

*Categories were not mutually exclusive; a minister informant could be classified in more than one category.

"a divine institution, everlasting and indestructable, in contrast to lodge, club, or political organization."
"God's instrument of reconciliation."
"The church is here to be the instrument of reconciliation in the estrangement between God and man."
"The church is man's instrument of service in God's name."
"A sacramental expression and channel of God's grace through which Word and Sacraments are conveyed, existent in its own right prior to the individual incorporated therein."

The body of Christ

"The church is centered in and governed by Christ." "The church is primarily a spiritual organization centered in Jesus Christ as our Savior."
"We are one body in Christ. All have not the same functions yet all are one body. The church is the body of Christ."
"The church is not simply an association of people but in a real way the body of Christ in which His will, if ever, will be expressed."
"The incarnation of God took human form in Christ for man's salvation. The church is the extension of the incarnation. It is the Body of which Jesus Christ is the head and all baptized persons are its members."

The evangel

"The church exists for the salvation . . . of man."

". . . there is only one central theme. Christ is the hope of the world and the savior of men."

"The church is people, the church has a special message, the church has a mission for the world, we declare a hope for another world."

"The church is made up of people whose task is to acquaint the unchurched with Christ . . ."

"People accepting Lord Jesus Christ as their personal savior."

The individualistic, or personal

"the love of God for man, the demonstration of that love in Jesus. The importance of the individual in the sight of God."

"Christ through the church is seeking to change the lives of individuals and it is only as individuals become whole in Christ and at peace with themselves and God that real and lasting good can be accomplished."

"The need for a personal satisfying relationship to an eternal God and Savior, response to a basic call within each individual; an individual's direct relation to his God."

"The basic element of personal faith and personal devotion to the Great Head of the Church."

"The necessity of personal religion, practiced with family members, business associates, etc." "I like to emphasize that the central matter is a personal experience of God that connects us with the source of our true life."

"Church membership is public affirmation of a personal relationship and of a desire to grow in Christ's spirit."

Fellowship or community

"The church, through Christians, offers adequate resources for satisfactory and reconciling relationships with others, covering the entire range of society, in response to the love and purpose of God who wills people to be consciously 'of his family.' The church builds upon the goals and accomplishments of all agencies within society and offers ultimate and complete relationship one with another in 'the Kingdom of God, on Earth, as in Heaven.' Hence the 'redemptive fellowship.' "

"The church is a fellowship of people who recognize the fundamental needs of their lives and believe that they can better meet those needs, as well as the needs of those around them by working and worshiping in fellowship rather than as so many independent units."

"The church is a fellowship with God and with likeminded men. In this fellowship there is power available for living—power from God and power from the personal contacts with others."

"In a city where organizations are legion, I desire the person to understand he is not coming into another mere organization, but that the church is unique in its fellowship."

"The church is the fellowship redeemed by our Lord—a saved and saving society whose principle functions are the worship of God, and helping others."

"The church is the community of believers that follow Christ. It will succeed as it develops a spirit of friendship that enables it to contribute to believers and unbelievers."

". . . the church is the profoundest understanding of community life that I have found. It strengthens individual personality, family life and group life because it accepts the judgment of the impossible and lives with it."

"The church is a community of believers having a common aim: developing the idea of Acts—'with one accord in one place.'

"The church is a dedicated community banded together to share experiences of faith and worship and to combine their talents for more effective service. It is an opportunity to draw upon the spiritual understanding and strength of the ages and to pass along the secular insights of the ages and the powers that we together experience under God."

The functional frame of reference

Pragmatic or relevance

"The relation (of) Christianity realistically to the business of living." "It depends on the person and what his problem is. We all have problems. In order for a person to understand the functions of the church (he) must see the joy of life and faith. I try to show him the relevance of worship to man's basic needs."

"I try to point out particular instances where the church has proven a help to individuals or to social life."

"The church is dealing with and has always dealt with the every-day issues of life. Our over-familiarity with theological vocabulary should not blind us to the fact that theological ideas and church organizations spring from human need."

"It depends on the person and the circumstances . . . Christian living is the most practical, satisfying way to live and the church's job is to help people find it . . . Everyone owes it to himself, to others, to God to be an active part of some church."

Social critic

"The church is concerned with the total life of the Christian and cannot ignore social nor personal implications of the Gospel."

"The need for the church to keep the community conscience sensitive to its needs and problems."

"(The) church must judge society and be the vehicle for God's mercy also."

"The church stands for positive wholesome principles in all areas: personal, social, economic, etc."

"The church is . . . for *all* kinds and conditions of men. It has something to say when the ethics and conduct of civil affairs, or any affairs, is below Christian standards, and has a right to say it, and as far as I am concerned shall say it."

Social action

"The church . . . has as its task the service, uplifting and fulfillment of the lives of other people."

The church is "a community of effort."

"The church is a group of people with whom we can work together to achieve some measure of our ideas for the community and to fulfill our own need for a sense of usefulness in service."

"(The church is) a world organization dedicated to building a better world under the guidance of the Holy Spirit."

"The church seeks to lift society through information and action in many areas of life."

Values

"One of the big functions of the church . . . is to remind people continually of the great eternal truths of life."
"The church affords opportunity for the expression of that which is best in human character; spiritual values are real and lasting."
"The church is a source of spiritual strength. One needs the church and its associations the same as a storage battery needs to be put on the 'charging line.' "
"The church is the foundation for morality, order, justice."
"The church gives people the proper perspective for realizing the true meaning of life and their own destiny."

Structural frame of reference

The structural dimension of the church includes the ecumenical and the denominational. In the latter concept the emphasis is on denominational loyalty. The church is a body of requirements for the members, and the structure of church government is important. One informant who holds the denominational view emphasizes "our denomination's concern with problems of social and civil importance as well as with the development of character in individuals; and the democratic principles it works out in Presbyterianism." In contrast, another informant who holds the ecumenical view reported: "The church is for all . . . denominations are secondary." Another stresses "the historical unity of the church since Christ's establishment . . . ecumenical progress." Ministers who differ in their commitment to the denominational as contrasted with the ecumenical theme, do not differ with respect to the theological and functional orientations. Ministers who are theologically oriented are not typically denominational or ecumenical; and neither are those who are functionally oriented.

Comparison of frames of reference

Using the three frames of reference regarding the church—theological, functional and structural—the ministers were classified as follows: Type I, those theologically oriented only; Type II, those both theologically and functionally oriented; Type III, those functionally oriented only; Type IV, those structurally oriented only; Type V, those who were not classifiable (Table 26). In each of the first four types a minister might mention one or more themes in the frame (or frames) of reference involved.

The theological themes were used in both Type I and Type II; the functional in Types II and III. The proportion of *theological* themes used in Type I in comparison to the proportion used in Type II is not statistically significant, using chi square. However, a comparison of the *functional* themes used in Types II and III does yield a difference that is highly significant statistically (.001 probability). Those who are both theologically and functionally oriented to the church tend to express the social critic and social action function to a greater extent than was expected. Those who are only functionally oriented tend to mention relevance and value more frequently than was expected. Type II clergy tend to have a different implementation of the functional orientation than do Type III clergy. In this case we may say that there is interaction between the theological and functional for Type II clergy; and perhaps also that the theological is more powerful when combined with the functional than is the functional orientation alone in relation to the

TABLE 26

CHURCH ORIENTATION TYPOLOGY

Type	Description	Percent (N = 1,111)
I	Theological only	52
II	Theological and functional	30
III	Functional only	15
IV	Structure only	2
V	Not classifiable	1

theological.

The parish minister is a symbol and an articulator of the theological view of the church. Since he is the professional leader of a congregation, he is responsible for the expression of the theological view of the church in the life of the parish. We assume that this needs to be based on both theory and practice if he is to fulfill the expectations associated with his professional leadership responsibilities. The Type II minister, having both orientations, may be described as having a more complete view and is better equipped to meet these responsibilities than are other types. Types I and III orientations are partial and incomplete understandings of the church. They are appropriate as theory or practice, as the case may be, but not of the application of theory to practice. If he articulates the structural orientation only, we assume that the minister is concerned primarily with organizational matters; and that the organization (the church) may be an end in itself rather than a means to an end. He has not internalized the theory of the church, and he is not concerned with the practical and operational functioning of the church in the lives of parishioners and in issues of importance in the community and the larger society.

Sermon themes

The minister, as the professional leader of the local church, is expected to explain its theological perspective and articulate its ideology; and by definition, to be able to do this in terms of Biblical and theological traditions to adherents as well as to outsiders.

The traditional way of implementing this ideological responsibility is by means of the preacher role, the chief ideologically-oriented act in which the clergyman engages, and to some extent by means of the teacher role. In the Protestant tradition the minister is free to use his pulpit as his view of his task may dictate; hence the sermon is a unique vehicle that the minister may use to share his own ideological orientation with his congregation. There is less opportunity for the minister to express his own views in the teacher role. He devotes very little time to it in the formal sense, as most teaching is done by lay leaders; and students (as well as teachers) in the educational program of the local church are provided printed curriculum materials published by a central agency for the denomination.

To gain insight on how the minister implements his view about the faith, informants were asked: "Please list the subject or theme of four recent sermons that you have preached and that best represent the message you feel should be preached." Sermon themes were then coded according to whether they concerned doctrines (such as the attributes of the deity, the works of the deity, the sin of man, faith, or the church) or practical application of doctrine. From the responses it was possible to classify the clergy according to the degree to which they preached on doctrinal and/or practical subjects.

It was expected that there would be a relationship between orientation toward the church and the extent to which sermons expressed doctrinal and/or applied religion themes. A cross-tabulation of these two factors indicated (.02) that those who were only theologically oriented to the church tended to preach on doctrinal subjects, and those who were only functionally oriented to the church tended to preach on practical subjects. Type I tended to preach about the person, attributes, and works of the deity to a greater extent than did Type II and Type III clergymen.

A minister's speaking is not limited to the four walls of his own church. He is by profession a public speaker who has many opportunities to address community groups which are not organized for religious purposes. Some of the people in such an audience will be associated with a religious group, but others will not. The religious group to which persons in community groups belong may or may not be that of the clergyman who is a visiting guest speaker. To some extent the minister is speaking to an outside group, and in an organizational context different from his own congregation. Nine out of ten ministers accept this type of invitation to speak. Educational groups and occasions were addressed by 21 percent of the informants, and twelve percent reported speaking to luncheon and fraternal groups. Most often the minister's substantive orientation in these talks was non-religious.

There are many occasions when the parish minister is invited to simply give a talk. It appears that many of these invitations do not require a focused address on a specific subject; however the most frequently requested subjects were family life, international peace, parent-child relations and marriage preparations.

The minister's orientation to the church, theologically, functionally and structurally defined, is the dependent variable in this chapter, and is analyzed in relation to the two series of independent variables: characteristics of the clergyman, and characteristics of the parish in which he serves.

Clergy Characteristics

The clergy characteristics which were cross-tabulated with church orientation typology and tested for significance are: personal (age, marital status, and number of children); personality (structure, emotional maturity, and attitude toward change); the minister's referents (status, mentor, and support); professional career (length of professional experience, tenure in present parish assignment, and occupational mobility); and criteria of effectiveness and success.

Of the three clergy personal characteristics we would expect that variability in the minister's orientation to the church is related to his age. Theoretically, the younger a minister is, the greater the tendency for him to be theologically oriented to the church; the older a minister is, the more likely that he will be functionally oriented in his view of the church. This was confirmed (.05 probability level). It would appear that the prospective clergyman is socialized with respect to theology in the seminary. As he enters the parish after ordination, he is increasingly socialized by parishioners and by the necessity of communicating his beliefs effectively to laymen in terms which they understand and appreciate. He is also confronted with the necessity of expressing beliefs about the church which permit the organization to fulfill its purposes. Of the three personality factors, awareness of change was the only significant variable in relation to church orientation (.05). Ministers who are only theologically oriented to the church tend to be aware or not aware, but others tend to be ambivalent about change.

Clergy referents, career factors, and the criteria for effectiveness and success were not statistically significant in relation to church orientation; however, date of ordination (or length of professional career) was significant (.001). The longer the professional experience, the more likely that a minister will be functionally oriented to the church; and the shorter his professional experience, the more likely that he will be theologically oriented to the church. Occupational mobility was found to be statistically significant at the .05 level. Clergymen who are highly mobile tend to be theologically oriented to the church, whereas those who are less mobile tend to be functionally oriented.

Organizational Factors

Characteristics of the parish in which the minister serves considered as independent variables were: denomination; regional location; type of community; size; and economics.

The clergymen in this study were all ordained by one of the cooperating denominational groups and had been professionally trained in colleges and seminaries to meet the standards of the denomination. The professional school offers instruction in the ideology or theology of the church and candidates for ordination are examined (usually with thoroughness) in their understanding of the commitment to this ideology. By tradition, denominations differ in the ideology that is held. By reputation they also differ in the way in which they function. Hence it would be expected that denomination would be a significant variable in both the theological and functional orientation to the church, as expressed by parish minister information. Denominational groupings were not found to be significant. However, when specific themes *within* the theological and functional orientations were analyzed by denominational grouping, statistical significance was found. The Lutheran, Methodist, Presbyterian, and Protestant Episcopal denominations stress theological themes to a much greater degree than do the Baptists, Disciples, Brethren, and United Church of Christ (.01 level of probability). The Lutherans and Episcopalians emphasized the church as God's instrument, an agent of grace and reconciliation. The Methodists emphasized the church as God's evangel and as a fellowship of believers. The Presbyterians also stressed the evangel theme, along with the church as the Body of Christ.

Specific functional themes (.001 level of probability) were emphasized by the Baptists, Disciples, the United Church of Christ, and the Methodists, rather than the Brethren, Lutherans, and Presbyterians. In particular, the Baptist-Disciples tend to stress the social action theme. This is also true for the Methodists, who in addition tend toward the social critic theme. The relevance-pragmatic theme was most typical of ministers in the United Church of Christ.

While the type of orientation a minister has toward the church does not vary by region nor by size of parish, it does vary by type of community. The more metropolitan-urban a community, the greater the number of ministers whose orientation to the church is functional; the more rural and non-metropolitan a community, the greater the chance that the minister will be theologically oriented toward the church (.001 level of probability).

The type of orientation (theological or functional) a minister holds about the church would not, in theory, vary in relation to the economics of the parish. It was found, contrary to this expectation, that the amount of the local budget was significant at the .001 level of probability. The smaller the budget, the greater the tendency of the clergyman to be theologically oriented toward the church; and conversely, the larger the budget, the greater the possibility of the minister being functionally oriented to the church.

Summary

This chapter has probed the minister's image of the church to gain understanding about the organization in which he works, and to examine the major ideas about the church which he wishes people to understand.

The minister is committed to practicing his profession in a theologically oriented social system. There is an expectation that he will not only articulate a theological interpretation of that system, but that he will himself conform to this theological orientation regarding the church. The conformity of the layman (or parishioner) to this view of the church is relative to other vocational and organizational commitments. The clergyman tends to view himself as being theologically literate regarding the church, and to view parishioners as being relatively illiterate theologically. This differential socialization of clergy and laity is a characteristic of the local church with which professional leaders and teachers are confronted.

The church has been operationally defined using as a criterion the way in which the minister would express a doctrine of the church in the day-to-day life of the parish. Recognizing the differing frames of reference which ministers have to the church, a series of five types of clergy views was developed: theological, both theological and functional, functional, structural (organizational) orientation, and those views which were not classifiable. The church orientation typology is the dependent variable in this chapter. As in the case of the master role analysis (Chapter IV), we assumed that ministers have a dual orientation to the church, ideological (or theological) and functional. We theorize that ministers who are both theologically and functionally oriented have the more realistic interpretation of the church for professional practice.

Since the minister is an articulator of the ideology of the church, it would seem that his public statements in sermons and speeches would differ as his orientation to the church differed. The theory was not sustained. The content of the minister's sermons and speeches do not vary with his orientation to the church. Ministers apparently sermonize and give addresses with about the same content regardless of their stated views of the church, which may differ.

Four clergy factors were significant in relation to church orientation. Younger ministers tended to be theologically oriented to the church; whereas older ministers were functionally oriented. Ministers who were either open or closed about change tended to be theologically oriented to the church, while those who were ambivalent about change were both theologically and functionally oriented. As the minister's professional experiences increased, his orientation toward the church tended to change from theological only to theological and functional, to functional only. The highly mobile are theologically oriented; and the less mobile, functionally oriented. It would appear that the socialization and re-socialization of the clergyman continues as his career pattern develops.

Organizational variables were not as significant as the findings regarding master role and theory would lead us to expect. Denomination was not significant for type of church orientation, but it was for specific theological and functional themes. The Baptist, Disciples and United Church of Christ ministers tended to be less theologically oriented than others. The Lutherans and Protestant Episcopalians tended to view the church as God's instrument, and the Methodists and Presbyterians used the evangel theme. The functionally oriented ministers emphasized the social action theme. Ministers in two denominations, Methodists and Brethren, tended to be ambivalent in their views of the church.

Type of community was a significant variable. Metropolitan-urban ministers tend to be functionally oriented, and non-metropolitan-rural ministers tend to be theologically oriented to the church. A related variable is size of local budget. Those ministers who are in churches which have small budgets tend to be theologically oriented; and those with large budgets, functionally oriented.

The minister who is theologically oriented to the church tends to have the following profile: young; open or closed to change; professional experience brief, highly mobile; Lutheran, Presbyterian or Episcopalian; serving a non-metropolitan-rural church with a relatively low budget. The characteristics of the functionally oriented are: older; ambivalent about change; relatively long professional experience; less mobile; Baptist, Disciples, or United Church of Christ by denomination; serving churches with relatively large budgets; located in a metropolitan-urban community. This profile suggests the theory that as a clergyman progresses in his career his orientation to the organization in which he works changes. His definition of the church as an organization and his career goals in the church both change.

X

RELATIONSHIPS WITHIN THE WHOLE
OF PROFESSIONAL PRACTICE

Each clergyman needs and has an image of himself. It consists of ideas and opinions that describe and explain his status and role in the church and in other social systems in society. It is his own view of his person and what he believes about himself as a professional religious leader and as a person with family, community and societal relationships.

We assume that the minister's self-image includes a feeling of what is expected of him as he functions in the church, and that this self-image motivates him to behave according to the expectations that actors in the church have of him; by the image that the public holds of him as well as by the picture he holds of himself.

The problem of the parish minister is to develop an image of himself which is adequate to his function; and within the social system in which he renders professional service to relate effectively to persons who also have images of clergymen. However, we seem to observe that there is some latitude about expectations concerning the role of minister. We are interested in the factors which are associated with this variability, with a view to greater clarification of the image of the clergyman and the *interrelatedness* of various aspects of his self-image. In addition we are interested in examining the degree to which an analysis of his self-image reveals that the minister has or does not have a common socialization to his profession, or that he has a unique socialization.

We have, in effect, in each succeeding chapter dealt with one facet of the self-perception of the clergyman. This is particularly the case for the master, integrative and practitioner role analyses. In addition, other dependent variables inform us about the minister's perception of his work environment, the church. We assume that all these aspects are interrelated parts of the minister's person, and our theory reflects the way in which these dependent variables are each a part of the whole.

In keeping with the interaction theory which is assumed in this report we theorize that segments of the minister's self-image are interrelated and that as a result of this interaction each minister will develop a wholistic view of parish professional practice.

Clergy roles have a multi-level structure: master role, integrative roles, and practitioner roles. This hierarchy of role generalizations implies that each structural level is related to the other two. For example, in Chapter VI it was noted that the minister tends to rate as important the practitioner roles that are supportive of his master role orientation, but performance and satisfaction evaluations did not vary with master role orientation. Specific integrative roles were found to be correlated with practitioner role satisfaction evaluation.

Theory about the role of the parish clergy suggests a relationship between the master and integrative roles. In theory a minister's orientation to his master role would be related to his integrative role. The latter would be derived from or supported by the former. Therefore, we theorize that a clergyman who was only theologically oriented to his master role would require a different integrative role than would the minister who was only functionally oriented to his master role. As the theory is elaborated, the minister who is both theologically and functionally oriented to his master role, or neither theologically nor functionally oriented, would hold unique integrative roles; and orientation to the master role would provide a rationale for the goals toward which his integrative roles were directed.

Relatedness among roles

The interrelationship between these roles (master and integrative) was analyzed for both the integrative role (traditional-contemporary) continuum and the specific integrative roles. A significant difference (at the .02 level of probability) was found for the specific integrative roles but not for the continuum. The believer-saint tended to be theologically oriented to his master role, the father-shepherd both theologically and functionally oriented, and the interpersonal relations specialists only functionally oriented. The evangelist, the parish promoter, and the general practitioner were neither theologically nor functionally oriented.

The relationship is close to theoretical expectations, with one exception. The evangelist, according to the theory, would be expected to be only theologically oriented to his master role. His message and activities usually imply a primary concern with the affirmation of belief and commitment to a new way of life. However, the data tend not to support the theory. One interpretation is that the evangelist is concerned with overt behavior related to his master role and perhaps his integrative role.

The relation between the master role orientation and the integrative roles would seem to be a fruitful one for further exploration.

The master role orientation of the parish minister is supported by his normative, but not by his performance and satisfaction evaluations of the practitioner roles.

The integrative role to which the minister is oriented is closely related to his satisfaction evaluation of the practitioner roles. The means he enjoys using are those that his goals in the ministry require. If the minister's goal is realistic in terms of the needs of the parish in which he serves, this motivation may be effectively used. However, if he selects his integrative role for personal reasons, he may follow a hobby.

We would expect on the basis of theory that the minister's concepts of his master, integrative, and practitioner roles are interrelated, and that his evaluation of the practitioner roles would vary in relation to his master and integrative roles. The relationship between the types of roles was tested by the chi square technique and by rank-order correlation. (See Tables 27 and 28.) Normatively the minister's master role orientation and the specific integrative role that was primary for him did not vary as expected. He tended to rate as important the practitioner role that was supportive of his master role orientation. However, the satisfaction and performance evaluations of the practitioner roles were not supportive of his master role orientation.

We theorize that if by definition the practitioner roles are performed by the minister as a means to an end or goal, then the integrative roles define the goal of the minister in his practitioner role behavior. Hence, if there is variability in the integrative roles, we theorize that there is also variability in the practitioner role behavior. Ministers will differ in the performance of the practitioner roles as their purposes differ. For example, the interest of one minister in preaching (a means-oriented practitioner role) may be to be persuasive to the non-believer, or to evangelize (a goal-oriented integrative role). Another may preach to instruct the believer, to edify, or to educate; still another may preach to bring judgment to the community, or to stimulate social action.

The integrative role pattern varies in relation to each of the practitioner role evaluations (normative, satisfaction and performance). The variation is highly significant for the *specific* integrative roles. The traditional-contemporary integrative role *continuum* is significant for the performance evaluation but not for the normative or satisfaction evaluations (Table 27). The degree of enjoyment or satisfaction a minister feels in fulfilling a practitioner role is correlated with the specific integrative role that is primary for him. The coefficient of correlation is .49 (Table 28). This would seem to have important implications for the motivation of the clergyman as a practitioner of religion.

TABLE 27

RELATIONSHIP OF PRACTITIONER ROLE EVALUATIONS TO MASTER AND INTEGRATIVE ROLES*

Practitioner Role Evaluations	Master Role	Integrative Role Continuum +	Specific
Normative	.02	—	.001
Satisfaction	—	—	.001
Performance	—	.02	.001

*Level of significance by chi square technique.
+ Traditional-Contemporary.

TABLE 28

CORRELATION OF PRIMARY ROLE WITH SPECIFIC INTEGRATIVE ROLE BY ROLE EVALUATIONS

Practitioner Role Evaluations	Master Role	Specific Integrative Roles
Normative	-.16	-.06
Satisfaction	-.07	.49
Performance	.02	.08

Roles, and concept of church

Theoretically it would be expected that the minister's concept of the church would be related to his concept of the master role, the integrative roles, and the evaluations that he makes of the practitioner roles. We would expect that those who are theologically oriented to the church would have differing views of their clergy roles than would those who are functionally oriented to the church. For example, we would expect that those who are only theologically oriented (Type I) to their master role would tend to be only theologically oriented (Type I) to the church. We would in theory say that those who have a Type I orientation to the church would tend to be oriented to the traditional integrative roles; and conversely, those who are Type III (Functional only) in their church orientation would tend to be oriented to the contemporary integrative roles. Following the same line of reasoning, we would expect ministers who are Type I in church orientation to evaluate the traditional practitioner roles most highly; ministers with a functional church orientation (Type III), conversely, would evaluate the contemporary practitioner roles most highly.

These relationships between the minister's orientation to the church and his concept of the clergy roles were analyzed by a series of two-way tables and were tested for significance using chi square and analysis of variance. Statistical significance was obtained for the church orientation in relation to the master role only (.001). Ministers who are theologically oriented to the master role also tend to be similarly oriented to the church; and functionally oriented ministers tend to be so for both their master role and their church.

The relationship between the master role and church orientation tends to confirm a common sense observation made frequently within the ministerial profession. Theology is conceived as a system. In many seminaries the discipline is called "systematic theology." Candidates seeking ordination in some denominations are asked to subscribe to formal creedal statements, or to the "system of doctrine" taught in the Bible. Disciplinary action is taken at times when ministers take exception to one or more doctrines in the belief system of a denomination. The social control mechanisms of denominations function to maintain conformity and consistency in doctrine.

The validity of theological norms for the clergy and the church is not examined, evaluated or questioned in this report. However, we do attempt to understand the *variable behavior* of the minister in relation to his stated theological norms. While we have been concerned in our analysis with both theological and non-theological factors, this is not a theological analysis. Rather it is a behavioral science interpretation of the minister which has taken into account the ideological views which the minister has of himself and of his work environment. It is seen as complementary to, rather than as a substitute for, a theological interpretation.

We have theorized in this report that the various aspects of the minister's self-image are interrelated. The findings regarding the church and community suggest that there are several sets of norms which operate in the life of a professional religious leader. We have argued that both theological and sociological norms are required for his effectiveness. The findings strengthen our argument. They lend credence to our assertions about the multiple sets of clergy norms, but they do not prove that his norms are related to or required for his effective functioning. This would require evaluative data and judgments about the minister which are not included in the purpose or design of the present research and anlaysis.

Conflict among roles

Socialization into the ministry is a process in which the prospective minister makes the religious culture an integral part of his way of life. He also learns those behaviors which are essential to his anticipated ministerial vocation. The minister whose socialization permits him to develop a mode of practice that is congenial to his personality and that is also appropriate to his profession will be able to resolve conflicts between his personal and professional life and between the traditional and contemporary interpretations of his roles. The personal-professional life conflicts may be more difficult of resolution than those of a traditional-contemporary nature. The former suggest the possibility that a minister has not fully accepted his status as a minister. Such a status necessarily impinges on one's personal life. While the Protestant minister's status as a professional is not total, as it tends to be for the Catholic priest and the orthodox Rabbi, there are expectations associated with the role which necessarily must be fulfilled. We would theorize that role conflict is related to the orientation a clergyman has to his own practice in the profession.

One aspect of our theory about a wholistic view of professional practice relates to role conflict. The requirements of ministerial practice would suggest that those who deviate from a wholistic view of their professional practice would have role conflicts to a greater extent than those who do not deviate. We would theorize further that those who tend to the theological, traditional orientation would have role conflicts involving the contemporary roles; and those with a functional orientation would have role conflicts involving traditional roles.

Since we assume that the various aspects of the minister's orientation to his role are interrelated, then in theory the role conflicts that a minister articulates would be related to his master and integrative roles and to his evaluation of the practitioner roles. It might be expected that the minister's concepts of role will vary in relation to the conflicts he experiences. In theory some conceptions of the master, integrative, and practitioner roles are less likely to be associated with role conflicts than are others.

The interrelationships between the various concepts of the roles of the minister and role conflict was analyzed. Variability in the master role concept was not significant in relation to the role conflicts articulated by the minister. However the integrative role was significant (.05) for both the traditional-contemporary continuum and the specific integrative roles in relation to role conflict. Ministers who identify their role conflict as AC (traditional-personal versus traditional-occupational) tend to be on the completely traditional end of the integrative role continuum, but those who identify no role conflicts are on the other end of the continuum (completely contemporary). In between these extremes the role conflicts may be arrayed from completely traditional to partially contemporary on the integrative role *continuum* as follows: AD, AC, CD, BD, and AB.* It would appear that the completely and partially traditional integrative roles tend to increase role conflict, and that the completely contemporary integrative roles tend to aid in resolving potential role conflicts. With respect to the *specific* integrative roles, conflicts tend to involve the believer-saint, father-shepherd, and interpersonal relations specialist to a greater extent than other roles. These integrative roles are oriented to persons rather than to groups, and two of them tend to be traditional. It would appear that from the perspective of the integrative role, conflict is associated with personal rather than organizational variables.

---

*Refer to Chart 1 for conflict model.

The role conflicts that a minister articulates vary significantly (.05) in relation to his normative evaluation of the practitioner roles. However, his satisfaction and performance evaluations of these roles are not significant in relation to the role conflict he articulates. Those who identified no role conflict or who have an evident AB conflict (traditional-personal vs. contemporary-personal), give primary normative evaluation to the preacher role. Those with an AD conflict (traditional-personal vs. contemporary occupational) give primary normative evaluation to the neo-traditional role of pastor. The contemporary practitioner roles are emphasized normatively by those who articulate BC (traditional-occupational vs. contemporary-personal), CD (traditional-occupational vs. contemporary-occupational), and AC (traditional-personal vs. traditional-occupational) role conflicts.

Theoretically, variability in orientation to the church and role conflict would be related to variability in the type of role conflict. Those ministers who articulate the traditional-personal vs. the traditional-organizational role conflict would tend to be more theologically oriented to the church; and those who articulate the contemporary-personal vs. the contemporary-occupational role conflict would tend to be functionally oriented to the church.

Role conflict may be interpreted as evidence that a minister has difficulty accepting a pervasive or monolithic approach to his professional practice. Role conflict and the dependent variables in this analysis are statistically significant in the integrative roles and in the normative evaluation of the practitioner roles. The A and B sectors of the role conflict model (traditional-personal and contemporary-personal) are involved more frequently than other sectors. Hence, in role conflict the personal life of the minister is an important influence more frequently than are the occupational aspects of his life. It is also to be observed that ideological questions are more important in role conflict than professional or occupational aspects.

Dependent and independent variables

Returning to our discussion of the interaction between dependent and independent variables, organizational factors are influential to a greater extent than are clergy factors. This is true for the master role, the practitioner roles and public affairs orientation. In the case of integrative roles, clergy and organizational independent variables seem to be equally important. The orientations a minister has to the church and to the community are primarily influenced by clergy variables. Overall, organizational variables tend to be the most influential, but some clergy variables are also strong.

It would appear that organizational variables influence the minister's behavior toward uniformity (or perhaps conformity); and that clergy factors influence behavior toward individual differences. When we examine the influence of clergy and organizational variables as they relate to role-oriented and work environment-oriented variables, about one-eighth of the clergy variables are important for both role and environment. Organizational variables influence role orientation and the environment about 30 percent of the time. The minister's self-concept of his role and his work environment does vary by clergy and organizational influences, but organization is by far the stronger.

We note that dependent variables are interrelated, but not totally so. There appears to be some latitude about the role behavior of the clergy. There is a common socialization among clergymen in some traditions, but there is also the possibility that some clergymen may be socialized into an uncommon or deviant tradition. Or we might say that clergymen share a common socialization, but that uniformity is neither prescribed nor pervasive, especially for Protestant clergy, and deviation is permitted and perhaps expected. Within limits the Protestant clergyman develops a wholistic approach to the practice of his profession.

There is a pervasive religious culture which informs the minister's orientation to his practice of the ministry. However, ministers differ somewhat in their understanding of and commitment to the religious cultures available. Their practice also varies in response to the social context of ministry, and the personal qualities and experience which they bring to a situation.

A review of the behavioral science literature on the clergy will reveal the paucity of knowledge about the image that ministers have of themselves and the image that laymen have of ministers. This book attempts to contribute to the clergy self-image literature. In this research the parish minister has been an observer and a reporter of his own actions and of his interaction with other actors in the church, the community and the society.

APPENDIX A

ACKNOWLEDGMENTS

Research is done by people. It is a social product, the result of interaction of many people. This report is no exception. Hence there are many acknowledgments that are made with gratitude and appreciation. First, the idea for the project was born before the author became associated with it. I am indebted to Dr. Donald Young and Dr. Leonard S. Cottrell of the Russell Sage Foundation, and to Dr. Henry P. Van Dusen and Dr. Arthur L. Swift of Union Theological Seminary, New York, for the inspiring way in which they shared their vision of the project and its possibilities for theological education throughout the duration of the project. Other members of the faculty advisory committee were Professors John C. Bennett, Searle Bates, Frank Herriott, Reinhold Niebuhr, Lewis J. Sherrill, Charles Matthews, and George W. Webber.

The administrators of the four other seminaries were: President Beauford Norris - Christian Theological Seminary; President Dwight Loder - Garrett Biblical Institute; Dean Jesse Trotter - Virginia Seminary; and President Frank Caldwell - Louisville Presbyterian Seminary. Other faculty members of the seminaries include Dean Kloman - Virginia Seminary; Dean Shelton - Christian Seminary; Professor Eugene Rector - Christian Seminary; and Professors Rockwell Smith and Murray Leiffer - Garrett Biblical Institute.

National Council of Churches Personnel:
Urban Church - W. J. Villaume; Joseph W. Merchant.
Town and Country Church - D. F. Pielstick; R. O. Comfort.

Denomination Representatives who selected the expanded panel of informants:
American Baptist Convention - Paul Madsen.
National Baptist Convention, U.S.A., Inc. - V. A. Edwards.
Church of the Brethren - Charles E. Zunkel; Edward Ziegler.
Congregational and Christian Churches - Stanley U. North; Ira D. Black; Thomas Alfred Tripp; Wesley A. Hotchkiss.
Disciples of Christ - Willard M. Wickizer; Dale W. Medearis.
Protestant Episcopal Church - G. Paul Musselman; Clifford L. Samuelson.
Evangelical and Reformed Church - John H. Shope; Claude J. Snyder.
Evangelical United Brethren Church - Roy D. Miller: Benjamin H. Cain.
Church of God (Anderson, Indiana) - W. H. Hunt.
Augustana Lutheran Church - S. E. Engstrom; Theodore E. Matson; Roswell V. Peterson.
Evangelical Lutheran, American Lutheran, and United Evangelical Lutheran - H. Conrad Hoyer; Walter Kloetzli; E. W. Mueller.
United Lutheran Church of America - Karl S. Henry.
Lutheran Church, Missouri Synod - Oswald C. J. Hoffman.
Methodist Church - Robert A. McKibben; Glenn F. Sanford.
Moravian Church in America - F. P. Stocker.
Presbyterian Church, U.S.A. - Harold H. Baldwin; Henry S. Randolph.
Presbyterian Church, U.S. - Hal Hyde; James M. Carr.
United Presbyterian Church of North America - James K. Leitch; George P. Kerr.
Cumberland Presbyterian Church - Hubert Morrow; E. Calvin Baird.
Reformed Church in America - Richard J. Vanden Berg.

Graduate students, Pennsylvania State University, who assisted in the conceptualization of the report and the technical analysis.
George A. Lee; Beryl B. Maurer; Kozabura Shimado.

Coding, punching, tabulating, Pennsylvania State University: Anna Wink; Ronald Strubble.

Typists: Shirley Downing Charpentier; Emiline Harpster.

Informal consultants:
Yale University Divinity School - Dean Liston Pope.
National Council of Churches - Dr. B. Y. Landis.
Board of National Missions, Presbyterian Church, U.S.A. - Dr. Herman Morse.
Columbia University - Professors Charles Y. Glock; Solon T. Kimball; Sloan Wayland; Robert C. MacIver.
Princeton Theological Seminary - Dean E. H. Roberts; Professor Hugh T. Kerr.
Pennsylvania State University - Professor Roy Buck.
Chicago Theological Seminary - President A. C. McGiffert; Professor Seward Hiltner.
Alfred University - Professor Luke Smith.
Meadville Theological Seminary - Professor James Luther Adams.

Finally, there are 1,111 acknowledgments that I wish to make, but the conventions of research prohibit the use of names of persons who have given me confidential information. So I must say to the parish ministers who furnished the materials for this report but who must remain anonymous, a thousand or more tokens of thanks.

As author of this report of a research enterprise in which many persons have participated and contributed ideas, I gratefully acknowledge their assistance. However, I must alone take responsibility for the interpretation presented.

Samuel W. Blizzard
1957

158

APPENDIX B

PARISH MINISTER'S TIME ALLOCATIONS (1955)
(N = 751)

Activity	Average (Mean) time per day Hours:Minutes
Traditional Roles	
Preaching	1:22
Regular service - own church	1:14
Conducting service	12
Preparing sermon	44
Other preparation	18
Special services - own church	02
Services elsewhere	06
Priestly	28
General worship	07
Communion, baptism, confirmation, confession	06
Weddings, funerals, and preparation	15
Church school teaching	10
Teaching	05
Preparation (alone)	03
Planning and preparation (with leaders and teachers)	02
Other Teaching	19
Confirmation class	05
Leadership training	01
Weekday religious education	05
Study and discussion groups	02
Preparation for teaching	06
Total Preaching and Priestly	1:50
Total Teaching	29
Total Traditional Roles	2:19
Neo-Traditional Role (Pastor)	
Visiting	2:02
Sick and distressed	46
Church members	58
New people	07
After meetings	04
By telephone	01
Other	06

Activity	Average (Mean) time per day Hours:Minutes
Counseling	19
Youth	01
Couples, families, premarital	05
Personal	13
Fellowship and recreation	
(individuals and informal groups)	14
Total Neo-traditional Roles	2:35
Contemporary Roles	
Local Church administrator	
Official board	12
Physical plant	10
Publicity	18
Clerical	1:12
Staff, committees, lay leaders	52
Budget promotion	02
General planning	03
Denominational administration	47
Interdenominational administration	10
General non-professional activities	07
Total local church administration	2:49
Total administration	3:53
Organizer	
Church organizations	40
Leadership	05
Participation	26
Fellowship and recreation	07
Planning	02
Community organizations	30
Civic and political	03
Educational	07
Youth and character	05
Health and welfare	05
Service clubs	06
Fraternal	01
Economic	01
Civil defense	01
General	01
Total organization	1:10
Total Contemporary Roles	5:03
Total professional working day	9:57

Activity	Average (Mean) time per day Hours:Minutes
Non-Professional Time Allocations	
Personal	
Spiritual growth	1:06
Intellectual development	26
Physical needs	1:44
Recreation (alone)	39
Family	
Spiritual life	07
Fellowship - recreation (family)	1:09
Family care	34
Business and maintenance	25
Total Personal	3:55
Total Family	2:15
Total Non-professional day	6:10
Total Waking Day	16:07

APPENDIX C

A COMPARISON OF CLERGY TIME ALLOCATION TO PRACTITIONER ROLES REPORTED IN TWO SURVEYS*

May 1934 Survey**			Russell Sage Foundation 1954-55 Survey***		
Practitioner role +	Hours and minutes allocated per week	Percent (N = 687)	Practitioner role	Hours and minutes allocated per week	Percent (N = 751
Ministerial and homiletical	38:42	49	Preacher, Priest, and spiritual growth-intellectual development	23:34	29
Pastor	19:30	25	Pastor	18:05	23
Administrative, civic and mechanical	16:00	21	Administrator and organizer	35:21	44
Educational	4:12	5	Teacher	3:23	4
Total	78:24	100		80:23	100

*This table was constructed from materials found in three sources: May (1934), Douglas (1935), and materials in the present report.

**May mailed questionnaires to approximately 2,000 ministers. His information about time allocation consisted of the useable replies received from 34 percent (687) of these ministers, 272 of whom were well-trained.

***The Russell Sage Foundation - Union Seminary Survey by Blizzard included ministers from varying denominations and differing types of communities; but all clergy were college and seminary graduates. All information was obtained by mail, and the rate of return was about twice that obtained by May.

+ The nomenclature used in the two surveys differs. The categories for practitioner roles used in this table are as comparable as the published data in the 1934 survey permit; however they are only approximate, they are not precisely alike. Douglass and Brunner (1935) give descriptions of the 14 ministerial functions that were compressed into 7 major types of ministerial duties by May. The tabulation in May (Vol. IV, Table 132) included additional details regarding the components of the compressed categories. These were re-grouped to conform to our categories for the practitioner roles. The May ministerial and homiletical categories were collapsed to compare with our priest and preacher category, and two components of our personal activities (spiritual growth and intellectual development) were added to make the collapsed preacher-priest category comparable. Our administrator and organizer roles were collapsed because it was not possible to distinguish these two practitioner roles in the May data. Also his mechanical category seemed to be comparable to the general church activities already included as one of the four components in our administrator role.

APPENDIX D

A COMPARISON OF CLERGY DAILY TIME ALLOCATIONS
(Hours and minutes per day)

Type of Activity	1944 Hartshorne & Froyd Study N = 152		1954-55 Russell Sage Foundation Study N = 751	
	Time	Percent	Time	Percent
Waking Day				
Personal and family	7:13	30	6:10	26
Working day*	8:47	37	9:57	41
Total Waking Day	16:00	67	16:07	67
Sleep	8:00	33	7:53	33
*Practitioner Roles				
(Working day)				
Preacher-Priest	1:41	19	1:50	18
Teacher	0:52	10	0:29	5
Pastor	2:24	27	2:35	26
Administrator	2:52	33	3:53	39
Organizer	0:58	11	1:10	12
Total, Practitioner Roles	8:47	100	9:57	100

APPENDIX E

40 TYPES OF MINISTERIAL ACTIVITY (AS RANKED BY HARTSHORNE AND FROYD - 1944) DISTRIBUTED AMONG THE RUSSELL SAGE PRACTITIONER ROLES.

Preaching and Priestly
    1   Church services - Sunday
    2   Church service - weekday
    4   Weddings and funerals
Teaching
    5   Sunday School
    6   Other work with children
    17   Teaching unspecified
    16a   Broadcasting
Pastor
    8   Pastoral calling
    9   Counseling
Administration
    10   Correspondence
    11   Clerical - calendar, budget, routine
    12   Church business meetings
    13   Church chores - upkeep, errands
    13a   Out of town meetings
Organization
    3   Church meetings - social
    7   Church choir
    14   Community service
    15   Services to schools - addresses, etc.
    16   Lecturing - unspecified
    18   Attending community affairs
    19   Civic organizations
    20   Meetings
    38   Travel was distributed among the "Practitioner Roles"
    40   Miscellaneous and unaccountable was distributed proportionately among the professional work day, personal and family affairs, and sleep.

APPENDIX F

QUESTIONNAIRE

PERSONAL JOB ANALYSIS

Before turning to the following pages, will you please help define the task or function of the minister. Please list below - *IN THE ORDER THAT THEY COME TO YOUR MIND* - the essential types of work that go to make up your personal job as a minister. There are no right or wrong answers and there is no right or wrong order. Your opinion is the most important thing. Use single words or short phrases in making your list. After you have listed them, place numerals in the column to the right, representing their *ORDER OF IMPORTANCE* in your ministry. Use the numeral (1) for the most important, etc. The higher the numeral, the lesser the importance in your ministry.

THE JOB	ORDER OF IMPORTANCE
1.	
2.	
3.	
4.	
5.	
6.	
7.	
8.	
9.	
10.	
11.	
12.	
13.	
14.	
15.	

If you need more space to list what you do as a minister, please use the next page.

What phases of your work do you think you are *most effective* in performing?

What aspect of the parish ministry gives you the most personal enjoyment?

What specific problems are you concerned about as you seek to be an effective parish minister? Please illustrate problems you face in the following areas:
  (a) your professional life;
  (b) the lives of your parishioners;
  (c) community life;
  (d) national life.

What aspects of your work seem to be the most irritating to you personally?

As you have worked out your ways of being the minister of a church, have you found it helpful to talk over problems with church members, church officers, community organization leaders, other clergy, other professional men (doctors, lawyers, and school principals), etc.? What type of person have you found most helpful when you wished to talk over problems?

As you observe the work of other parish ministers, what practice(s) do you see them follow that you would criticize?

When you are explaining the church to people (church members, and prospective members, adherents of other religions, newspaper men, etc.) what are the major ideas you seek to have them understand? What do you talk about in this situation?

When you are explaining the work of a minister to people (whether church members or non-members, friends or strangers, clergymen or laymen), what is the major picture, image, or conception that you seek to give them?

As you now see your church, what facts about the social life, economic life, groups and social divisions, and other aspects of the community in which it is located are *you* most likely to take into consideration in developing an adequate program that will meet its religious needs?

Are there some things you feel you need to know about your community that are not available to you? What?

Please indicate your professional experience as a clergyman *prior* to your present pastorate.

Position	Institution	Location	Dates
_____	_____	_____	
_____	_____	_____	
_____	_____	_____	
_____	_____	_____	

As you think of these experiences, what understandings or insights about the function of the minister did you gain?

What problems seemed to be most urgent in these previous ministries? These may have been personal, church, community, denominational, or other problems.

What occupational experience (including student and summer assignments) have you had in positions other than that of a clergyman?

Position	Type of Business or Industry	Location	Dates	Full or Part Time
_____	_____	_____	_____	_____
_____	_____	_____	_____	_____
_____	_____	_____	_____	_____

What has this occupational experience contributed to your present understanding of the work of the minister? Are you aware of any ways in which these previous occupational experiences influence the way you now do your ministerial work?

YOUR EDUCATIONAL BACKGROUND:

Institution	Location	Major	Dates Attended	Degree
_____	_____	_____	_____	_____
_____	_____	_____	_____	_____
_____	_____	_____	_____	_____
_____	_____	_____	_____	_____

How do you evaluate your pre-theological training in terms of its usefulness to you as a minister? For example, how adequate or inadequate do you now feel your training in the humanities (languages, literature, philosophy, history, etc.) was in preparing you for your present work?

How do you rate in relation to your needs in the parish the adequacy of your pre-theological studies in the sciences (chemistry, biology, mathematics, etc.)?

How adequate or inadequate were your pre-theological preparations in the social sciences (sociology, psychology, cultural anthropology, economics, political science, government, etc.) as you now evaluate them in the light of your experience as a parish minister?

If your pre-theological undergraduate training was *not* in a liberal arts college, but in engineering, business, agriculture or education, etc., how do you feel about its advantages or disadvantages in preparation for the parish ministry? Would you recommend that other preministerial students select the same course?

As you now see it, what experiences (recreational, travel, military life, family background, or community life, etc. excluding formal education) contributed most to your effectiveness as a parish minister?

Looking back on your reading since you finished seminary, what books, magazines, or newspapers have *changed* your ways of being a parish minister?

Please name any person(s) whom you admire as a leader(s) or who has (have) greatly influenced the ways you think and act as a minister. Why do you admire him (them), or how have you been influenced?

Outside the membership and activities of your church, in what activities and organizations do you usually participate?

What type of persons (identify by their occupation or some other social fact) do you seek to know?

Please list the subject or theme of four recent sermons that *you* have preached and that best represent the message you feel should be preached.

What are some subjects or themes that you have used recently in addressing community groups outside the church?

Where do you seek information if you are preparing to preach about an issue that some parishioners might consider controversial?

What are two or three of the controversial issues in your community in the last two months on which you have felt free to speak or to take a stand?

Describe one or two typical social questions or ethical issues that have come up in the last month or two in your pastoral work.

On what issues have you found persons and resources in your community that were helpful in solving problems? Please specify.

Are you aware of any way in which members of your parish desire to change the program of the church?

Are you aware of any way in which non-members of your church who live in the community think that the program of your church should be changed?

What are the personality traits or characteristics of ministers that seem to lead to effective parish work?

What are the ways that ministers conduct themselves that seem to assure their success in your denomination?

Has your experience in the pastorate made you feel a need for more thorough preparation in any of the types of training that you received in the seminary? Please specify.

Has your experience in the pastorate made you feel a need for adding to the seminary program any new types of training that were not available when you were a student? Please specify.

If you had an opportunity to offer suggestions on how you think (in the light of your experience) the seminary training of the prospective parish minister could be improved, what are the major points you would stress? What would you tell a committee of theological professors who were seeking your advice on this subject?

YOUR NAME _____

ADDRESS _____
              Street or R.F.D.   Town or City   State

AGE _____   YEAR ORDAINED _____

MARITAL STATUS _____ NUMBER OF CHILDREN _____

YOUR PRESENT CHURCH OR CHURCHES: (If you serve a multiple-church parish, please give data for each church separately.)

CHURCH _____DENOMINATION _____

LOCATION: _____
              Street or R.F.D.   Town or City   State

Number of Communicants _____ Number in the church

                              school _____

Local expense   Benevolence

budget per year $_____budget per year $_____

How many years have you been the minister of this congregation? _____

USE ONLY IF you serve more than one church:

    CHURCH _____ DENOMINATION _____

    LOCATION _____
              Street or R.F.D.   Town or City   State

Number of communicants _____ Number in the
church
school _____

Local expense   Benevolence

budget per year $_____budget per year $_____

How many years have you been the minister of this congregation?
_____ If you serve three or more churches, use the back of this page.

Please list those members of the church staff (janitors, dieticians, choir directors, directors of religious education, associate or assistant ministers, etc.) who receive remuneration from the church budget.

       POSITION   *FULL OR PART TIME**

_____   _____

_____   _____

*Please indicate part time work in fractions (¼, ½, etc.)

APPENDIX G

A STUDY OF THE FUNCTIONS OF THE PARISH MINISTER

The purpose of this project is to discover how the parish minister functions in modern society. We are interested in the demands that are made on your time. How do you use your time in any one day as a parish minister? To help us get a picture of the choices that you make in the use of your time, will you give us a diary of your activities on the day before you receive this questionnaire. If you receive this questionnaire on Monday, please report your activities on Saturday, Sunday. Please report your activities even though the day may not be typical or spent in ministerial activities. Your report will be integrated with that of a panel of informants. In reporting your actual activities, you will help us get a cross section of the activities of the panel. Please record *all* of your professional activities including reading. Block off time devoted to family life, eating, recreation, etc., also. If other persons or groups were involved, kindly identify them by title or position and/or type of group.

DATE_____

  Month   Day   Year

Do you consider this a typical or a non-typical day?

_____

Time Period	Description of Activity	Place of Activity	Persons and/or Groups Involved
Before 7 A.M.			
7:00			
7:30			
8:00			
8:30			
9:00			
9:30			
10:00			
10:30			
11:00			
11:30			
12:00			
12:30 PM.			
1:00			

:30

:00

:30

:00

:30

:00

:30

:00

:30

:00

:30

:00

30

00

30

00

30

:00

:30

:00

ter

P.M.

:00

REFERENCES

Abelson, R. P.
1959   "Modes of resolution of belief dilemmas." Journal of Conflict Resolution 3:343-352.
Adorno, T. W., Else Frenkel-Brunswik, Daniel J. Levinson, and R. Nevitt Sanford
1950   The Authoritarian Personality. New York: Harper and Brothers.
Ackerman, Nathan W.
1951   "Social role and total personality." American Journal of Orthopsychiatry 21 (January):1-7.
Baker, Oren H.
1949   The Problem of Professional Training for the Ministry. Report of the workshop on theological education. Evanston, Illinois: Garrett Biblical Institute.
Beard, Augustus F.
1946   The Story of John Frederic Oberlin. New York: The Christian Rural Fellowship.
Bennett, John L.
1957   "The faculty re-examines its work." Union Seminary Quarterly Review 12 (January):25-29.
Berckman, Edward
1956   "Correspondence: Ministry under tension." Christianity and Crisis 16 (December):172.
Bernard, Chester I.
1938   The Functions of the Executive (chapter 17). Cambridge: Harvard University Press.
Bizzard, Samuel W.
1955   "The roles of the rural parish minister, the Protestant seminaries, and the social sciences of social behavior." Religious Education 7 (November-December):382-392.
1956a   "The role of the rural minister in community and cultural change" in New Horizons for Town and Country Churches (October):26-40. New York: National Council of Churches, Department of Town and Country.
1956b   "The training of the parish minister." Union Seminary Quarterly Review 11 (January):45-50.
1959   "The parish minister's self-image and variability in community culture." Pastoral Psychology 10 (October):27-36.
Bloom, Samuel W., et al.
1960   "The sociologist as medical educator: A discussion." American Sociological Review 25 (February):95-101.
Brooks, Robert M.
1960   The Former Major Seminarian: A Study of Change in Status. Unpublished Ph.D. dissertation, University of Notre Dame.
Brown, Emory J.
1953   "The self as related to formal participation in three Pennsylvania rural communities." Rural Sociology 18 (December):315-318.
Burchard, Waldo W.
1954   "Role conflicts of military chaplains." American Sociological Review 19 (October):528-535.
Campbell, Ernest Q., and Thomas F. Pettigrew
1959   "Racial and moral crisis: The role of Little Rock ministers." The American Journal of Sociology 64 (March):509-516.
Carr-Saunders, Alexander M.
1955   "Metropolitan conditions and the traditional professions." Pp. 280-283 in Robert M. Fisher (ed.), The Metropolis in Modern Life. New York: Doubleday and Company.
Carr-Saunders, Alexander M., and P. A. Wilson
1933   The Professions. Oxford: Clarendon Press.
Chaffee, Edmond B.
1933   The Protestant Churches and the Industrial Crisis. New York: The Macmillan Company.
Chapman, Stanley H.
1944   "The minister, professional man of the church." Social Forces 23 (December):202-206.
Cottrell, Leonard S., and Eleanor B. Sheldon
1963   "Problems of collaboration between social scientists and the practicing professions." The Annals of the American Academy of Political and Social Science 346 (March):126-137.
Coxon, Anthony P. M.
1965   A Sociological Study of the Social Recruitment, Selection and Professional Socialization of Anglican Ordinands. Unpublished Ph.D. dissertation, University of Leeds, England.

Davies, Horton
1959   A Mirror of the Ministry in Modern Novels. New York: Oxford University Press.

Donovan, John D.
1951   The Catholic Priest: A Study in the Sociology of the Professions. Unpublished Ph.D. dissertation Harvard University.
1958   "The American Catholic hierarchy: A social profile." The American Catholic Sociological Review (June):98-112.

Douglass, H. Paul, and Edmund de S. Brunner
1935   The Protestant Church as a Social Institution. New York: Harper and Brothers.

Duncan, H. G.
1932   "Reactions of ex-ministers toward the ministry." Journal of Religion 12 (January):100-115.

Evans, Thomas Q.
1960   The Brethren Pastor: Differential Conceptions of an Emerging Role. Unpublished Ph.D. dissertation Ohio State University.

Falk, Lawrence
1962   The Minister's Response to Perceived Conflict between Self and Other's Expectations of his Ro Unpublished Ph.D. dissertation, University of Nebraska.

Farmer, Herbert H.
1947   God and Men, pp. 11-70. New York: Abingdon-Cokesbury Press.

Foley, Albert S.
1955   "The status and role of the Negro priest in the American Catholic clergy." American Catholic Sociol cal Review 16:83-93.

Frenkel-Brunswik, Else, Daniel J. Levinson and R. Nevitt Sanford
1947   "Anti-democratic personality." In T. M. Newcomb and R. L. Hartley (eds.), Readings in Social Psyc ogy. New York: Henry Holt and Company.

Getzel, J. W., and E. G. Guba
1954   "Role, role conflict, and effectiveness: An empirical study." American Sociological Review (April):164.

Glock, Charles Y., and Philip Roos
1961   "Parishioners' views of how ministers spend their time." Review of Religious Research 2 (Spring): 175.

Gough, H. G.
1951   "Studies in social tolerance." Journal of Social Psychology 33:237-246.

Gross, Neal, Ward S. Mason, Alexander W. McEachern
1958   Exploration in Role Analysis: Studies of the School Superintendency Role. New York: John Wiley Sons.

Gullahorn, John T., and Jeanne E. Gullahorn
1963   "Role conflict and its resolution." The Sociological Quarterly 4 (Winter):32-48.

Gustafson, James M.
1954   "An analysis of the problem of the role of the minister." The Journal of Religion 34 (July).

Hammond, Phillip E.
1966   The Campus Clergyman. New York: Basic Books.

Hartshorne, Hugh, and Milton C. Froyd
1945   Theological Education in the Northern Baptist Convention. Board of Education of the Northern Ba Convention.

Henry, William E.
1949   "The business executive: The psychodynamics of a social role." The American Journal of Socie pp. 286-287.

Hepple, Lawrence M.
1958   "The church in rural Missouri." Part III, Clergymen in Rural Missouri. Research Bulletin 633c: 221 Agricultural Experiment Station, University of Missouri.

Hudnut, William H.
1956   "Are ministers cracking up?" Christian Century 7 November.

Jenkins, Daniel T.
1947   The Gift of Ministry. London: Faber and Faber.

Johnson, F. Earnest, and J. Emory Ackerman
1959   The Church as Employer, Money Raiser and Investor. New York: Harper and Brothers.

Jones, Arthur R.
1963   Aspects of the Career Pattern of Clergywomen: A Study in the Sociology of Professions. Unpubl M.A. thesis, Louisiana State University.

dd, Gerald J., Edgar W. Mills, and Genevieve W. Burch
1970   Ex-pastors: Why Men Leave the Parish Ministry. Philadelphia: Pilgrim Press.

ausner, Samuel Z.
1964   Psychiatry and Religion. Glencoe, Illinois: The Free Press.

ng, Frederick R.
1958   "A study of testing as related to the ministry." Religious Education 52 (May-June):246.

ndis, Benson Y. (ed.)
1960   Year Book of American Churches. New York: National Council of Churches in the U.S.A.

ffer, Murray H.
960   The Role of the District Superintendent in the Methodist Church. Evanston, Illinois: Bureau of Social and Religious Research.

ner, Daniel, and Harold D. Laswell
951   The Policy Sciences. Stanford University.

ert, R.
932   "A technique for the measurement of attitudes." Archives of Psychology 140:52.

ely, Anne O.
958   A Survey of Mission Workers in the Indian Field. Mimeographed report. New York: National Council of Churches.

tie, Dan C.
959   "Laymen to Lawmen: Law School, careers and professional socialization." Harvard Educational Review 29 (Fall):352.

ch, James G., and Herbert A. Simon
958   Organizations. New York: John Wiley and Sons.

son, Ward S., Robert J. Dressel, and Robert K. Bain
959   "Sex role and the career orientations of beginning teachers." Harvard Educational Review 29 (Fall):370-383.

y, Mark A.
934   "The profession of the ministry: Its status and problems." The Education of American Ministers, Volume II: 143-175, and Volume IV (Appendix B to Volume II):180-188. New York: Institute of Social and Religious Research.

ton, Robert K., and Alice S. Kitt
950   "Contributions to the theory of reference group behavior." Pp. 41-42 in Robert K. Merton, and Paul F. Lazarsfeld (eds.), Continuities in Social Research: Studies in the Scope and Methods of 'The American Soldier.' Glencoe, Illinois: The Free Press.

s, Edgar W.
966   Leaving the Pastorate: A Study of the Social Psychology of Career Change. Unpublished Ph.D. dissertation, Harvard University.

nell, Joseph
968   "Methodist superintendency: Not so general." Christian Advocate 12 (March):12-13.

re, James B.
57   "Why Young Ministers are leaving the church." Harpers Magazine (July).

phy, G., and R. Likert
38   Public Opinion and the Individual. New York: Harper and Brothers.

rs, C. Kilmer
57   Light and Dark Streets. Greenwich, Connecticut: Seabury Press.

uhr, H. Richard
56   The Purpose of the Church and its Ministry. New York: Harper and Brothers.

uhr, H. Richard, and Daniel D. Williams
56   The Ministry in Historical Perspective. New York: Harper and Brothers.

s, Wayne (ed.)
61   The Minister's Own Mental Health. Great Neck, New York: Channel Press.

a, Thomas F.
61   "Five dilemmas in the institutionalization of religion." Journal for the Scientific Study of Religion 1 (October):32-39.

ons, Talcott
49   Essays in Sociological Theory: Pure and Applied. (First Edition) Glencoe, Illinois: The Free Press.

ons, Talcott, and Edward A. Shills (eds.)
54   Toward a General Theory of Action. Cambridge: Harvard University Press.

son, Roy
56   "Why ministers break down." Christianity and Crisis (October):144.

Poll, Solomon
 1962   The Hasidic Community of Williamsburg. Glencoe, Illinois: The Free Press.

Potter, E. Bruce
 1963   A Comparison of Perceptions Regarding the Role of Senior Pastor and the Role of Associate Pastor Unpublished M.A. thesis, University of New Mexico.

Reiss, Albert J.
 1955   "Occupational mobility of professional workers." American Sociological Review 20 (December):69- 700.

Russell Sage Foundation
 1947-1948   Annual Report, pp. 13-14. New York.
 1952-1953   Annual Report, pp. 31-32, 42. New York.

Sarbin, Theodore R.
 1954   "Role theory." In Gardner Lindzey (ed.), Handbook of Social Psychology. Cambridge, Mass.: Addison Wesley Publishing Company.

Scherer, Ross P., and Theodore O. Wedel (eds.)
 1966   The Church and Manpower Management. New York: National Council of Churches, Department of the Ministry.

Schmidt, Armin L.
 1959   Mission Board Executives: Expectations for the Role of the Agricultural Missionary. Unpublished M thesis, Ohio State University.

Shimada, Kozaburo
 1958   Role Conflict and Authoritarianism in a Sample of Protestant Parish Ministers. Unpublished M thesis, Pennsylvania State University.

Shrader, Wesley
 1956   "Why ministers are breaking down." Life Magazine (August):95. Also in Reader's Digest (November):55-58.

Siegel, S.
 1954   "Certain determinants and correlates of authoritarianism." Genetic Psychological Mongraph 49:1- 229.

Simpson, Ida Harper
 1956   The Development of Professional Self-Images among Student Nurses. Unpublished Ph.D. dissertation, University of North Carolina.

Sittler, Joseph
 1959   "The maceration of the minister." The Christian Century (June).

Sklare, Marshall
 1955   Conservative Judaism: An American Religious Movement. Glencoe, Illinois: The Free Press.

Smith, James A.
 1964   The Developing Roles of the General Superintendent in the Methodist Church. Unpublished doctoral dissertation, Boston University.

Southard, Samuel (ed.)
 1959   Conference on Motivation for the Ministry, pp. 51-55. Louisville, Kentucky: Southern Baptist Theological Seminary.

Sperry, Willard L.
 1946   Religion in America. New York: Macmillan.

Stamm, F. K.
 1935   "Perils of my profession." Reader's Digest (October):9.

Stouffer, Samuel A.
 1949   "An analysis of conflicting norms." American Sociological Review 14 (December):707.

Stouffer, Samuel A., and Jackson Toby
 1951   "Role conflict and personality." American Journal of Sociology 56 (March):395-405.

Sutcliffe, J. P., and M. Haberman
 1956   "Factors influencing choice in role conflict situations." American Sociological Review (December):695-703.

Toby, Jackson
 1952   "Some variables in role conflict analysis." Social Forces 30 (March):323-327.

United Presbyterian Enterprise in Theological Education
 1959   Council on Theological Education, General Survey Committee, Herman Morse (chairman). United Presbyterian Church in the U.S.A.

Vollmer, H. M., and D. L. Mills
 1966   Professionalization. Englewood Cliffs, New Jersey: Prentice-Hall.

Wallace, James E.
1964   Law and Religion in American Society. Unpublished Th.D. dissertation, Princeton Theological Seminary, Princeton, New Jersey.

Wardwell, Walter I., and Arthur L. Woods
1956   "The extra-professional role of the lawyer." American Journal of Sociology 61 (January):304-307.

Whitman, Ardis
1968   "The view from the pulpit." McCalls magazine (February):83.

Williams, Daniel D.
1956   "In correspondence: Ministry under tension." Christianity and Crisis 16 (December):169-172.

Wilson, Bryan R.
1959   "The Pentecostal minister: Role conflicts and status contradictions." American Journal of Sociology 64 (March):498.

Wood, Charles L.
1964   Function of the Parish Priest in the Episcopal Diocese of New Jersey. Unpublished doctoral dissertation, Rutgers—The State University.

West, M. Dwayne
1959   A Study of Protestant Agricultural Mission Service and how to Prepare for it. Unpublished M.S. thesis, Ohio State University.

Young, Donald
1955   "Sociology and the practicing professions." American Sociological Review 20 (December): 641-648.

BIBLIOGRAPHY

Blizzard, Samuel W.
1954   "The church and its community." Shane Quarterly Review 15 (October):153-168.
1954   "Social science in the training of the parish minister." Inaugural lecture in the Union Seminary Quarterly Review, Special Issue (January):39-43.
1955-
1956   "New areas of opinion research I: Research on institutions." Public Opinion Quarterly 19 (Winter):427.
1956   "The minister's dilemma." Pp. 74-78 in Robert C. Johnson (ed.), The Church and its Changing Ministry. Philadelphia: General Assembly of the United Presbyterian Church in the U.S.A.
1956   "The role of the rural minister in community and cultural change." New Horizons for Town and Country Church 16 (October):26-40.
1959   "The layman's understanding of the ministry." Pp. 50-65 in Samuel Southard (ed.), Conference on Motivation for the Ministry. Louisville Kentucky: Southern Baptist Theological Seminary.
1967   "Role conflicts of the urban Protestant parish minister." Pp. 212-217 in Richard D. Knudten (ed.), The Sociology of Religion. New York: Appleton-Century-Crofts.

Blizzard, Samuel W., and Charles E. Mathews
1957   "Criteria and skills of professional practice." Pp. 108-120 in J. Christy Wilson (ed.), Ministers in Training. Published by the Directors of Field Work in the Theological Seminaries of the Presbyterian Church, U.S.A.

Davis, Jerome
1936   "The social action pattern of the Protestant religious leader." American Sociological Review 1 (February):105-114.

Dittes, James E.
1962   "Research on clergymen: Factors influencing decisions for religious service and effectiveness in the vocation." Religious Research 57 (July-August):S141-S145.

Fulton, Robert L.
1961   "The clergyman and the funeral director: A study in role conflict." Social Forces 39 (May):317-325.

Gist, Noel P., and L. A. Halbert
1956   Urban Society, pp. 440-456. New York: Thomas Y. Crowell Company.

Glock, Charles Y., and Benjamin B. Ringer
1956   "Church policy and the attitudes of ministers and parishioners on social issues." American Sociological Review 21 (April):148-156.

Glock, Charles Y., and Rodney Stark
1965   Religion and Society in Tension, pp. 170-184. Chicago: Rand McNally and Company.

Johnson, Douglas W.
    1963   The Minister's use of his time. Unpublished M.A. thesis, Boston University.

Lenski, Gerhard
    1961   The Religious Factor, A sociological study of religion's impact on politics, economics, and family life, p 268. Garden City, New York: Doubleday and Company.

Maurer, Beryl B.
    1958   A Study of Selected Factors Associated with the Professional Behavior-image of Protestant Parish Ministers. Unpublished Ph.D. dissertation, Pennsylvania State University.

Olson, Arnold O.
    1952   The Social Attitudes and Social Action of Some Ministers of the New York State Conference of the Methodist Church. Unpublished Ph.D. dissertation, Yale University.

Olson, Philip
    1964   "Rural American community studies: The survival of public ideology." Human Organization 2 (Winter):342-350.

Ringer, Benjamin J., and Charles Y. Glock
    1954-
    1955   "The political role of the church as defined by its parishioners." Public Opinion Quarterly 1 (Winter):337-347.

Shissler, Henry
    1957   "An experiment in attitude outcomes resulting from seminary courses in 'The church and the community.' " Rural Sociology 22 (September):250-257.

Stein, Maurice R.
    1960   The Eclipse of Community. Princeton, New Jersey: Princeton University Press.

Vidich, Arthur J., and Joseph Bensman
    1958   Small Town in Mass Society: Class, power and religion in a rural community. Princeton, New Jersey Princeton University Press.

Winter, Gibson
    1955   "The church in suburban captivity." The Christian Century 72 (September):1112-1114.

Wispé, Lauren G.
    1955   "A sociometric analysis of conflicting role-expectations." The American Journal of Sociology (September):134-137.

SUBJECT INDEX

Actors in a theologically-oriented system
Ministers as, with many roles...........30, 117
Non-ministerial..........................31
Age, and
Church orientation.......................142
Goals...................................78
Role conflict............................129
Time management 103, 111
Analysis of clergymen
Limitations of...........................133
Methodology used in....................23-24
At one point in time......................25
And role conflicts.....................123-129
Apparel as status identification 32
Apparent role conflict model.............127-128
Attitude toward change, source of data for......42
Authoritarian personality
Defined................................40
And integrative role......................78
And role conflict 129
Blizzard papers..........................24n
Careers for theologically trained persons
Lay assumptions about....................29
In research sample 44
Types of 23, 29-30
Changes in society
In the behavioral sciences 20
To which ministers respond 35
In parishioner's expectations of clergy roles....19
Structurally..............................19
In theological thinking.....................20
Church, the
Comparsion of frames of reference to 140-142
Data for analysis of minister's concepts of 136
Functional frame of reference to 137, 139
Minister's image of, and orientation to 135-138
Operational definition of 136
Roles, and concept of.....................150
And sermon themes 141
Structural and theological frames of
reference to...........................136-140
Variability in church typology by clergy and
organizational factors................142-144
Citizenship role...........................37
Clergy characteristics analyzed by role
Criteria of professional effectiveness and
success 59, 78
93, 105, 131
Personal 57, 78, 103, 129
Personality..............57, 78, 104, 129-130
Professional experience........59, 78, 105, 130
Referents.......................58, 78, 104
Clergy evaluations of practitioner roles
Normative/importance 86-88
Performance/effectiveness...............89-90
Satisfaction/enjoyment..................88-89

Clergy factors
Described...........................39-48
Influence behavior......................152
Complexity of ministers' roles..............31-32
Concept of self 32
Constellations of role conflict
Identified.........................120-122
Interaction pattern......................122
Contemporary roles
Integrative............................70-75
Practitioner............................85
And time management 102
Content analysis 39n, 65, 81, 83, 123, 136
Covert behavior...........................83
Denominational affiliation, and
Integrative role......................79-80, 82
Master role............................60
Orientation to the church 144
Practitioner roles 93-95
Role conflict 131-132
Time management 106
Denominations participating in the study 48
Dependent variables.......................39
Doctrine, use of by ministers.................136
Dual organizational status and role conflict 118
Economics of parishes studied, and
Integrative role...........................81
Master role............................62
Time management 109
Effectiveness as criteria of technical
competence...........................32
Effectiveness, feelings of, and
Clergy criteria........................45-46
Concept of the church 136
Integrative role..........................78
Master role............................59
Practitioner roles 89
Ranked with other evaluations..............102
Emotional maturity
Continuum.............................41
And master role.........................58
And role conflict 130
Evaluations of practitioner roles
By clergy.............................86-93
Are contradictory.......................102
And integrative role......................148
And operational requirements of parish.......102
Evident role conflicts
As dependent variables................128-129
Number of, held by ministers...............123
Functional analysis of the minister 23
Functional frame of reference to the
church 136-137, 139, 141
Future research suggested 38, 133, 148, 153
Goal orientation
Contemporary.................65-66, 70-75, 77

General practitioner 65-66, 75-76
Traditional 66-70, 77
Ideological orientation to master role 52-54
Image of a minister
  Development of 30
  Lay actors in the system contribute to. 33, 147
Independent variables 39
Integrative roles
  Contemporary 70-75
  Definition of 65
  General practitioner 75
  Primary/secondary 65, 77, 81
  Related to practitioner roles 148
  And role conflict 151
  And structure of goal orientation 65
  Traditional 66, 70
  Variability in, analyzed 78-81
Interaction theory in professional practice . .147, 151
Language as problem in bi-discipline research . . .24
Lay persons
  Define ministry 29
  Have images of ministers 33
Leadership expected of minister 37
Master role
  And concept of church 150
  Data source of analysis of 52
  Definition of 51
  Ideological and functional orientations to 53-56
  And integrative roles 65, 148, 151
  As total status 51
  Typology 56
Mentor referent .43, 104, 114
Methods of analysis 23
Minister, the
  Behavior of, influenced by clergy and
    organizational factors 152
  Church orientation of 136-142
  Classified into master role types 56
  As described historically 25
  Lack of systematic knowledge about
    self-perceptions of 25
  Leadership expected of .37
  As symbol to the community 38, 141
Minister's use of time: See Time management.
Ministry, the
  As occupational group .24
  As sub-culture 24
Mobility, professional 44, 105, 111, 130, 143
Neo-traditional practitioner role
  Described 84
  And time management 102, 113
Nomenclature used to designate clergy 31
Non-professional activities
  In clergy use of time 110-111
  In competition with professional activities 115
  Described 98, 99
  And organizational factors 115
Normative evaluation of practitioner roles
  Described 86-88
  And master role 148

As ranked with other evaluations 102
And role conflict 152
Open-ended nature of questionnaire 39n, 41
Ordination of clergy in study 44
Organizational characteristics of parishes
analyzed by clergy role
  Denominations 60, 79, 93, 106, 131-132
  Economics of parish 62, 81, 95, 109, 132
  Organizational complexity 61, 80, 95,
                                                    107, 111, 132
  Regional location 61, 80, 95, 106
  Type of community 61, 80, 95, 107
Organizational factors of parishes
  Described 39, 48-50
  Roles influenced by 152
Overt behavior 65
Parishioners' expectations of ministers 19-20,
                                                    25, 109-110, 135
Parish minister
  As career type 29
  As central actor in the system 117
  As reporter of own perceptions 26
Performance (effectiveness) evaluation of
  practitioner roles 89-90
Personal characteristics of clergyman
  Analyzed by role 57, 78, 93, 129
  Description of, in research sample 39
  And time management 104, 111
Personality characteristics of clergyman
  Analyzed by role 57, 78, 93, 129
  And authoritarianism 40
  Awareness of desired change 42
  Description of 40-42
  Emotional maturity 41
  And time management .111
Practitioner roles
  Contemporary 85
  Data source for analysis of 83
  Described 84
  Evaluation of, by clergy and non-clergy . .83, 86-89
  Evaluations of, compared 89-92
  Interaction pattern of 86
  Level of generalization .83
  Related to other roles .148
  Traditional and neo-traditional 84
Primary/secondary integrative roles . . .65, 76, 77, 81
Princeton Theological Seminary, Speer
  Library 24n, 52n
Professional activities
  Classified by practitioner role 99
  Extra-professional relationships 37
  And role conflict 152
  Time allocation to 99-100
Professional experience
  And integrative role 78
  And master role 59
  And mobility 44, 105, 130, 143
  Of parish minister 44
  And role conflict 130-131
  And time management .105

A wholistic view of.........................147
Professional personnel
  Non-ministerial............................30
  Status of................................30
Profession, definitions and types of.............30
Quotations from clergy participants in Blizzard survey, on
  The church..........................136-140
  Contemporary orientation to goals 71-75
  Denomination 140
  Effectiveness.............................46
  Orientation to master role 54-55
  Problems observed in parishioners 136
  Referents...............................43
  Role conflict........................124-126
  Self-understanding 34
  Success..............................35
  Traditional goals.......................67-70
Referent groups.................42, 58, 78, 104
Regional location of parishes 49, 61, 80, 95, 111
Research to study parish minister
  Approaches to 21-22
  Denominations participating in..............48
  Functional method of analysis in............23
  Language used in.......................24
  Researcher's own frame of reference for . . .24, 26
  Sample description.......................39
  Self-images of ministers as focus for......25, 38
  Union Theological Seminary's participation in . .21
Role conflict
  Analysis of evident and apparent types of.............................123-129
  And dual organizational status..............118
  Model 120-121
  And normative evaluations.................152
  Related to clergy characteristics and organizational factors................129-132
  Related to incompatible personal expectations, 117
  And social norms 118
  Theory of.............................117
  Time management difficult.................115
  And a wholistic view of professional practice.........................151-152
Role constellations
  Conflicts identified....................120-122
  Interaction pattern.......................122
Roles
  Are complex for minister...................32
  Extra-professional.......................36-38
  Lack of knowledge about 25
  Of minister being redefined 19
  Multi-level structure of.....................147
  Non-professional.......................36-37
  As performance of actors in system..........31
  Relatedness among..................148-149
  Theory about, useful to study professions......20
Russell Sage Foundation study
  Initiated..............................20-21
  Studies of ministers compared with......101-110, 164, 166, 168

Satisfaction evaluation
  And integrative role......................148
  Of practitioner roles.....................88-89
  As ranked with other evaluations............102
Self-image
  Necessary to function adequately............33
  Of Protestant minister 34, 39, 147, 150
  And understanding related to goals..........34
Self-reported data
  Limitations and advantages of 26
  Use of, a committee decision...............39n
Seminaries
  Alumni as respondents in research 26
  Confidential reports to.....................26
  Participating in research....................26
  Self-evaluation by 26
Sermon themes.......................141-142
Social relationships for the minister.............37
Social sciences related to practice of ministry. .20-23
Structural frame of reference to the church...................136-137, 140-141
Success, feelings of, and
  Criteria for............................45-48
  Integrative role 78-79
  Master role.............................59
  Practitioner roles.........................93
  Role conflict............................131
  Time management 105
Symbols identifying clergy 31-32
Technical competence 32
Tenure 44
Theological education
  Function of social sciences in.............21-23
  Implications of research for 19
Theological orientation to the church
  Expressed by respondents 136-138
  Minister symbolizes, to community 141
Theoretical model, development of...........25-26
Time management
  And clergy role evaluations 101, 102
  And day of week, season of year............112
  As a major problem for clergy 97
  And non-professional activity............98, 111
  Parishioner perception of 109-110, 112
  Source of data for 98
  And typicalness of reported time 113
  Variability in, analyzed by clergy and organizational factors................103-109
  "Work day" studies compared 101, 164, 166
Traditional goal orientation 66-70
Traditional and neo-traditional practitioner roles described 84
Types of community of parishes in research.......................49, 61, 107
Typical parish 50
Union Theological Seminary as base for study . . .26
Wholistic view of professional practice 147

AUTHOR INDEX

Abelson, R. P. 120
Ackerman, J. Emory 29
Ackerman, Nathan W. .117
Adorno, T. W. 41
Bain, Robert K. 51
Baker, Oren H. 40
Barber, Bernard 13
Baxter, Sandra 9
Beard, Augustus F. 73
Becker, Howard S. 13
Bennett, John L. 26
Bentz, W. Kenneth 13
Berckman, Edward 119
Bernard, Chester I. 119
Blanchard, Dalla S. 7, 11
Blass, Jerome H. 5
Blizzard, Samuel W. . . . . .v, vii, 1, 24n, 26, 27
Bloom, Samuel W. 21n
Bonn, Robert L. 4n
Bouma, Gary D. 1, 7, 13
Brooks, Robert M. 51
Brown, Emory J. 32
Burchard, Waldo W. 40, 51, 118, 120
Burch, Genevieve W. 7, 119
Campbell, Ernest Q. 8, 52, 119
Carroll, Jackson 4, 6, 10, 11
Carr-Saunders, Alexander M. 25, 30, 76
Chaffee, Edmond B. 73
Chapman, Stanley H. .30
Coates, Charles H. 9
Converse, Philip E. 4
Cottrell, Leonard S. 21n
Coxon, Anthony P. M. .94
Cumming, Elaine 13
Cummings, Des, Jr. 8n
Davies, Horton 33
DeLuca, Joel R. 12
de S. Brunner, Edmund 95, 106, 107, 108
Donovan, John D. 29, 33, 51
Douglass, H. Paul 95, 106, 107, 108, 164
Doyle, Ruth T. 4n
Dressel, Robert J. 51
Dudley, Robert L. 8n
Duncan, H. G. 119
Dyble, John E. . . . . .7, 8 n
Etzioni, Amitai 8
Everett, Robert F. 8n
Falding, Harold 11n
Falk, Lawrence 119
Farmer, Herbert H. 56
Ference, Thomas P. 10
Fichter, Joseph H. 6, 10
Fishburn, Janet F. 12
Foley, Albert S. 119
Frenkel-Brunswik, Else 40
Froyd, Milton C. 5, 101, 166, 168
Fukuyama, Yoshio 11n

Gannon, Thomas M. 13
Getzel, J. W. 117, 118, 120
Glass, C. Conrad, Jr. 7
Glasse, James D. 11, 12
Glock, Charles Y. 9, 10, 109, 110
Goldner, Fred H. 10, 11, 13
Goldstein, Sidney I. 5
Gottlieb, Avi 2
Gough, H. G. 41
Greeley, Andrew M. 9n
Gross, Neal 117
Guba, E. G. .117, 118, 120
Gullahorn, Jeanne E. .120
Gullahorn, John T. 120
Gustafson, James M. 10, 33
Haberman, M. 120
Hadden, Jeffrey K. 6, 7n, 8
Hammond, Phillip E. 29
Hargrove, Barbara 6
Harrington, Charles 13
Harris, John C. 11
Hartshorne, Hugh 5, 101, 166, 168
Hastings, Philip K. 10
Hendricks, Polly 8
Henry, William E. 40, 46, 57
Hepple, Lawrence M. .106
Hoge, Dean R. . . . . .vi, 1, 7, 8n, 10
Hudnut, William H. 119
Hughes, Everett C. 13
Hultgren, Dayton D. 7
Ingram, Larry C. 11n
Jarvis, Peter 13
Jenkins, Daniel T. 12, 20, 23
Johnson, Douglas W. 10
Johnson, F. Earnest 29
Jones, Arthur R. 29
Judd, Gerald J. 7, 119
Kelly, Henry E. 9n
Kistler, Robert C. 9
Kitson, Gay C. 7n
Klausner, Samuel Z. 29
Kleinman, Sherryl 11
Kling, Frederick R. .7, 86
Landis, Benson Y. 29
Laswell, Harold D. 20
Lehman, Edward C., Jr. .6
Lehman, Edward W. 8
Leiffer, Murray H. 29
Lerner, Daniel 20
Levinson, Daniel J. .40, 41
Likert, R. 41n
Lively, Anne O. 29
Longino, Charles F., Jr. .7n
Lortie, Dan C. 36
Luecke, David S. 8n
Luecke, Richard Henry 9
Lummis, Adair 6

McEachern, Alexander W. 117
Madron, Thomas W. 8
March, James G. 118
Marty, Martin E.. 10
Mason, Ward S. 51, 117
May, Mark A. 5, 33, 91, 101, 106, 107, 164
Merton, Robert K. 42
Mills, D. L.. 35
Mills, Edgar W.. . . . . .7, 8, 9, 11, 119
Mitchell, Joseph 29
Mitchell, Robert E. 12
Moore, James B.. 119
Murphy, G.. . . . . .41n
Myers, C. Kilmer 73
Nauss, Allen 5, 8n
Nelsen, Hart M. .vi, 8, 9
Newman, William M.. 7
Niebuhr, H. Richard 6, 23
Oates, Wayne 119
O'Dea, Thomas F.. 114
Parsons, Talcott. 34, 53
Pearson, Roy.. 119
Pettigrew, Thomas F. 8, 52, 119
Polk, David T. 7, 8n
Poll, Solomon 51
Potter, E. Bruce. 29
Quinley, Harold E.. 8
Reilly, Mary Ellen 9
Reiss, Albert J. 30
Riche, Martha Farnsworth 10
Ritte, Richard 10
Roof, Wade Clark 9, 10
Roos, Philip 9, 10, 109, 110
Roozen, David A. 10
Sanford, R. Nevitt 40
Sarbin, Theodore R. 117
Scherer, Ross P. 29
Schmidt, Armin L.. 29
Schoenherr, Richard A. 9n
Schreuder, Osmund 9
Schuller, David S. 11
Sheldon, Eleanor B. .21n
Shills, Edward A. .34, 53
Shimada, Kozabura 41, 120
Shrader, Wesley 119
Siegel, S.. . . . . .41n
Simon, Herbert A.. 118
Simpson, Ida Harper. 51
Sittler, Joseph 119
Sklare, Marshall 33
Smith, James A. 29
Southard, Samuel. 33
Sperry, Willard L. 30
Stamm, F. K.. 119
Stouffer, Samuel A. 117, 118, 120
Stout, Robert J.. 12
Stryker, Sheldon 2
Sutcliffe, J. P.. 120
Sweetser, Thomas. 11
Switzer, David K.. 12

Toby, Jackson 117, 120
Trillen, Calvin.. 12
Turner, Ralph H. 2, 12
Vollmer, H. M. 35
Wallace, James E. .4, 85
Walsh, Mary Paula 9
Wardwell, Walter I. 36, 37
Webb, Sam C.. 7
Wedel, Theodore O. 29
Whitman, Ardis 119
Williams, Daniel D.. 119
Wilson, Bryan 5, 119
Wilson, Robert. 6
Winter, J. Alan.. . . . . .8, 9
Wood, Arthur L.. 36
Wood, Charles L. 94
Wood, James R.. .8n, 10
Wuthnow, Robert.. 10
Yankelovich, David 10, 12
Yokley, Raytha L.. 8
Yost, M. Dwayne 29
Zald, Mayer N. 8n